Garrison Keillor

Twayne's United States Authors Series

Frank Day, Editor
Clemson University

TUSAS 624

Garrison Keillor
Photograph by Carmen Quesada

Garrison Keillor

Peter A. Scholl

Luther College

Twayne Publishers ■ **New York**

Maxwell Macmillan Canada ■ **Toronto**

Maxwell Macmillan International ■ **New York Oxford Singapore Sydney**

Garrison Keillor
Peter A. Scholl

Twayne Publishers   Maxwell Macmillan Canada, Inc.
Macmillan Publishing Company   1200 Eglinton Avenue East
866 Third Avenue   Suite 200
New York, New York 10022   Don Mills, Ontario M3C 3N1

Library of Congress Cataloging-in-Publication Data

Scholl, Peter A., 1945-
    Garrison Keillor / Peter A. Scholl.
    p.   cm. – (Twayne's United States authors series; TUSAS 624)
    Includes bibliographical references and index.
    ISBN 0-8057-3987-4 (alk. paper)
    1. Keillor, Garrison – Criticism and interpretation. 2.
Humorous stories, American – History and criticism. 3. Pastoral
fiction, American – History and criticism. 4. Lake Wobegon
(Imaginary place). 5. Minnesota in literature.. I. Title. II. Series.
PS3561.E3755Z87   1993
813'.54 – dc20   93-10599
                                                                             CIP

10 9 8 7 6 5 4 3 2

Printed in the United States of America.

To Titus and Charlotte

Contents

Preface

So important is humor to our collective sense of identity in the United States that for at least a century the nation has maintained, though unofficially to be sure, the post of the Humorist Laureate. A chronologically ordered list of hypothetical honorees would include the names of Mark Twain, Will Rogers, James Thurber, and since 1985 (should anyone be so rash as to make such a list in these days of canon-bashing), Garrison Keillor. In that year Keillor's face, superimposed across his fictional town of Lake Wobegon, Minnesota, appeared on the cover of *Time* magazine. Though the cover story coincided with the publication of *Lake Wobegon Days*, *Time* was not profiling Keillor just because he had authored a sudden best-seller. Rather, the publication of the book offered a fitting occasion to celebrate his achievements as a "radio bard" and host of "A Prairie Home Companion," the radio variety show on which he had originally told the stories that provided the basis for the book. During its peak years in the mid-1980s, the show had a weekly listener tally that rivaled the total number of copies (four million) that the book eventually sold. Speaking for the board of directors of the American Public Radio network, William M. Dietel said in 1989 that Keillor "singlehandedly restored the medium of live radio variety show."[1] Yet throughout the two decades during which his radio career unfolded, Keillor published humorous sketches and fiction in the *New Yorker*; his double mastery of the arts of storytelling and writing was perhaps most compactly symbolized in the choice of the *Lake Wobegon Days* set of cassettes (1986) for the Grammy awarded for the best spoken-word recording of 1987.

His contributions to radio notwithstanding, some have suggested that Keillor's popular success as a writer is somehow diminished because the sales of his books were boosted by his prominence as the Shy Companion of the airwaves on his nationally broadcast show. *Leaving Home: A Collection of Lake Wobegon Stories*, published shortly after Keillor said farewell to his radio show in 1987, sold another two million copies or so, and although none of

Keillor's three other books have sold nearly so well as the two most closely associated with "A Prairie Home Companion," the sales of all of them have numbered in six figures. That his fame and exposure via radio was crucial to the remarkable sales of his books is undeniable. But Keillor's success in two media enhances and in no way diminishes the distinctiveness of his work in both. Furthermore, he had distinguished antecedents: Twain went on the first of many successful tours as a comic lecturer and storyteller before he had published his first book; Rogers was also famous for his radio performances and even acted in films; Thurber not only wrote "the gray stuff around the cartoons" in the *New Yorker* but became a famous cartoonist himself.

Keillor's enormous popularity in the eighties as the down-home Companion from the prairies shows that Will Rogers was not the last nationally famous Crackerbarrel Philosopher. But though he assuredly continues that venerable tradition, Keillor is not a parasitic revivalist of bygone comic roles and literary forms, for if he attained his widest acclaim as a yarnspinner in the nineteenth-century traditions of local color and literary comedy, he also revitalized those traditions and modes at one moment, but stepping around them a moment later, he adopted comic modes and played roles that had little precedent in eras other than his own. Moreover, his skill and achievements as a *New Yorker* writer affected the structure and nuance of his oral, vernacular tales so that they are, rightly considered, hybrid forms, the products of literary cross-pollination between the traditional modes of oral storytelling and the verbal artistry practiced by not only the "classic" *New Yorker* writers Keillor admired so highly in his youth – Thurber, S. J. Perelman, A. J. Liebling, and E. B. White – but also later experimentalist writers such as Donald Barthelme.

The name Garrison Keillor is a pen name that Gary Edward Keillor began using when he was about 13. The implicit distance between Gary and Garrison not only denotes the separation of son and private individual on the one side and writer, showman, and, later, celebrity on the other; this internal division also corresponds to an external division between Keillor's public career as a radio performer and his more solitary life as a writer. At least four times – perhaps first in 1968 when he left KUOM-AM (University of Minnesota) and most recently in 1987 when he left "A Prairie Home

Companion" – he has quit his positions in radio to devote himself more exclusively to writing. This oscillation between two callings reveals a complex ambivalence in Keillor's career – a complexity that, for convenience' sake, I have abbreviated as a series of suggestive dialectical pairings that complement the paradigmatic Gary/Garrison and radio performer/writer oppositions: the biscuit/the croissant, the Lonesome Lutheran/the New Yorker, the Shy Person/the monster of greed and ambition, the Prodigal Son/the Prodigal's elder brother, the Yarnspinner/the postmodernist.

While these paradoxical pairings are somewhat hyperbolic, they nevertheless suggest why so many people have been fascinated by Keillor's life as well as his work. Additionally, some of them call attention to the arresting qualities of his published work: although much of it is oral, social, and participatory, it can, at another extreme, be primarily visual, silent, and fundamentally textual, its meaning unfixed and playful. The utterance-based material is more spontaneous, emotional, and sentimental, while the writerly material is more satirical, witty, and experimental. Likewise, as a performer Keillor draws his listeners close into a communal circle, but he has also repeatedly abandoned his audience to live – like a latter-day Thoreau – the deliberate, anonymous life of a writer.

Chapter 1 includes a summary of Keillor's early life, and the subsequent chapters tend to follow chronologically the shape of his dual career. I chose this structure not intending to discover the nature and meaning of Keillor's life but believing that an examination of the pattern of his career would provide a context to better understand and appreciate his work. Nevertheless, since Keillor has played so many public roles that seem so close to his true identity and has written so much about his life, it is often difficult to separate analysis of the work from analysis of the author. Keillor's negative capability is formidable: he proliferates avatars of himself in both the third and first persons, in performance and in print, in fiction and nonfiction. Some seem closer than others to his core identity – some are peripheral and others are playful inversions (as my discussion of many of his works, especially *Lake Wobegon Days* and *WLT: A Radio Romance*, demonstrates).

My method for anatomizing and discussing this panoply of poses and personas relies most heavily on literary and rhetorical analysis. I am especially indebted to Mr. Keillor for assisting my research by allowing me to interview him and for generously providing access to his manuscripts and papers and the vast archive of tapes at Minnesota Public Radio in St. Paul and at his American Humor Institute in New York. I have listened to most of the radio broadcasts of "A Prairie Home Companion" from 1980 to the end of that show and to nearly all from the first three seasons of "American Radio Company," and to many other occasional performances as well. I had to content myself with sampling tapes of Keillor's morning show and of "A Prairie Home Companion" for 1974-79, however, since much of that material was either no longer available or too fragile to be used for research.

I am also grateful to William Kling, president, and Tom Kigin, vice president and general counsel, for their cooperation with this project, and I thank all the other MPR staffers who have helped me, especially David O'Neill and Kate Gustafson. Jennifer Howe, Ann Stonehill, and Elizabeth Murray, who all worked for Keillor's American Humor Institute, also provided valuable assistance. I am especially grateful to Rosalie Miller who piloted me through the vast store of Keilloriana over which she presided while she worked for MPR. I am also indebted to the competence of the staffs of the Wilson Library of the University of Minnesota and the Preus Library at Luther College, especially Elizabeth Kaschins and Ruth Reitan.

My spring 1992 seminar on Samuel Clemens and Keillor helped me to many new insights. I have been influenced at every stage by the work of many scholars, reporters, and writers in a wide array of articles and books, and while I have tried to acknowledge my intellectual debts with references, I have undoubtedly understated my indebtedness in many instances; among the scholars, I am deepest in debt to Judith Yaross Lee for her *Garrison Keillor: A Voice of America*, which appeared as I entered the last phase of this project. At Twayne, Frank Day, the series field editor, amazed me with his celerity and buoyed me with good cheer, and Barbara Sutton expertly smoothed the rougher places in the manuscript. Editors Liz Fowler, Jacob Conrad, and Mark Zadrozny also helped out along the way.

I am grateful to Luther College's Committee for Faculty Development and Research and to the Paideia Endowment for their support of my research. And to all my colleagues and friends, and especially my wife, Diane, for listening and appearing interested.

Acknowledgments

I would like to thank Penguin Books USA Inc. for permission to quote from the following titles:

From *Happy to Be Here: Even More Stories and Comic Pieces*, by Garrison Keillor. Copyright 1970, 1971, 1972, 1973, 1974, 1975, 1976, 1977, 1979, 1980, 1981, 1983 by Garrison Keillor. Used by permission of Viking Penguin, a division of Penguin Books USA Inc.

From *Lake Wobegon Days*, by Garrison Keillor. Copyright 1985 by Garrison Keillor. Used by permission of Viking Penguin, a division of Penguin Books USA Inc.

From *Leaving Home*, by Garrison Keillor. Copyright 1987 by Garrison Keillor. Used by permission of Viking Penguin, a division of Penguin Books USA Inc.

From *We Are Still Married: Stories and Letters*, by Garrison Keillor. Copyright 1982, 1983, 1984, 1985, 1986, 1987, 1988, 1989, by Garrison Keillor. Used by permission of Viking Penguin, a division of Penguin Books USA Inc.

From *WLT: A Radio Romance*, by Garrison Keillor. Copyright 1991 by Garrison Keillor. Used by permission of Viking Penguin, a division of Penguin Books USA Inc.

Macmillan Publishing Co. has granted permission to quote from stories included in *Happy to Be Here: Stories and Comic Pieces*, by Garrison Keillor (New York: Atheneum, 1982). Copyright 1970, 1971, 1972, 1973, 1974, 1975, 1976, 1977, 1979, 1980, 1981, 1982 by Garrison Keillor.

I am grateful to Minnesota Public Radio and its Vice President and General Counsel, Thomas J. Kigin, for making available to me archival manuscript material of "A Prairie Home Companion." Rosalie Miller, a former assistant producer of "A Prairie Home Companion," kindly assisted me in my research in the MPR archives. Kay Gornick, Mr. Keillor's assistant, also was most generous with her time.

I would also like to thank Gordon Mennenga and Howard Mohr, writers for "A Prairie Home Companion," who answered a number of my questions about the show.

Finally, I am most grateful to Garrison Keillor for permitting me to quote from his published writing and from transcriptions of his radio shows.

Chronology

1942	Gary Edward Keillor born 7 August to John Philip and Grace Ruth (Denham) Keillor in Anoka, Minnesota.
1947	The family buys a lot in semi-rural Brooklyn Park, Minnesota, where Gary's father begins building the house for the family that would grow to six children and where Gary would live in until age 18.
1955	Uses the name "Garrison Keillor" for the first time when submitting poems to his junior high literary magazine.
1957-1960	Attends Anoka High School.
1960-1966	Attends the University of Minnesota, graduating with a B.A. in English.
1960	Takes first job in radio with WMMR-AM, a university radio station.
1962-1963	Drops out of school and spends four months working for the *St. Paul Pioneer Press*.
1963	Returns to the university and takes a job with university radio station KUOM-AM; is fiction editor on the student literary magazine, the *Ivory Tower*.
1964	Serves as editor of the *Ivory Tower* from October until resigning in January 1966.
1965	Marries Mary C. Guntzel on 11 September.
1966	Wins first prize in the university's American Academy of Poets Contest; graduates with a B.A. in English and in the summer hitchhikes to the East Coast to interview for jobs at the *New Yorker* and the *Atlantic*.
1967-1968	Takes courses toward an M.A. in English at the University of Minnesota while continuing to work at KUOM.

1968   Leaves job as public affairs director for KUOM to con-
            centrate on writing.

1969   Son, Jason, born in the university hospital; the family
            resides in a farmhouse in Freeport, Minnesota, when
            he begins working as an announcer on an early-
            morning show for Collegeville-based KSJR-FM, the first
            radio station run by Minnesota Educational Radio
            (MER), the name of Minnesota Public Radio (MPR)
            until 1974.

1970   Publishes first pieces in the *New Yorker.*

1971   Leaves radio station KSJR and tries to support his fam-
            ily with freelance writing but resumes early morning
            show over MER's new station, KSJN-FM, in St. Paul, in
            October.

1973   In November leaves radio station KSJN to write.

1974   Travels to Nashville to write about the "Grand Ole
            Opry" for the *New Yorker.* Returns to work on KSJN;
            the first Saturday evening "A Prairie Home Com-
            panion" ("PHC") show is taped in May, and the first
            live show is broadcast 6 July.

1976   Is divorced from Mary Guntzel Keillor. In July resumes
            weekday morning radio show (which he left in 1973).

1977   *G.K. the DJ* is published by MPR and offered as a pre-
            mium for supporters of the network.

1979   *The Selected Verse of Margaret Haskins Durber,* a se-
            lection of poems, is offered as a premium for sup-
            porters of MPR.

1980   In May "PHC" begins regular national live broadcasts
            via satellite; the show wins the George Foster Peabody
            Award.

1982   First edition of *Happy to Be Here* is published by
            Atheneum; in April Keillor quits his morning show to
            work on *Lake Wobegon Days.*

1983   *Happy to Be Here,* revised and enlarged paperback
            edition, is published by Penguin.

1985   Attends twenty-fifth reunion of Anoka High School
              class and sees former classmate, Ulla (Strange)
              Skærved, for the first time since 1960. In October *Lake
              Wobegon Days* is published by Viking and on 4
              November he is featured on the cover of *Time* maga-
              zine. On 29 December he and Ulla are married in
              Holte, Denmark.

1986   On 26 April the reopening of the completely refur-
              bished World Theater in St. Paul is commemorated,
              and "PHC" is televised for the first time.

1987   The last shows and the final performance of "PHC" on
              13 June are televised by the Walt Disney Company;
              Keillor leaves Minnesota for Denmark in June. *Leaving
              Home* is published, and in September Keillor takes up
              residence in New York City, where he works as a staff
              writer for the *New Yorker*. The *Lake Wobegon Days*
              set of cassettes wins a Grammy for best spoken-word
              recording of 1987.

1989   *We Are Still Married* is published by Viking; in
              November begins broadcasts of "American Radio
              Company of the Air" (later called "American Radio
              Company" ["ARC"] for MPR over the American Public
              Radio network).

1990   Keillor is the voice of Walt Whitman and other histori-
              cal characters in the PBS television documentary series
              The Civil War, produced by Ken Burns. Begins second
              season with "ARC."

1991   *WLT: A Radio Romance* is published in the fall by
              Viking, and Keillor begins his third season doing
              "ARC."

1992   Keillor announces that "ARC" will return to the World
              Theater for 18 weeks of the next season and that he
              has purchased a log cabin on a wooded lot near River
              Falls, Wisconsin, within commuting distance of the
              Twin Cities.

Chapter One

Gary Edward and Garrison Keillor

I made up my mind that the most wonderful thing in the world would be to be a storyteller.[1]

Gary Edward Keillor was born in Anoka, Minnesota, on 7 August 1942, the third of six children of John Philip and Grace Ruth (Denham) Keillor, and by the time he was seven or eight he knew he wanted to be a writer.[2] His early decision and consistent dedication to that end make for a narrative that conforms readily to the pattern of nonconformity in the biographies of many famous American writers on the way up. His story rehearses the contradiction of being raised in a close and stable family yet feeling smothered and deprived as he grew older by the very bonds that kept the family tight. Never lacking parental affection, he suffered from a sense of social isolation, alienation, and personal inferiority – conditions that nourished a stubborn determination to free himself from the constrictions of heritage, upbringing, and circumstance and that goaded him toward the discovery of ways to turn his personal liabilities into literary capital. "I still feel this little engine of ambition whirring at my back that started whirring back when I lived in Anoka,"[3] he said 30 years after leaving.

Home

The author's paternal grandparents, James and Dora (Powell) Keillor had immigrated from Canada to Ramsey Township, near Anoka, and bought a farm in 1880 that was still owned by Keillors a century later. While many fans of "A Prairie Home Companion" ("PHC") assumed that he was born a Norwegian-American and raised as a Lutheran like so many Wobegonians, Keillor is a Scottish name, and although his mother was born in Minneapolis, her father was an immigrant

1

from Glasgow. He was raised in a Protestant fundamentalist sect, the Plymouth Brethren, the model for the Sanctified Brethren as depicted in *Lake Wobegon Days*. Keillor's father, one of eight children, left the farm and serving in the army during World War II, lived with his young family in Bettendorf, Iowa. After short stints in St. Paul and Minneapolis, in 1947 the family purchased a one-acre lot in Brooklyn Park, eight miles south and across the Mississippi River from Anoka. John Keillor worked as a clerk in the Railway Mail Service on the St. Paul–Jamestown, North Dakota, run, supplementing his income with freelance carpentry, and he built the house where Keillor lived until he left home for the University of Minnesota.[4] Although both Anoka and Brooklyn Park became bedroom communities to the Twin Cities, Keillor describes growing up in "a lovely green place with a cornfield across the road, a deep twisting ravine behind the house and a dry creek bed with big rocks where we made camps and forts, and just over the hill, the Mississippi to swim in and skate and skip stones."[5]

Keillor devoted himself earlier and more persistently to writing than to performing, starting his own newspapers in elementary school – the *Sunnyvale Star* at Sunnyvale School in nearby Dayton and the *Riverviewer* at Riverview school, closer to home.[6] In these juvenile journalistic ventures he was already writing humor: "Mainly crazy stuff about grown-ups and teachers. I'd put them in ridiculous situations. . . . It was a way of making my friends laugh, of making myself popular. I got a lot of mileage out of it" (Nelson). When he was 16 he published in the 25 September 1958 Anoka *Herald* his first for-pay story, "Tornadoes Swamp Ramsey 40-0," an account of his Anoka High School's football triumph, and he continued to report on sports and other local stories for that newspaper.[7] His burgeoning literary activity had already caused frowns at home, since from his parents' fundamentalist perspective the life of a writer was "fraught with temptation."[8] They were not so concerned about journalism, but Keillor says that when he published a poem, they were quite upset: "They felt it was a shame on the family. . . . I don't feel like an outcast now, but I recall vividly a time when I did" (Letofsky).

The Plymouth Brethren "set themselves apart from the world out of religious conviction" and early on Keillor's parents proscribed television along with dancing, drinking, smoking, and other "worldly temptations" (Beyette, V2). When a neighboring family bought a television set, the Keillor children lobbied hard to have one as well, but their parents resisted on the grounds that the family was too poor and, more importantly, that television was the moral equivalent of the movies. Radio was always permitted, however, and Keillor remembers sitting on an uncle's lap sharing the headphones to his crystal set and hearing an announcement that World War II was over. Later, the whole family listened together, the six kids (J. Philip, Judy, Gary, twins Steven and Stanley, and Linda) on the floor around the big Zenith console to shows from as close as WCCO in Minneapolis to as far away as those on "short-wave stations in strange languages and we hung on every incomprehensible word until the signal faded away."[9]

At the University of Minnesota Keillor wrote a piece of "reverse cultural snobbery" in which he fondly remembered network radio shows including "Fibber McGee and Molly," "Gangbusters," "My Little Luigi" and his local favorites such as "Cedric Adams and the Aquatennial radio shows, Cedric Adams and Stairway to Stardom, Good Neighbor Time on WCCO [recalling the days] when you could go down to the studio and see Wally Olson's band and hear all that corny music live" (the studio visits were recounted in his 1976 story "Drowning 1954").[10] The ban on television was lifted when Gary was in the ninth grade not because he persuaded his parents that there was no essential difference between radio and television since so many of the old radio shows had simply moved to the fuzzy screen but because his younger twin brothers and sister got sick with the chicken pox and then mumps in unbroken succession. The television kept them quiet. By that date, however, Gary felt there was a stigma attached to watching television and could never wholly enjoy it ever since a high school friend had registered his admiration, believing that the Keillors had no television because they were intellectuals, not because they were fundamentalists.[11] Keillor's early ambivalence about television persisted, and while he allowed the televising of "PHC" near the end of its run, he regretted the decision, writing that "radio was so sensual and delicious and it injured the show and insulted the audience to allow cameras to tromp around in it."[12]

Nom de Plume

Nearly everyone else in the fifth grade at Benson School laughed at imitations of Jackie Gleason after seeing him on television the night before, but the general hilarity meant nothing to Gary, "except that our family was odd" ("TV," 40). It was at least as odd for a teenage boy to write poetry, and when he submitted poems to his junior high school literary magazine at the age of 13, he felt a powerful need for a nom de plume. "I looked in the dictionary," he says. "I was looking for a way to lengthen my name. So I looked under g – gar – and, uh, there it was gargoyle, garrison and Gargantua."[13] He chose it because "it sounded mighty, formidable, like someone not to be trifled with" (Letofsky). His legal name remains Gary Edward, and he thinks of himself as Gary: "That's a good reason for having a name like that [Garrison] – you can distinguish between the person that strangers know and the person who you are, which is always a good idea" (McConagha).

Keillor's early self-rechristening signals at once a consecration to his calling and the establishment of a defensive perimeter around his core identity, set in place to resist further encroachments by threatening forces – his peers, the schools, or the even more formidable Christian soldiers in his family. Additionally, since Garrison is also the name of a small Minnesota town about 100 miles north of Minneapolis, the name connects Keillor to Minnesota in the way Samuel Clemens was linked with the Mississippi River by his pen name of "Mark Twain," which was adopted from the riverboat phrase meaning "two fathoms deep." By his junior year at Anoka High, according to his English teacher and mentor Deloyd Hochstetter, the tall, slouching boy who seldom said a word in class discussions was submitting reams of articles, assigned and unassigned, to the school paper under the byline "Garrison Edwards" (Fedo, 18). Hochstetter also remembered that Keillor's mother shared with him her concern over her son's reclusive habits, staying in his room writing all the time. The teacher advised her, "Just let him do that. One day something special's going to happen" (Fedo, 17).

Taking up this pen name was an unmistakable declaration of more than literary independence, flags fluttering from the battlements; yet in naming himself a writer and in becoming a performer he was also carrying on familial traditions and modeling himself on those nearest to him. The flight of the Prodigal, unawares, imitated that of the boomerang John Keillor once made and gave to his son for Christmas.[14] He would attest many times that his desire to become a storyteller was inspired by the examples of his storytelling relatives – by his great uncle, Lew Powell; his aunt, Ruth (Keillor) Blumer; and his grandfather, James Keillor. And surely the urge to "raise people up a little bit" with his stories and to make them laugh has more than a whisper of the evangelical spirit.[15]

On a special Thanksgiving broadcast in 1977, Keillor described the amusements his family would pursue at a holiday family gathering, including hymn singing and his father's enthusiastic declamation of household poems and ballads, such as Henry Wadsworth Longfellow's "The Wreck of the Hesperus" and "Paul Revere's Ride" or Oliver Wendell Holmes's "The Deacon's Masterpiece; or, The Wonderful 'One-Hoss Shay.'" "All of those poems that you and I and ordinary people may know the first stanza of," Keillor said, "my father knew all the way to the end."[16] He would write scores of humorous songs and ballads in similar poetic genres, performing most of them on his radio shows, interspersed with many of the same hymns and ballads that had entertained his family's gatherings.

His virtuoso memory received the same compulsory training that his father's had undergone – working up Bible verses each week. In a very early "PHC" talk (back when he referred to Brooklyn Park or Freeport rather than Lake Wobegon as his hometown) he reassured his audience that they should not worry if he ran out of things to say since he had a number of Bible verses memorized in reserve, a precaution necessitated by his youthful habit of putting off the obligatory weekly duty until the family was actually en route from Brooklyn Park to the meeting a half-hour away in Minneapolis.[17] The spontaneous prayers and preaching of the Brethren – his tradition values preachers who speak what is "on their heart" – certainly colored his own storytelling manner, and he often described his feelings about talking on the radio in revivalistic terms. About his work on his early morning show from 1969 to 1973, for example, he wrote that sometimes "I truly believed I was doing the Lord's work, leading the choir, goosing the downhearted, helping along with the rejoicing."[18]

Writing for the *New Yorker*

Having realized his ambition of becoming a staff writer, Keillor said in 1987, "I have written for *The New Yorker* since high school, though they weren't aware of it at the time" (*WASM*, xiii). He first discovered the magazine in either the Anoka or the Minneapolis Public Library (details vary slightly in different tellings), and he found it "a fabulous sight, an immense glittering ocean liner off the coast of Minnesota, and I loved to read it." He bought his first copy when he was 15 and smuggled it home because "my people weren't much for literature, and they were dead set against conspicuous wealth, so a magazine in which classy paragraphs marched down the aisle between columns of diamond necklaces and French cognacs was not a magazine they welcomed into their homes."[19] In honor of its writers – so many of whom signed their names with two initials, including E. B. White, A. J. Liebling, S. J. Perelman – Keillor said he signed himself "G. E. Keillor for a while, hoping lightning would strike" (*WASM*, xiii).

He admired the writing, and E. B. White was his particular hero, but he also used the magazine to "impersonate the qualities of money and present myself in the very best light," carrying it around in high school as "a sign of class." In this context, his assumption of a pseudonym correlates with the motif of the Prodigal Son, especially since his youthful ambitions are discussed under the rubric "The betrayal of the working class by its own children" ("What Do You Do?," 31-32). The voice of the Sojourner from Lake Wobegon that he would develop during the course of "PHC" was close to home, but long before that voice had fully evolved he experimented with other voices on the air, and in his writing he created dozens of narrative voices for the pieces he published in the *New Yorker* and other magazines. The wide variety of these voices testifies to Garrison Keillor's negative capability – the depth and versatility of his imaginative power and the acuity of his ear – but before the publication of *Lake Wobegon Days* (1985) few of the narrative voices in his *New Yorker* pieces sounded much like Gary Keillor or the Sojourner. At the height of the popularity of "PHC" when *Lake Wobegon Days* was getting its first reviews he said, "As I get older, more and more often I hear my father's voice coming out of me, and I find myself saying things he would say, I write things that seem to be something my father would have said, or my Uncle Lou [*sic*] would have said – sort of an apotheosis of what they would have said if they had been writers. I find the satisfaction in doing that, that I don't get from writing funny stories."[20]

Tradition

While Keillor's fierce independence, single-mindedness, and dedication to freedom of expression and individuality propelled him to distance himself from his family's Christian fundamentalist subculture, he has often implied that in attending to the beat of a different drummer he was also following in the footsteps of his schismatic forebears. In an essay celebrating the Declaration of Independence, he explained that his "great-great-great-grandfather was Elder John Crandall, who left England in 1634 and settled in Rhode Island .... [and] accompanied Roger Williams to London in 1663 to obtain a charter from King Charles II guaranteeing the inhabitants of Rhode Island Colony political and religious freedom."[21] Writing one year later in opposition to President Bush's proposal of a flag-burning amendment to the Constitution, he characterized the branch of his family that arrived in 1680 as "good Puritan stock who came here to enjoy greater restrictions than they were permitted under English law." When the Revolution came along, these forebears expressed their independent spirit by remaining loyal to the King, and they paid for that decision by fleeing to Nova Scotia. This second emigration cost them dearly in material terms, and when grandfather James Keillor arrived in Anoka in 1880, all the cheap, good land was taken.[22]

Though he has said "Minnesota was a repressive place to grow up" (*WASM*, 127), Keillor admires his fundamentalist family for their refusal to be conformed to the ways of the world around them and for the rigor of their convictions. Though he officially joined the Evangelical Lutheran Church of America (a mainline, nonfundamentalist Protestant denomination) in 1990,[23] he has on many occasions refused to distance himself from some key tenets of Plymouth Brethren belief and seemed to take vicarious pleasure in explaining how in 1831 the Brethren (in Great Britain) revolted against Anglicanism "for its worldliness, its lack of prophetic vision and lack of millenialist fervor for the Second Coming of Christ, its unholy union with the state" (*WASM*, 179). Though his fundamentalist upbringing made him "conspicuously different," he said that he "also felt very secure. We were so separated from the world with our restrictions and discipline that it encouraged us to have greater love for each other – which was more than I have found in any other kind of church."[24] Indeed, in certain "PHC" monologues and in the story "After a Fall" (1982) he clearly indicates that his understanding of comedy is theologically grounded and enabled by the fundamental drama of redemption.

The U of M

When Keillor graduated from Anoka High School in 1960, he knew he wanted to be a writer but had not really planned to go to college. Even though friends had been busy applying not just to the regional universities but to places like Dartmouth, Stanford, and Carleton, Keillor had applied to none, and in the summer following his senior year he took a job at the Salvation Army–run Evangeline Residence for Women in Minneapolis (a job he enjoyed, judging from the use he made of it in the "Home" chapter of *Lake Wobegon Days*). "It was only then, working in the scullery as a dishwasher that I lost my nerve, and I applied to the University," he says.[25] Keillor said in 1976 that he thought college had a "corruptive influence" on his development as a writer (Letofsky), and while he no longer felt so strongly that this was the case in 1990, he recalled that his decision to attend involved

> a compromise of two strong loyalties. One was loyalty to my class. . . . My rela-
> tives worked for the post office or were auto mechanics or worked in offices as
> secretaries – nobody in our family had gone to college – except my brother
> [J. Philip, eldest of the Keillor siblings]. . . . It also represented a departure
> from loyalty to my faith, which became tangled and complicated after that.
> (Interview, 10 August 1990)

Since high school and probably before, Keillor had shown clear signs of scholastic potential, but his energies were not directed toward earning an impressive academic record to win a college scholarship. His ambivalence for course work continued at the university, where his gradepoint average reflected the consequences of working to pay for his schooling, as a parking lot attendant (1960-62) and in radio – during his freshman year on the University of Minnesota's WMMR-FM and later at KUOM. But it was flagging motivation and a matter of priorities more than the pinch of financial exigency that allowed his grades to fall.

When Keillor dropped out of school in 1962, it was not only because he was "broke," though this was one reason he gave. "I was restless in school, felt useless, and had romantic ideas about newspapering," he later wrote (*WASM*, 140), and so he spent four months working as a copy aide at the *St. Paul Pioneer Press*. After Keillor had become well-known, his former city editor on that job opined that Gary's "mind seemed to be elsewhere. He just didn't seem cut out to be a newspaperman."[26] Although Keillor took courses in journalism and was soon working at close quarters with the student staff of the *Minnesota Daily*, the former editor's negative assessment of his suitability for a career in the press rings true. Very few of the pieces he subsequently published were straight or routine newspaper stories; his on-the-job experience, however, provided him with ammunition for satirical assaults on newspaper writing and writers that began appearing soon after he returned to the campus.

Ivory Tower

In the fall of 1963 Keillor became fiction editor of the *Ivory Tower*, a monthly literary magazine (cataloged as a supplement to the *Minnesota Daily*) in which he had previously published two poems. He got the job of editor the following year, and continued in this prestigious, for-pay position from the beginning of his junior year in fall 1964 to the first semester of his senior year. He resigned from the editorship when he went on academic probation, owing to the conversion of some incomplete grades into F's – a situation he managed to turn about when the chips were down by earning straight A's, "even an A in Public Health."[27]

From his perspective as a writer who had already published 23 pieces in the *New Yorker* and was being referred to in the local press as a "cult hero" for his two-year-old Saturday evening radio show, "A Prairie Home Companion," Keillor somewhat ruefully recalled that in his *Ivory Tower* pieces he "pretended to . . . a sort of juvenile sophistication" and satirized the "wrong things": "The satire was against lower middle-class people, Minnesota as part of the Bible Belt, fundamentalists, small town culture" (Letofsky). The man who was becoming famous for posing as "just a biscuit" (in his Powder-milk Biscuit spots) had earlier tried to present himself as a croissant – not just a "croissant from the Dales" but a croissant from far away.[28] (The "Dales" – as in the names of Twin Cities malls Ridgedale and Southdale – referred to mall-centered suburbs every-where.) "In my writing," he says, "I pretended I was a stranger here, that I came from New York and I was commenting on this strange, outlandish behavior of the residents" (Letofsky).

Actually, Keillor's university writing shows considerable maturity and remarkable skill in various genres and modes. And he wrote a lot: in the *Ivory Tower* alone (the main, but not the sole, outlet for his talent) he published at least 53 pieces from 1962 to 1967 (19 signed and probably more than 34 unsigned).[29] And while the narra-tive persona in about 15 satires or parodies corresponds roughly to the pose of spurious sophistication he later described, there are also a few pieces in which the first person narrator anticipates the self-deprecatory tones of the biscuit from Lake Wobegon. Furthermore, the generic spectrum covered by his pieces was wide, and only 23 or so of the total (fewer than half) can be classified as satirical (including parody and burlesque) or humorous prose. Fourteen of his contributions are poems, but only two of these qualify as humor-ous or light verse. Of the remainder, there are three short stories; four reviews; two in-depth, "color" sports features (on hockey); two earnest editorials (one criticizing President Johnson's Vietnam pol-icy); and five miscellaneous pieces, including personal reminiscences and a memorial tribute to a teacher.

Of the pieces that do seem to carry a tone of precocious sophis-tication, many were written for the *Ivory Tower*'s regular feature, "Broadsides of the Tower," a potpourri of unsigned commentary, reportage, and satire mostly on topics having to do with campus life, arts events, or academic politics. Some of his pieces in the editorial "we" do seem to be written from the perspective of Eustace Tilley, the monocled dandy who poses above the headline for "The Talk of the Town" in each issue of the *New Yorker*. Other signs that Keillor may have been imitating aspects of his favorite magazine appear in

the form of his variations on the "newsbreak," in which some published solecism or ambiguity is exposed to ridicule, often by means
of a clever tag line. The feature was a specialty of Keillor's literary
exemplar, E. B. White. In "The Green Goose Awards for Impenetrable Prose," for example, he pulled passages from the *Minnesota
Daily* and wrote comic tag lines that were funny but stung the targeted authors sharply enough that they still smarted a bit 22 years
later (Fedo, 42).[30]

The *New Yorker*'s longtime editor, Harold Ross, was famous for
editorial fastidiousness and strict factual accuracy, and Keillor's similar standards were in evidence even before the first issue under his
editorship had appeared. In a letter Keillor chastised the *Minnesota
Daily* for misquoting him. He never said the *Ivory Tower* was "an
outlet for literary attempts by members of the University community"; it is an "edited magazine," and its stories and articles arrive
"not as the waters of genius and imagination washing away the sands
of apathy and flowing forth unto the sea of life" but as
"contributions," which are carefully selected on the basis of craft
and merit.[31] In a satirical piece on another student periodical, Keillor
targeted not the political opinions in the passages he quoted but the
author's style and usage, striking a fairly Jovian pose to say, "I am
struck by the page upon page of turgid prose stirring up the sands of
jabberwock as the clouds of mindlessness shed the rains of inconsis-
tency upon the King of the Inscrutable Sentence."[32]

He tore into the major Twin Cities dailies more than once, and a
little over a year after leaving his job at the *Pioneer Press* he pilloried
the *St. Paul Dispatch* for what he characterized as its complicity in a
hypocritical, self-promoting campaign against pornographic magazines in that city. He lambasted the St. Paul mayor and the paper in
particular for their disproportionate rhetoric, reducing to absurdity
the notion of a "war on smut" by comparing such language to World
War I scare headlines about "What Huns Would Do if City Were Captured," digressing from the primary target to strafe the newspaper's
fundamental addiction to mindless trivia and "consistently bad writing."[33] (Ironically, the *Dispatch*, an evening paper, would merge in
1985 with Keillor's old employer, the morning *Pioneer Press*, to create the *St. Paul Pioneer Press Dispatch* – the paper Keillor would
accuse in 1987 of making it impossible for him to remain in the Twin
Cities.)

Keillor would target newspaper writing and government or other brands of jargonspeak in many of his subsequent parodies and burlesques in the *New Yorker*. But by that time the acerbic, sometimes intemperate pose of the smart young stranger from the East had largely given way to a variety of first person narrators who tended to betray their own inadequacies with every word they wrote. And in his pose as the Sojourner in the middle and later "PHC" monologues, Keillor avoided biting satire, preferring a gentler irony that can admit both sides of the question while deftly undercutting one in favor of the other. The distance he traveled beyond the juvenile sophistication pose he affected in the mid-1960s can best be gauged by comparing a satirical "Broadside" from 1964 to a popular "PHC" monologue from 1985.

In his leading piece for the first issue under his editorship, he skewered the Campus Crusade for Christ in four crisp paragraphs. Planting the presumption that what this organization had done was a desperate maneuver, he first invited the reader to imagine he or she was the Crusade's program chair trying to raise the dismal attendance at the meetings. In this context Keillor reported the offense that had inspired his article – the advertisement for "One of America's Leading Illusionists . . . the Story of How the Man Who's Never Been Fooled by a Magician Found the Reality in Christianity." Keillor then imagined what might come next: a child evangelist, a faith healer, and "Bob 'Big Gunner' Verrell, Former Major League Baseball Star Who Found Christ in the Outfield in Yankee Stadium." In conclusion, lest the barb had not struck home, he offered the straightforward assertion that the organization's program "is charlatan Christianity, a mockery of intelligent Christians and an insult to the campus."[34]

Twenty years later he sketched a scene in which dismal attendance plagued the Wednesday night prayer meetings of Lake Wobegon Lutheran Church. The program chair, Val Tollefson, responded by booking the World's Tallest Evangelist, a group of six that played 36 instruments, and a former Mr. Minnesota who had developed his neck muscles to the point that they constricted his breathing. He had died from this condition but was revived after a few minutes to become an evangelist. The scenario unfolded in the same way as in the *Ivory Tower* satire, but without acid. And in place of a condemnatory coda Keillor launched into a detailed account of the performance of Ernie and Irma Lundeen's Gospel Birds, in tones of slightly ironized admiration at how they played hymns on bells, impersonated the animals entering a model of Noah's Ark, and took up a collection on the wing – satirizing such chancel chicanery but managing somehow to preserve the possibility that grace can descend even on the wings of charlatan birds.[35] The subject remains the same, but the narrative perspective is that of the Sojourner, as I have called the composite narrative persona of the Man from Lake Wobegon who narrates the monologues from around 1981 on. How Keillor negotiated the replacement of the superior, imaginary New Yorker with the companionable Sojourner from a hick town "where smart doesn't count for so much" as his most familiar narrative voice is the main subject of the next two chapters.[36]

Stories and Burlesques

Not all of Keillor's humorous pieces for the *Ivory Tower* are satires written in the pose of Eustace Tilley. Three or four of his funniest pieces are not precisely satirical but anticipate Keillor's later proclivity toward parody and burlesque – those subtypes of the satirical form that target a literary form or a style rather than an objectionable person, a bad idea, or an oppressive institution. "The Vulgarians," for example, opens with a quotation from what is presumably a real letter to the *Minnesota Daily* by a citizen roused to indignation by the disparity between the money the university spent on athletic rather than academic activities. The letter deplores the salaries – many times what "distinguished professors" earn – paid to Minnesota's coaches, "many of whom are vulgarians." A sophisticated young stranger from the East might well be expected to agree with the letter writer and whip up derision for such Philistine priorities. But what follows is a minidrama, a scene in high diction played out between battling distinguished professors and a vulgarian coach – very much in the fashion of S. J. Perelman, who in the *New Yorker* often took off on his flights of whimsy from just such "serious" opening quotations. While Keillor depicts the coach as a tattooed brute, lashing his secretary with a whip while dressed in a velvet waistcoat over a silk vest, ornamented with "two fox-skins which serve as a sort of breech clout," there is no suggestion of moral indignation. Rather, the target of the piece is the style and clichéd sentiment of the complaint letter, gleefully reprinted since it allows an occasion to wax farcical.

In an adjacent unsigned article Keillor paid tribute to another of his *New Yorker* favorites, A. J. Liebling (1904-63), summarizing Liebling's 29 years with the magazine and reviewing his major subjects – boxing, city life, the war, the lives of sharp operators – a writer whom he would celebrate again in 1989 in a Foreword to a collection of humor pieces featuring one of Liebling's favorite con artists. Keillor recalls that in college he found Liebling "laugh-out-loud-pee-in-your-pants funny . . . ; a comic outsider and a rebel against convention and at the same time a man of the world who enjoyed himself hugely and whose best stuff was all about himself and having a hell of a good time."[37]

Keillor contributed only three short stories to the *Ivory Tower*, all of which are the sort of undergraduate writing, skillful as it is, that would cause people like the parents of Johnny Tollefson, the under-graduate contributor to the St. Cloud State *Cumulus*, to close their eyes and shake their heads (*LWD*, 307). "The Man Who Locked Him-self In" explores sexual anxiety and repression as experienced by Howard Berdie, a neurotic "little man" character who is losing badly in what the famous *New Yorker* humorist James Thurber called "The War between Men and Women." Howard has locked himself into a bathroom at a church during his daughter's wedding. The story has flashes of wit and the situation is basically comic, as are Howard's recollections of seeing his wife magnified many times her normal size in the car windshield one night – an image that duplicates Thurber's cartoon "House and Woman" – but the mood is dark and the piece no funnier than Thurber's lesser-known little-man stories about marital persecution, divorce, and even spousal murders.[38]

Keillor's second story, "The Courtship of Eve," describes an ironic quest through a surreal landscape that culminates in a con-frontation with a woman the young male protagonist calls Eve – a hideous, witchlike hag. Rather mysterious and grotesque, the tale fairly bulges with elusive allegory and is finally something of a head-scratcher.[39] Keillor did, however, write a realistic story, "Frankie," in his senior year; it is about a high school boy who has an accident in the family Buick on the way to see his girlfriend. Many Lake Wobe-gon stories would treat the lives of similar characters and would explore the same territory of teenage anxiety over sex, self-worth, and friendship. Yet, like the others, this story is not calculated chiefly to amuse, and it seems likely that at age 24 Keillor still lacked the requisite perspective that would later enable him to turn such materials into humor.[40]

A Bearded Poet

The pen name of Garrison Keillor was first used to designate the author of poems when he was 13, and even as late as March 1974 a Twin Cities newspaper identified him as a poet.[41] In a 1965 pen-and-ink portrait in the *Ivory Tower* Keillor wears a full beard and handlebar moustache and even looks like the stereotypical poet of the era, save for the scholarly aspect of a pair of hornrim glasses drifting down his nose. (Later he sported granny glasses and kept his thick beard most of the time until 1981.) His initial and all but one of his first eight contributions to the *Ivory Tower* (between spring 1962 and the following fall) were poems; indeed, his first appearance in a nationally known periodical came under the heading "Young Poets" in the *Atlantic* in 1968 – "Some Matters Concerning the Occupant."[42] That poem, like several of his *Ivory Tower* poems, exposes the impersonality of bureaucracy by ironically mixing the language of an official notice with religious metaphors and biblical echoes.

Many of Keillor's humorous songs, ballads, mock-commercial jingles, and odes are well-known; he wrote hundreds of these verses, many of which have been published as performed on his recordings, often accompanied by the texts in liner notes or inserts; many have been collected in *We Are Still Married* and elsewhere. Yet only two of the 14 poems in the *Ivory Tower* qualify as light or humorous verse, although several satirize such language as the pretentious talk of graduate students, academic criticism, or advertising copy. Most of the rest address the nature and function of poetry and other arts or explore religious themes. Keillor took courses from or associated with several poets at the university, including Allen Tate, James Wright, Reed Whittemore, and Roland Flint; John Berryman published a memorial tribute to a faculty colleague in *Ivory Tower* during Keillor's editorship.[43]

Keillor won honorable mention in the university's annual American Academy of Poets Contest in 1965 for two poems with religious themes, "On Waking to Old Debts" and "Nicodemus" (which, like his first poem in the magazine for 30 April 1962, "My Child Knew Once Who He Was," seems to demonstrate how his faith had "become tangled and complicated"). As a senior the following year he won first prize in the same contest for "This Is a Poem, Good Afternoon" and "At the Premiere" – poems that reveal his early and persistent animus against "pretentiousness," whether it be couched in the language of officialdom, advertising, the arts community, or academia.[44] "This Is a Poem, Good Afternoon" is a short dramatic monologue in which the speaker, "an associate poet of poetry," quotes a poem-within-the-poem and offers his analysis of it, inadvertently indicting himself as a bloodless critic as he attempts to articulate the unparaphrasable essences of poetry. "At the Premiere" is set in an elegant orchestral hall where high-toned women (in the Prufrockian tradition of those who "come and go, / Talking of Michelangelo") are fawned over and fêted. Describing a procession, Keillor metaphorically conflates the empty pageantry and show of High Church ritual with the gilt trappings of wealth that imprison art and demean artistic expression; the women are shown to their seats

> Led by a gypsy violin,
> The elder priest and his tiny page
> In ancient colors artfully dressed
> With a chrysanthemum over his heart,
> Swinging silver bells recently blessed
> By the archbishop of art.

Keillor's schismatic Protestant and working-class sensibility informs his depiction of these wealthy consumers of culture and their religion of art – an idolatrous cult of empty forms and opulent display. True art may be languishing, since as the ladies leave for tea the orchestral hall is on fire.

After he graduated with a B.A. in English in 1966, the long-haired, bearded poet made a summer pilgrimage east to land a job on the *New Yorker* or, failing that, with the *Atlantic* in Boston. Fortunately, he did not slam the door behind him, as both magazines turned him down. He returned to the Twin Cities where he spent the following two years taking graduate courses in English and working at KUOM until quitting in 1968 to concentrate on his writing. (In his opening remarks of an "American Radio Company" performance 2 May 1992 at the University of Minnesota's Northrup Auditorium, he said he had stayed in graduate school to avoid the Vietnam War draft.)

Keillor's last piece in the *Ivory Tower* is not a poem, but in it he describes himself as a poet – or at least as the author of "a large collection of unpublished poems." "How Can I Be Happy When I Can't Play Hockey like I Wanna?" is a mock-autobiographical humor piece very much in the tradition of Thurber's more familiar little man stories, such as "The Secret Life of Walter Mitty." The narrator confesses how he has labored diligently to live out the advice that in sports, "spirit *works*; mere talent is neurotic, self defeating." This credo is remarkably similar to that of a hockey coach whom Keillor had portrayed in a long sports article about the Minnesota – North Dakota rivalry two years earlier. Yet the comic butt of this piece is neither the coach nor his inspirational advice but the talentless first-person narrator himself. He claims that he has taken the coach's advice literally and that he has done all he could to become a hockey player by sheer strength of spirit. Though he describes himself as a bespectacled frequenter of the Reserve Reading Room and poet, he purports to have finally mastered the mental transformation into a defenseman, "a hard-nosed individual, part thug and a bit of a mucker." But he coyly admits that the spiritual transformation may be all he can manage, since he is "just under eight feet tall . . . and I cannot stay on my feet when I skate." Here at last is a glimpse of a Garrison Keillor who shows the early signs of the future Companion and rustic Yarnspinner on the radio prairie, marking off this "portrait of the artist as a young mucker" as a very early prototype of his most familiar persona, that of the Sojourner.[45]

Jason's Birth

In his junior year Keillor married Mary Guntzel, a music major at the university. She was an organ student of Heinrich Fleischer, whose campus recital Keillor had extravagantly praised in a 1963 review. (In 1965 Guntzel published "The Unabridged Heinrich Fleischer," a profile of her teacher in the *Ivory Tower*.) Although Keillor seldom mentioned his first wife in print, he wrote and read on the radio a moving account of the spring 1969 birth of their son, Jason. (After his parents' divorce in 1976, Jason lived primarily with his father.) The young couple struggled through more than 48 hours of labor at the university hospital, and toward the end Keillor had a premonition that the child would be lost. After they were home with Jason and finally satisfied that their son was whole and safe, Keillor tried to write a poem to express his joy and praise. But it would not come:

> The poems that I had written were all poems about myself and how I felt. . . . I could only write a poem about some of the strangeness and the incongruities of those two days standing . . . beside the bed of a woman who is writhing in labor and looking down in the night at the couples who were strolling into a dance in the student union. But it wasn't strange; it wasn't incongruous. It was a miracle. We felt that we were lifted up by many unseen people, and never let go of.

At 26, a husband and a father, the writer confronted his occupational curses of narcissism and pride, the same dogged hazards he would name over the years. And in this account of his struggle to write a "poem of great praise," a poem that spoke of matters beyond the horizon of his personal feelings, he struck a theme that seems to lie close to the center of his view on the meaning of life and the role of the artist:

> The inability to give praise, a kind of a spiritual dejection, or just plain sullenness we might call it – is a deadly sin . . . and probably is an offshoot of the sin of pride because it is at the heart of it a refusal to pay attention to things: to see what is there to see and to see miracles and gifts for what they are, miracles. Pitiful to be so absorbed by our own desires . . . that we cannot recognize those small and frequent miracles by which we live.[46]

Freelance Writer

With the exception of the short period during World War II when his family lived in Bettendorf, Iowa, Keillor never lived outside Minnesota until 1987, when he departed for Copenhagen. After leaving Brooklyn Park, however, he moved more than a dozen times within the state, residing most of the time in the Minneapolis – St. Paul area but also in St. Cloud, rural Freeport, and, some years later, in the small town of Marine On St. Croix (near River Falls, Wisconsin, where in 1992 Keillor placed a century-old cabin on an 80-acre wooded lot). By quitting his job at KUOM and moving to Stearns County (St. Cloud and also a brick farmhouse near Freeport), Keillor was already demonstrating the restlessness that had prompted him to drop out of school in 1962. His double career would describe a wavelike cycle over the next two decades, as he would quit radio work to concentrate on his writing and subsequently return to the air. In 1969, having landed a poem in the *Atlantic* but still unpublished by the *New Yorker*, he had an interview with William Kling for an announcing job on KSJR-FM in nearby Collegeville. Joking about this encounter, Keillor recalled that Kling, looking "like a loan officer for a bank," said to the bearded writer, "I hear you write poetry." Keillor replied, "Not so much anymore; I'm getting over it," and accepted an early-morning time slot. Within the year he was mentioning a town called Lake Wobegon, Minnesota, on the air.[47]

Chapter Two

"A Prairie Home Companion"

It occurred to me that I needed a hobby. . . . I'd like to say funny things that couldn't be edited, that no researchers would examine' – and that led me to live radio.[1]

Thus Keillor described the motives that culminated in the creation of "A Prairie Home Companion," which aired live most Saturday evenings from 6 July 1974 until 13 June 1987. He was speaking particularly of the periods between 1968 and 1971 when he tried to support himself and his small family by freelance writing while living in the farmhouse near Freeport, Minnesota. Yet his characterizing live radio as a sociable, avocational activity, in contrast to the lonely, disciplined work of writing, corresponds to the long-standing distinction between radio performance and writing that he has made throughout his career.

Keillor took his first job in radio as a freshman in 1960 at the University of Minnesota's WMMR-AM. In 1963, after a year away from school and at the *St. Paul Pioneer Press*, he joined the university's educational and outreach station, KUOM, where he was public affairs director by the time he left in 1968. From 1969 to 1982, with a number of interruptions, he hosted live morning slots on public, noncommercial radio; they were called "The Morning Program" (1969-71), "The Old Morning Program" (October 1971 to December 1971), "A Prairie Home Companion" (December 1971-73), and "The Prairie Home Morning Show" (1976-82). It was on these early-morning programs that he developed a large regional following for his eclectic blend of recorded music, guest musicians, readings, greetings and announcements, comedy routines of various kinds, radio dramas, and mock-commercials for Jack's Auto Repair in Lake Wobegon. He honed his oral techniques and unconsciously laid the groundwork for the Saturday show before it premiered in 1974, and he did both the morning show and the Saturday broadcast for fully six years (1976-82), during which he was responsible for 12 hours of live air time in every typical week.

A Temporary Performer

While Keillor says that live radio seemed recreational in prospect, he demonstrated considerable ambivalence for such work over the years, leaving to write and returning when the need for reliable income proved irresistible. He quit the University of Minnesota's KUOM to devote himself more fully to writing, but he soon found another radio job in 1969 with KSJR-FM, the Collegeville station that was the first outpost of Minnesota Educational Radio (MER), later reborn as Minnesota Public Radio (MPR).[2] Keillor left his early-morning announcer's job at that station in 1971 to live "in virtual poverty" in the Freeport farmhouse, writing exclusively for the *New Yorker*. Nine months later he was in St. Paul starting up "The Old Morning Program," which he soon rechristened "A Prairie Home Companion." Now he was working out of a makeshift studio in the basement of the St. Paul Arts and Sciences Center for KSJN-FM, an affiliate of KSJR, which had just been upgraded from a retransmitting station for KSJR/Collegeville into a broadcasting facility destined to become the flagship station of the MPR network. Even though he was allowed considerable artistic freedom, Keillor left again in 1973 to give more time to writing, "only to discover that he wasn't writing that much more" (Letofsky). He was back in the spring, and on 6 July 1974 he hosted the first broadcast of his live Saturday-evening show, "A Prairie Home Companion" ("PHC"). In July 1976 he also returned to his morning slot, hosting "A Prairie Home Morning Show" until November 1982, when he needed time to write what became *Lake Wobegon Days* (though he continued working on the Saturday evening show). Two years after Keillor left the morning show for good, John Bream reported that "Keillor never thought he'd make his living talking. He never thought of radio as a real profession. Returning to his daily radio show is not in his plans. In fact, if it weren't for 'A Prairie Home Companion,' he doubts that he'd still be in radio. 'I'd still be writing.'"[3] Nearing the end of the 13-year run of "PHC," Keillor told *Writer's Digest*, "I'm a writer who is temporarily a performer. As a writer, I have gotten onto a track of writing material, for performance, which I feel only I can perform. But I'll get off that track."[4] When Keillor left "PHC" in 1987, one of his stated reasons was, "I want to be a writer again." Yet on 25 November 1989, a little over two years later, he premiered "American Radio Company of the Air" live from Brooklyn, New York.

In the same interview in which he spoke of live radio as a "hobby" he also indicated that entering radio as a career was a Hobson's choice. Of his unsuccessful attempt to land a job with the *New Yorker* or the *Atlantic* in 1966, he said, "I had a choice between radio and writing. . . . I never got a writing job, so I chose radio" (Traub, 112).

Perhaps radio work would have remained just a way to support his writing if Keillor had not been granted room to experiment and develop his own brand of live radio, especially in the years from 1969 and through the early years of "PHC." But while he often ridiculed the cultural pretentiousness and educational tone of public radio, he was allowed to go his own way, and to go that way substantially enough that his performative, "fun" work in live radio contributed directly to his major achievements as a writer. The time stolen from his lonely writing table to speak into a microphone was well-invested in the development of an imaginary space that he started calling Lake Wobegon as early as 1969 on his morning show out of KSJR in Collegeville. While he claims it was his reputation as a *New Yorker* writer that allowed him to get away with as much as he did on public radio, his best-known books, *Lake Wobegon Days* and *Leaving Home*, derived essentially from the material he composed for performance and not from what he wrote expressly for the printed page.

Keillor's immense popularity and concomitant financial success as a writer was made possible in large part because he had a huge, enthusiastic following from his radio shows. That the horse of the radio show should pull the cart of his greatest literary success is an irony fully discernible only in light of Keillor's early and singular devotion to the task of writing words for the permanence of print, as opposed to those he wrote to fly away over the air.

Talking for Pay

Keillor had planned on being a writer from an early age but entered radio more or less on the spur of the moment: as a freshman at the University of Minnesota in the fall of 1960 he saw the Danish Royal Ballet perform and, charged with fond memories of "a Danish exchange student at Anoka High School," "got the dreamy idea of interviewing lovely pale long-legged Danish girls for the student radio station, WMMR. I went up to the studio . . . , screwed up my courage and slipped in and proposed my radio idea, 'The Danish Royal Ballet: A Portrait in Sound,' not knowing how short-handed they were. They made me a staff member on the spot and gave me a daily fifteen minute noontime newscast a few minutes after I arrived."[5] The exchange student was Ulla (Strange) Skærved, whom Keillor would fall in love with and wed just months after first seeing her again at the twenty-fifth reunion of their Anoka High School class of 1960, after they each had pursued careers in their own respective countries and had raised children from previous marriages. WMMR was a "closed circuit student radio station," and he went from there to KUOM, which broadcast to the wider community (Fedo, 34).

It was at WMMR where Keillor first experienced the worst technical difficulty that can befall a radio broadcaster: after months of pronouncing difficult foreign words in his brand new radio voice, an engineer informed him that the transmitter had been dead since he didn't know when – "since November" he guessed – leaving Keillor a Bartleby of the airwaves. (He told different versions of this cautionary tale over the years, and it probably underlies a similar incident in *WLT: A Radio Romance* [210].)[6] Explaining why he continued to work in radio, he talked about the salary; strapped for money, he saw an ad in the fall of 1963 "offering an announcing job at the university radio station for $1.85 an hour – 50 cents more than I received parking cars. . . . I liked radio just fine even though I was so shy I could hardly bear to be looked at when I was on the air."[7]

MER was always pleased to have a bona fide writer on board; for example, an October 1971 notice in the station's publication, *Preview*, which announces Keillor's resumption of the morning program, proudly alludes to his early publications in the *New Yorker*. As the station grew, it employed his literary talent by offering contributors collections of his work as premiums. In one of these, *G.K. the DJ*

(1977), Keillor managed in brief compass to both mock and praise public radio and convey that persistent ambivalence that dogged his radio career: "Most of these pieces . . . were written *against* radio, with a mind towards escaping from the studio and becoming an artist. I considered that my art was good workmanlike art, the carpentry of prose sentences, and no relation to what passed for art on radio: cueing up Schubert and pronouncing him 'Shoe*bear*.' The timid formalism of announcing classical music. . . . What a relief to quit and leave it behind" (*DJ*, 2).

Keillor's style as a radio announcer has never been characterized as "timid formalism," and while he played classical music, early on he played almost every other kind as well. Marvin Granger was station manager at the University of Minnesota's KUOM during the mid-1960s and alternated as host with Keillor on a variety program called "Radio Free Saturday." Granger remembers how upset the director of the university broadcasting service had been one week when Keillor played the entire Beatles album, *Sgt. Pepper's Lonely Hearts Club Band*, on the show. "Rock and roll," he is reported to have said, had no place on such a station. Granger also remembers a whimsical "hot-air-balloon traffic report," hilariously accomplished with the aid of a tape loop for realistic sound effects behind Keillor's calm voice-over (Fedo, 35).

Reminiscing on those early days in radio, Keillor emphasized how he was awakened to the power of folk music: "A concert by Pete Seeger or Jean Redpath was the next thing to going to church. . . . The U.S. government was corrupt, dishonest, but the culture of the American people was honest, decent, and profoundly sane, and the germs of this sanity were carried by folk songs." He listened to the records of university friends after arriving on campus in 1960 and discovered "all the corners of folk music," including "Almeda Riddle, Dock Boggs, Mahalia Jackson, Pete Seeger, Mississippi John Hurt, The New Lost City Ramblers, Lester Flatt & Earl Scruggs, the Carter Family, and Jean Redpath." A frequenter of the countercultural cafés and coffeehouses, he became acquainted in 1968 with Marcia and Jon Pankake, who were then graduate students and performers in a string band. Keillor credits the Pankakes with initiating him into the mysteries of the truly unusual music that later leavened the standard classical repertoire on all the public radio stations for which he would work.[8]

Neither rock-and-roll nor folk was savored by many of the regular contributors to the struggling public station that specialized in news and the classical repertoire. Some letters from listeners complaining about Keillor's departure from the classical format appear even in the November 1969 *Preview*, which is the first issue of the station's monthly organ to identify him as the host of "The Morning Program." Early staffers recall that William Kling (who returned from a leave of absence to be president, first of MER in 1971, and later of MPR) encouraged him: "Why don't you play a little Joni Mitchell once in a while," he said. "Garrison played the Beach Boys instead, and the rest is history."[9]

A Cowboy at the Prayer Meeting

In the month before Keillor's arrival on the scene, *Preview* indicated that henceforth, program listings would be detailed for "The Morning Program." Listings for October show exclusively classical music and news. But whereas Keillor's first program listing for 3 November 1969 includes classical recordings only (Dvorák, Beethoven, [Claude] Paul Taffanel, Telemann, Joseph Gungl), it opens whimsically: "Will the sun rise today? asks this continuing dramatic series. News at 8." The next day gave more classical listings, preceded by, "The waters of Walden Pond lapping in the background." Indications of what music was to be played dropped out entirely by 25 November, but the whimsical statements continued: "Where the beautiful people gather to brush their teeth" (2 December); "On Dec. 19, 1732, the first issue of 'Poor Richard's Almanac' was published by Benjamin Franklin. Late to bed, up at 6:45 makes you feel stupid and barely alive" (19 December 1969). For more than a week, each daily listing was a limerick:

> There was a young priest from Osakis
> Who got into a doctrinal fracas,
> Whether God, in his bounty,
> Included Todd County
> When he said He would never forsake us.
>
> (1 December 1970)

One listener wrote that Keillor's radio voice was "most enjoyable. His delivery is generally impeccable." But, this listener claimed, most listeners are "not interested in his discourses into unrequited love and the denier of the hair in Leadbelly's navel – and the music played to illustrate these theories."[10]

After hearing many such complaints, station manager Mike Obler sent Keillor a memo indicating that he could not be responsible for the loss of support from one particularly heavy contributor; severely irked, Keillor left the station in January 1971 to live on the royalty checks for the stories he had just started to sell to the *New Yorker*. A columnist reported that it had been "bluegrass that precipitated Keillor's departure from the station": driving to work from Freeport to the KSJR studio in Collegeville, he had listened to southern mountain stations and wanted to play the same sort of thing on his own show. "They put a note in my box one day telling me not to play so much country music," Keillor said. "I didn't like it that they would tell me such a thing in the first place, and I didn't like it that they did it by putting a note in my box. That's the way you fire someone, so I took it that I was fired."[11] Some longtime MPR staffers still chuckled 20 years later over a parody of *Preview* that Keillor produced around this time (*Preview* became a section within *Minnesota Monthly* in 1976). Keillor named names and let air out of the educational, esthetic, and high-cultural aspirations of the station as reflected in the features and program listings; the privately circulated parody may have been a sort of parting shot from this round peg in what seemed at the time a very square hole.

Keillor's allure to many of his fans (and bane to his detractors) on the early morning shows was his unpredictability, his unique blend of hipness with a paradoxically populist spin. He has frequently talked of hating the pretentiousness of public radio, and often felt miscast as an announcer on educational and public radio: "I started doing a classical music show, 6 A.M. to noon," Keillor said in 1976 of his days at KSJR. "But it was pretentious of me to sit and play music I didn't know, and to sit there and play opera and try to guess at the pronunciations. So I started playing other music I did know" (Letofsky).

The root of the problem was not merely the programming; it struck much deeper, having everything to do with the cultural and personal nuances of his radio persona. He was powerfully attracted by the gravy-smooth tones of professional radio announcers and learned to imitate them well. Yet he was also disgusted with his own tendency to indulge this admiration and perfect the "educational radio voice" at KUOM. Such voices, he came to believe, were artificial and, moreover, did not accord with his own origins and native associations. In 1989 he entertained Public Radio Conference participants by telling them how on his first radio shows he "developed a voice . . . that was basically Midwestern . . . but a Midwesterner who had lived in New York for a while and had spent a lot of time in Oxford and who maybe had a French mother."[12] Cultivating such a voice was vain, he gradually realized. He did not want to sound like an oracle but "to be perceived as a person sitting in a studio reading wire copy, like somebody sitting across the breakfast table from you reading an item." On his morning show he began to use his "Stearns County voice," replete with the down-home inflections and nonstandard grammar presumably used by "ordinary people" – the voice that sounded to him increasingly like that of his father (Letofsky).[13] (Stearns County is roughly 60 miles northwest of Minneapolis, and Freeport, Collegeville, St. Cloud, and Sauk Centre are all within its boundaries; if Mist County, in which Lake Wobegon is placed, were not wholly imaginary, it would certainly border Stearns.)

Keillor's radio voice has been described as "warm and supple as the soft nap of old corduroy," as a "slow midwestern voice," as "thick as molasses and soft as a sigh," but Keillor's characterization of the voice of Walter "Dad" Benson – a Crackerbarrel Philosopher and star on the fictional radio station WLT – best captures what Keillor's own voice came to sound like on the air.[14] It was Dad's voice that made "Friendly Neighbor" thrive from the start: "that warm dry Minnesota voice with a slight burr, a little catch in it, a little hesitation that got the listener leaning forward."[15]

KSJN in Downtown St. Paul

Keillor has been called moody or even dictatorial, and throughout his career he has been prickly at times and has insisted on considerable autonomy. Kling and others at MER recognized his talent, however, and contrived to find a slot for him in their programming mix.

That slot was filled with something on the order of comic relief. He was a combination comedian and genius-in-residence, given to fits of oddity or excess, which troubled or alienated many important station supporters, yet attracted even more new listeners, among them a great many who were not previously devotees of public radio. Some such logic must have guided the negotiations that led to Keillor's return to morning radio in October 1971, as he was offered more leeway and more resources when he came back. According to Marvin Granger, Kling had recognized Keillor's "genius" and had sent Granger out to the farm in Freeport to beg him to return to the new, more strategically situated KSJN broadcast facility in St. Paul (Fedo, 60).

In a fictionalized account of his return in *Preview*, Barry Zarathustra (Granger?), an advertising agent for Jack's, came out to Freeport and persuaded Keillor to return since research had convinced Jack that to reach his market KSJN needed "a type of person who never fully grew up and who needs a steadying influence in the dim pre-consciousness hours." In this humorous first-person essay Keillor portrays himself as a sort of rustic simpleton, easily bamboozled by the slick ad man from the city: "So long as Jack's had such confidence in me, I felt I could do the job so I sold the White Rocks, moved to the metropolis, and tried to bring a little certitude to the airwaves. . . . I got to believing that I was a real radio announcer and not just an ordinary fellow from Freeport, with a voice that made men and women buy Jack's products."[16]

The new morning show, briefly called "The Old Morning Program" and from December 1971 "A Prairie Home Companion," took the air in October 1971 from 6:30 to 9 A.M. over KSJN and the growing network of affiliated public radio stations. *Preview* heralded Keillor's return, using one of Keillor's on-air personae in the title, "Harley Peters Returns!": "Harley Peters (alias Garrison Keillor) the extension sex agent whose advice columns recently appeared in the *New Yorker*, and whose 'Sex Tips' show was heard over KSJR/KSJN regularly until last January, returns to the air this month. . . . Harley will team with Jack of Jack's Auto, Mr. Fist and other personalities to co-host 'The Old Morning Program' . . . beginning October 1."[17] Keillor was apparently impersonating a variety of comic personae. He would do the voice of Jack on occasion and also Mr. Fist, "a man who when the world yells at him he yells back." Keillor's pieces in the *New Yorker* abound in parody and are often written in the first person; analogously, his Mr. Fist routine was delivered as an oral parody of public service radio announcements. In his testimonial Mr. Fist encourages listeners to be "hard-nosed" and to complain, for example, about bad food in restaurants; he promises that "whenever somebody is making life hard for you, call for Mr. Fist. I'll be there in a minute, invisible, putting new energy into your body and fresh insults into your mouth."[18]

Announcing Keillor's return to the morning program in 1971, columnist Will Jones wrote, "A chastened management not only will allow Keillor to play country music if he wants to, but is listening to his suggestions about bringing groups . . . into the studio for live sessions." When Jones asked Keillor how he reacted when called "weird and far out," he said he was surprised: "With the radio program, I set out deliberately to be warm and folksy and Middle American and down to earth. It's the most down-to-earth thing I've ever done, and I have to believe people are putting me on when they say it's far out." The following week Jones reported that the "the returned, revived, retreaded Garrison Keillor . . . has proved to be a safety menace. I nearly drove off the road twice yesterday morning, on the way Downtown, cracking up as Keillor began his second Annual Chicken Music Festival, featuring chicken-themed music all the way from a 16th-century German 'The Little White Chicken' to the Beatles to Mississippi John Hurt doing a song in which he spells C-H-I-C-K-E-N to Tiny Tim singing 'Chickery chick' " (Jones, 6D). The list of guest musicians who would be appearing with Keillor on the live show included his old friends Marcia and Jon Pankake and Butch Thompson, the jazz pianist and clarinetist who would be a "PHC" regular.

Three years before the first live broadcast of his Saturday evening show Keillor had already developed many of its basic elements, including Jack's spots, Lake Wobegon, live performance with guest musicians, and informal banter, often abandoning his Announcer's voice and posture and assuming various comic roles and poses.

All Tracks Lead to Jack's

Given wider scope to follow his whims, Keillor also began to expand
the dimensions of Lake Wobegon, which on one occasion he said he
started using "simply as a way of putting my relatives and people I
had grown up with in a fictional context, so as not to hurt their feelings. I liked the word 'woebegone.' To me it sounded vaguely like an
Indian word, so I could use it and also get some of the English
meaning of the word – you know, 'bedraggled' – and still claim that
it meant something else."[19] More frequently he explained the origins
of Lake Wobegon as an afterthought, a place to situate Jack's Auto
Repair, the first and most famous of his imaginary sponsors during
his tenure at KSJR (1969-71). "I dearly love public radio," he told an
interviewer in 1982, "but to me radio isn't radio without commercials."[20] Keillor reportedly has said that the name of his first sponsor
was inspired by a real Jack's Auto Repair, a shop made over from a
church building that he passed whenever he drove Highway 10
between Freeport and the Twin Cities (Fedo, 63). When fans started
sending photographs of various real Jack's Auto Repair shops, "I
could see if I didn't come up with a location, I was going to be in
trouble," said Keillor. "So, I came up with Lake Wobegon. Then
someplace along the line I started telling stories about the people
who live there. God knows, it was nothing I had planned out. . . .
The whole show is just a hobby that got out of hand" (Radel, B9).

It is clear, in any case, that Keillor named the town and impro-
vised its history, geography, and traditions as he went along, and this
process began a good while after he had started making jokes about
small-town life. Even after he coined the name, however, he did not
exclusively identify Lake Wobegon as the show's location or the site
of the imaginary businesses he would promote. One morning, for
example, he greeted his listeners, "Good morning, this is Clive
Sedlak speaking from the front porch, 1423 Maple Street in Your
Town, U.S.A. where once again it's time for 'A Prairie Home Companion.'" In a station identification spot he warned that any
rebroadcast "or its use in slide presentations, lectures, or private
conversations without written consent of Jack's Auto Repair of
Freeport is expressly forbidden." Yet in a sign-off bit on the same
program Jack's location is given as Lake Wobegon but "Mr. Keillor's
socks [are] courtesy of Clifford's Sock Boutique of Freeport."[21]

Keillor's identity as host of the morning shows from 1969 and into 1973 was a riddle to many listeners; he was impossible to pigeonhole, and his comic inventiveness aroused the amused wonder of regional listeners. However "warm and folksy" Keillor's morning-show banter may have seemed to listeners, it was not called nostalgic. Indeed, it seemed almost racy considering the format of KSJR in 1969, which, according to journalist Mike Steele, was "that of an old lady, merrily spinning Beethoven between soft, but ever so earnest, appeals for contributions." Steele called the program "provocative," saying that it had been a "much-talked-about and chuckled-over addition to early-morning listening, especially when [Keillor] did his political satires or switched to Jack's Auto Repair where Jack, worried about a right-wing takeover, was offering humanities night courses with his tuneups."[22] Apropos of Jack's multifariousness Keillor says, "I wanted to keep Jack's garage. But I kind of ran out of ideas. I don't know that much about cars" (Letofsky). Jack was soon in publishing as well as education, selling anything from Christmas cards, gifts, and clothing to power bracelets and terror-fighting lessons. The mock-commercials were not sentimental but witty – the show sparkled along, seeming to listeners unconventional, hip, and almost countercultural: a whiff of the anti-establishment odor of the 1960s lingered about it. The small-town material seemed a kind of "put-on," a send-up of the sticks from a citywise perspective. And though it was not curmudgeonly or bitter, neither was it laced with heartwarming insights about the durable values and perseverance of provincial characters.

Keillor retrospectively characterized "PHC" as a "hobby that got out of hand," but he may well have been speaking in one of his favorite early roles, that of the Amateur, making the origins appear more serendipitous than they actually were.[23] Not only had Keillor grown up listening to radio, but there is evidence that he was a conscientious student of old-time radio, as well as a talented improviser. In the summer of 1973, for example, Keillor reviewed tapes of 30- and 40-year-old radio programs, including those of Bob DeHaven, Cedric Adams, and Gene Autry that included storytelling and exotic sound effects. "Twin Cities radio archivist" Bill Lund played such tapes to Keillor (Fedo, 71). Such research probably provided him with material for his WLT stories (and *WLT: A Radio Romance*) and also prepared him for "PHC." Even so, the evolution of Lake Wobegon and its creator's persona in fact did have much to do with the improvisational spirit of the early morning and the Saturday-evening shows on into the 1980s.

Prairie Home Previews

Many of the most popular "PHC" shows and monologues were those that dealt, often very emotionally, with civic and religious holidays. While the Keillor of the pre-1976 morning show was not known for personal, intimate, emotional reminiscence, these dimensions are discernible in three special programs he recorded in the studio during 1973. There is "Baseball" (aired 4 July 1973), "A Minnesota Thanksgiving" (aired 22 November 1973 and rebroadcast in 1974 and 1975), and "Home for Christmas" (aired 25 December 1973). None of the three were performed before a live audience, but together they demonstrate how KSJN had begun to make use of Keillor's abilities as a versatile host-announcer and raconteur whose range exceeded what the morning, drive-time radio slot afforded.

The "Baseball" show made use of live performances of turn-of-the-century baseball music by Vern Sutton (who sang on both the first and the last and many other "PHC" broadcasts) and Philip Brunelle (another "PHC" mainstay) on harpsichord. Keillor introduced baseball songs, interviewed a colorful old-time ballplayer, and near the end of the show delivered a first-person tall tale about his own glory days with the Freeport Flyers. In his best Stearns County voice, in the unhurried, pseudosincere intimacy of the deadpan Yarnspinner, he tells how back in the twenties they called him "Old Hard Hands"; the lies grow richer as he recalls the time his team substituted animals for human players, and in the gathering dark the opposing team could not see that it was an Aberdeen angus on the mound and that the fly balls were caught in mid-air by a chicken-hawk. Later on "PHC" many of the mock-commercials and talks about Lake Wobegon were equally tall, and in one pre-1984 monologue Keillor told of a softball game in which animals were substituted. It was not until roughly 1980, however, that Keillor consistently narrated his Lake Wobegon monologues in the first person, portraying himself as an ex-smalltowner who personally experienced the events he narrated. Keillor is a fan of the Minnesota Twins, and on the evening show he frequently reported the exploits of the Lake Wobegon Whippets, who would sometimes play the Freeport Flyers in Wally "Old Hard Hands" Bunsen Memorial Field.

Both the Thanksgiving and the Christmas specials include seasonal and religious music and Keillor reading poems or telling historical anecdotes and "just talking" or storytelling in a warm, heartfelt manner that anticipates the mood of holiday monologues of the eighties. The voice is essentially that of the public-radio announcer, less given to Stearns County inflections and less spontaneous and conversational. Without the presence of a live audience Keillor's talk about the origins and history of Thanksgiving celebrations risks sounding didactic and lacks the fuller sense of personal responsiveness, the "companionship" that had so much to do with the success of his monologues on "PHC." The Thanksgiving show is notable for the personal and nostalgic reminiscence of Keillor's childhood memories. After playing "Blest Be the Tie That Binds" he softly tells about how his grandparents came to farm in Anoka County in 1880, raised eight children, suffered good times and bad. In meditative tones he details what was eaten at the Thanksgiving meal and how the adults talked afterward about hard times, the harvest, the virtues of Fords as compared to Chevrolets. Such talk about holiday celebrations in days gone by, family histories, menus, and automobiles was often the typical substance of the "PHC" monologue, but it took six to seven years before the personal, much less the intimate, tonalities, the meditative and confessional elements, began to rival the more usual drolleries and jokes about small-town life.

Another topic of great importance in the monologues of the middle and late "PHC" was the importance of storytelling, especially within the family circle. Here at the end of the Thanksgiving reminiscence Keillor tells how guests went home late because grandfather Keillor was a great storyteller, and he evokes a wistful mood as he characterizes the nature of James Keillor's stories, "whose real glory and strength is not in their plot line or in the structure of them but rather in a fine sense of detail, characterization, and mimicry of voices. And on Thanksgiving Day, after dinner with friends and relatives around him, feeling kind of mellow and receptive – he must have been in fine form out there in the living room with the smell of goose grease in the air."[24] Just as the storyteller in Keillor's narrative provided a center around which the family circle coheres, so Keillor would later pose as a storytelling father who could reconstitute the studio and the vast, unseen "PHC" audience of the as one large family during the spell of the monologue.

Keillor's departure from his morning show in late 1973 was in actuality a leave of absence from daily radio work, as plans were already afoot at MER as early as the summer of 1973 when Bill Kling mentioned the possibility of "a Saturday version of 'Prairie Home Companion' specializing in live music from across the state."[25] During that year he had already been bringing guests into the studio on his morning program, but, as Kling recalled in 1987, Keillor "thought that the show might get a bit of a lift if we did some live music from a theater or concert hall." The first such show (Kling was not speaking of the three special shows described above) was broadcast from "the cold, alley-like auditorium of the Arts and Science Center in St. Paul": "A very few people gathered that morning to listen to an array of performers that could charitably be called 'eclectic' – including a Western singer who sang 'Old Shep' and a glass-harmonica player."[26]

In the early 1970s Keillor had been giving public poetry readings, sometimes on the same bill with such poets as Robert Bly and Michael Kincaid, and more frequently with Robin Raygor, Gregory Bitz, and Tom Arndt (Fedo, 66-68). "The Minnesota Grain Show," a stage show that had three performances in January 1974 at the Walker Art Center in Minneapolis, anticipated the "PHC" format and content in several ways. In addition to "Jack's Autoharp spot," "Jack's School of Humor spot," and "Jack's Auto Repair Lecture on Poetry," Keillor read his "Ode to the Street System of Southwest Minneapolis" (a humorous poem included in *G.K. the DJ* [1977]) and talked about WLT, presumably drawing on "Friendly Neighbor," the first of his stories about the old-time radio station that had only recently appeared in the *New Yorker*. Bitz and Arndt offered a movie and slide show, and other performers included Judy Larson and Bill Hinkley, later "PHC" regulars, doing musical numbers such as the Beach Boys' "Help Me Rhonda" (a familiar song on the morning shows and "PHC"), bluegrass, and dance numbers. Keillor emceed, and a reviewer commented that "if the Twin Cities intellectual community has a folk hero, it is Garrison Keillor."[27]

Before the end of 1973 Keillor had already assembled most of the components that would go into the Saturday evening show. By his own account he had not yet conceived of the idea for the evening show and was not consciously planning the "PHC" format. Nevertheless, his use of live music and his interaction and banter with musicians and other guests on his morning show had evolved substantially. On the morning show he had experimented with the concert-hall productions involving live music, and through his various experiences with Robin Raygor and others involved in "performance poetry," he had gained experience with staging, emceeing, and performing before a live audience, as demonstrated especially by the Walker Art Center shows in January 1974. On stage and on air, his repertoire of humor, sentiment, and self-presentation already adumbrated most of the comic poses, moods, themes, and subjects that would find expression on "PHC."

A Show like the "Opry"

The account of the origins of "PHC," as it has been told many times by Keillor and repeated by others, emphasizes the importance of Keillor's trip to cover for the *New Yorker* the move of the "Grand Ole Opry" out of its old gospel temple and into the glitzy Opryland in March 1974 (published that May).[28] His account of his experiences in Nashville became part of the legend of the show's origins:

> Sitting in a hotel room one Saturday night listening to it, I found it as wonderful as when we pulled it in on the old Zenith. It made me think of starting up a show like that back in Minnesota, and there in the Sam Davis Hotel, I made a list of musicians I particularly liked. . . . I went home, talked to Kling, and he took it hook line and sinker.[29]

The Damascus Road suddenness of his inspiration seems surprising in hindsight, yet Keillor's account of this moment of illumination in the hotel expresses what is certainly an emotional truth. For although his morning show, the experiments during 1973, and his Walker Art Center shows in January 1974 had prepared him for such a show, when asked about "PHC" origins and models Keillor insisted as late as May 1990 that, regardless of what MER had been planning, "the show remained unformed in his own mind until his visit to the Opry" (Lee, 191*n*15).

A 1974 chronology of "PHC" in the MPR archives indicates that three 90-minute shows were taped for later broadcast at the Walker

Art Center in Minneapolis on 7 April 1974. Performers included Vern
Sutton, Philip Brunelle, Becky Riemer, the Herrick Quartet, and the
Wolverines Classic Jazz Orchestra. The rundown indicates a particular title for the second show, "Faded Photos, Parlor Music and Old
Jazz," and thereby indicates how, from its inception, "PHC" aimed
to re-create old-time radio. Keillor presides as host, talks "about old
things," promotes *The Fallen Person: What Can You Do?* (a book
from Jack's Press), and does a spot for Art's Baits in Lake Wobegon.
The "talk" segments are brief; the Jack's spot – by far the longest – is
only several minutes long. The spots are, of course, parodies of radio
commercials and would have been familiar in form and content to
listeners of Keillor's morning shows. The spots are performed exu-
berantly and continue to be especially peppy and unpolished in the
early years of "PHC," often involving dialogue, with musicians reading parts and laughing uninhibitedly at their frequent miscues and
bloopers. The preposterous products and the spirited and unprofessional performance of the spots contribute to one of the intended
effects of the show as a whole: to sound like an informal gathering, a
casual Saturday evening get-together of friendly folks and family,
determined not to educate or improve but just to have a good time.
It was as if they had been coached by the ex-restaurateur, inventor,
and amateur media-theorist Roy Soderbjerg, who believed that radio
"was too simple a medium for adults. Spontaneity was what the doc-
tor ordered for radio – and the more mistakes the better! Goofs were
better than anything you could plan. 'Innocence must instruct
experience'" (*WLT*, 157).

Chapter Three

The News from Lake Wobegon

Nobody clapped at the end of 'em. You sat there without moving. Until when you finally got up hours later your legs had gone to sleep and you'd fall over. That was a sign of success for a storyteller. My uncle if he told his two stories back to back and told the extended versions, when he got to the end of 'em, whole roomful of people'd stand up and pitch forward. ("PHC," 4 December 1982)

The narrative about Lake Wobegon – which was at first not included in the format at all and in the early years appeared intermittently and typically lasted only three to six minutes – gradually became the most celebrated "PHC" feature. It lengthened to 15 and even 30 minutes and took a central, undeviating place in the show's lineup.[1] By the early 1980s critics hailed the monologues as the show's centerpiece: "This segment of the show," wrote one reviewer in 1982, "just might be the most remarkable fifteen minutes in American broadcasting."[2]

But the importance of this feature was not evident in the first "PHC" recording made available to listeners, *A Prairie Home Companion Anniversary Album* (1980), which includes four mock-commercials, a Keillor ballad, and 23 songs and musical numbers but only one "Lake Wobegon spot." No Lake Wobegon monologues had been published in *G.K. the DJ* (1977) or *Happy to Be Here* (1982, 1983). The word *monologue* does not seem to appear in rundowns of "PHC" performances until 13 June 1982, and before and even after that date the "News" segment is indicated most commonly only as "GK spot." Such a designation fails to differentiate it generically from the various mock-commercials, such as Jack's Auto Repair or Powdermilk Biscuits, which appear as "Jack's spot" and "PMB spot." By 1983, however, the importance and distinctiveness of the monologues had long been obvious to all concerned, and that year MPR produced the first set of four audiocassettes ("in a butter box") titled *News from Lake Wobegon*, which included only monologues, no songs or mock-commercials. Soon thereafter, from February 1984 to the end of "PHC" in 1987, the rundowns consistently employed the rubric "Lake Wobegon monologue" (or an abbreviation of the same), and by this point the feature had stopped moving around and took its own time slot shortly after the mid-point intermission. Fans now could set their radios and recorders for 6:10 P.M., CST, and be sure to catch the monologue.

Broadcasting Nationwide

In May 1980 MPR began live national broadcasts of "PHC" via the public radio satellite system, collecting a fee from the stations that chose to air it. Soon the show was no longer a regional phenomenon: in October 1980 it won the George Foster Peabody Award for broadcasting excellence, and its popularity and commercial viability contributed in large measure to MPR and four other public radio stations being able in 1982 to form American Public Radio (APR), a national network of stations to facilitate nationwide acquisition and distribution of that show and others without relying on National Public Radio (NPR). The head of NPR, Frank Mankiewicz, had in 1979 turned down MPR's request that NPR carry "PHC" nationally; he reportedly told Bill Kling the humor was too regional and would have insufficient appeal outside the Midwest. But "PHC" proved a hot enough item in the early 1980s that APR member stations had to pay an extra fee for the rights to air it.[3] Most were glad to pay, since the popularity of the show more than paid for itself when pledge week rolled around. After media reports of rivalry between NPR and APR, Mankiewicz denied that he had condemned "PHC" and paid it a backhanded compliment by saying that "if Garrison Keillor were to get laryngitis tomorrow, no station would carry APR."[4] When "PHC" aired its tenth-anniversary broadcast on 7 July 1984, it was heard by an estimated three to five million listeners over 218 stations "from Alaska to Key West."[5]

Keillor had become a radio celebrity, but the success of the monologues prompted him to cut back on the time he was allotting to his two radio shows, and he resigned from his morning show in April 1982, giving the same reason he had for leaving it in 1971 and again in 1973: to devote more time to writing for publication. The book he published three years later has remained the one for which he is best known, *Lake Wobegon Days*.

Though Keillor divided his time between writing the book and writing, planning, and rehearsing his remaining radio show, composing *Lake Wobegon Days*, *Leaving Home*, and parts of *We Are Still Married* was more than a matter simply of writing radio scripts with an eye toward subsequent publication. Keillor did take the manuscripts of his Lake Wobegon books through various stages and revisions, but much of his composing was a matter of cutting back and quarrying out from the sedimented mass of manuscripts originally written for performance on the air. And although he talked about Lake Wobegon on his morning program prior to 1971, the town portrayed in the book was not substantially like that portrayed on the radio for many years. The mythos of Lake Wobegon accumulated as layer upon layer of spots for imaginary merchants was delivered, as news notes, rustic letters, and eventually coherent stories were told week after week over the air.

How and why did Keillor move from jokes and humorous bur-lesques of small-town news to the sometimes poignant, local-color realism of some of the later monologues? What changes in form, tone, and narrative method and point of view took place? When and how did such changes come about? Answers to such questions must be given before the genesis of *Lake Wobegon Days* and *Leaving Home* can be understood.

High and Delicate Art

As Mark Twain explained in "How to Tell a Story," the humorous story differs structurally from the common joke or witty story in that the former "may wander around as much as it pleases, and arrive nowhere in particular; but the comic and witty stories must be brief and end with a point." But apart from the structural differences, what makes the humorous story "strictly a work of art – high and delicate art" is that "only an artist can tell it." It is "told gravely; the teller does his best to conceal the fact that he even dimly suspects that there is anything funny about it."[6] Nineteenth-century masters of the art named by Twain included Artemus Ward (Charles Farrar

Browne, 1834-67), Bill Nye (Edgar Wilson Nye, 1850-96), and James Whitcomb Riley (1849-1916), more widely remembered as a poet. To this short list of literary comedians (as these humorists of the period 1855-1900 are called in literary history) Mark Twain (Samuel L. Clemens, 1835-1910) must be added at the head.[7]

In carrying forward this tradition in the latter quarter of the twentieth century, Garrison Keillor must be recognized not only for his exceptional abilities as a literary comedian – such as his blurring of the narrative persona with the identity of the humorist, his mimicry of dialect, and his comic wordplay – but also for what Mark Twain believed was more crucial and most rare: a mastery of the art of *telling*. Keillor's affinity with the literary comedians is most evident in his writing and performance on the morning show and in the early years of "PHC." The genres that most closely link him to this tradition include his burlesques of commercial and public service announcements, his doggerel verse, his tall tales, and his humorous essays or speeches.

Like Twain, however, Keillor cannot be casually lumped in with one "school" or tradition. If some features of his narrative manner encourage comparisons with the literary comedians, others – his evocation of Lake Wobegon as a place and his investing it with the status of myth, his depiction of regional culture and characters, his characteristic use of a frame for his stories – invite comparisons to that other nineteenth-century literary tradition: local color (1867-1900). Prominent writers of humorous local color include Harriet Beecher Stowe (1811-96), Edward Eggleston (1837-1902), Joel Chandler Harris (1848-1908), and Twain.

The local colorists continued the tendency toward realism already evident in the writing of even earlier regional humorists who wrote about Yankee life Down East or about the raucous world of the Old Southwest (both groups are dated 1830-67): "Like the earlier humorists . . . and like the later humorists [literary comedians] in certain moods, the local colorists usually regarded themselves as truthful depicters of the life of a section of America during a certain period" (Blair, 126). Their careful representation of dialect and local customs, and their general concern for accuracy and detail in their portrayal of regional manners and native characters link these humorists with such later writers as Sherwood Anderson, O. E.

Rölvaag, Sinclair Lewis, and William Faulkner, all of whom have been mentioned in analyses of Keillor's Lake Wobegon material.

The key difference between the Lake Wobegon monologue and the assorted modes of other humorous talk on "PHC," from Keillor's own point of view, is that the monologue is a story and the other forms are not. In a press release prepared for the occasion of his announcement of the end of "PHC," Keillor discussed the reasons behind his movement toward storytelling, saying that he "wasn't much good at . . . the zippy stand-up monologue that we associate with variety shows, but I figured that comedy at least is a form of *writing* so I would stand a chance. Over the first couple years, failure as a stand-up comedy [*sic*] drove me towards storytelling."[8] From the beginning Keillor had more in common with the platform manner of the literary comedians and his storytelling relatives than with contemporary standup comedians; the literary comedians who performed on stage actually told stories, while today's standup comics are usually compelled to deliver a series of one-liners since the pressure to be unremittingly funny has increased and there is little tolerance for the slower-paced and less direct comedy of the humorous lecture, comic story, and tall tale. In a voiceover introduction to a television special in the fall of 1991 he said that what he does is humor, and "humor is comedy in slow motion."[9] Keillor never forsook joketelling, however, and continued to write snappy spots; he did not fail at this sort of comedy, but he tired of its constraints and eventually supplemented the episodic spots and mock-commercials with longer stories. The jokes in the early years were not satisfying to him, he said some years later; moreover, he came to feel that

> they were patronizing and tended to be sort of flat. Flat in the sense of being two-dimensional and not that interesting to do. Since I hit middle age and had a child and got a little older, I've had a dread of standing on a stage and just telling jokes. To be somebody like David Letterman I would consider a sort of performing Hell. To stand up there and simply do comedy off in this very detached and ironic position. All the people . . . , the writers who I care about and have thought about are not writers who adopted a straight comic voice. Mark Twain was a man who, both in his writing, his essays, and also his platform appearances, commanded quite a wide range and was able to tell funny stories and be witty but also was able to express all manner of feelings; to feel grief and rage and bitterness and a great deal more. (Interview, 10 August 1990)

He had told a first-person tall tale on his 1973 "Baseball" special and had celebrated his grandfather, James Keillor, as a vernacular storyteller on his 1973 Thanksgiving special, in the context of a first-person, autobiographical reminiscence about the warmth of home at the holidays. But home in the tall tale was Freeport, and in the Thanksgiving reminiscence it was Anoka/Brooklyn Park. On the morning show and for years on "PHC" he kept considerable ironic distance between the narrative persona and Lake Wobegon, and only gradually did he diminish that distance to nothing, presenting himself ultimately as a sometimes-nostalgic native son. In Keillor's hindsight accounts, his desire for greater artistic range seems to have driven him straight past the detached poses suitable for telling rube jokes and spots and toward the less ironic postures that developed with the longer tales. Yet before he gained widespread national recognition as the Sojourner from Lake Wobegon, a Crackerbarrel Philosopher in a new key, he spent six years experimenting with his "talks" on "PHC," varying form, content, and his own self-presentation.

Trying It Out on the Dog

During his days on the lecture circuit in the late 1860s Mark Twain learned the value of rehearsing and revising his material by touring the small towns for a month before coming into Boston. There the reaction of an audience of 2,500 would determine the lecture's commercial value. He told how in Boston he once watched an over-confident humorist flop dismally because he had come so highly touted that the management of the tour allowed him to skip the obligatory month of "trying it out on the dog." Though Twain started touring as a humorous lecturer in 1866, it was only after 1873 that he really began to move away from "more or less coherent discourse on a single topic" and started telling stories of the sort and in the anecdotal manner that he described in "How to Tell a Story."[10] It was as late as his 1884-85 tour with George Washington Cable that he made the discovery that he had to abandon the book and memorize his selections, since "written things are not for speech; . . . they are stiff, inflexible, and will not lend themselves to happy and effective delivery with the tongue – where their purpose is to merely entertain, not instruct; they have to be limbered up, broken up, colloquialized, and turned into the common forms of unpremeditated talk – otherwise they will bore the house, not entertain it."[11]

Keillor evidently understood this principle from the outset. Still, considering the many years Twain had been performing before he learned to throw away the script, it is not surprising that Keillor's first six years on "PHC" can be seen as, if not an apprenticeship, at least a journeyman period, replete with frequent tours around the Minnesota small-town circuit, including the April 1977 "Death March to the Prairie," 16 shows in 16 different locations in 16 days – almost as exhausting as the tour of The Shepherd Boys gospel quartet depicted in *WLT: A Radio Romance*.

Look Who's Coming through That Door

The first live broadcast performance of "PHC" was in the concert hall of the Janet Wallace Fine Arts Center of Macalester College in St. Paul, 4:30-6:00 P.M., on Saturday, 6 July 1974, before an audience of 12.[12] Musicians included Vern Sutton, Philip Brunelle, Bill Hinkley, Judy Larson, Ernie Garvin, and the Brescian String Quartet, performing a mix of old music-hall numbers, patriotic tunes, the Minnesota fight song, and classical music. In imitation of the radio variety shows of an earlier age, Keillor presided as host and master of ceremonies and opened with the theme song, followed by welcomes, previews of the contents, and introductions of the principal guests. The theme song, "Hello Love," first recorded in 1974 by country-western singer Hank Snow and ostensibly sung by a lover addressing an old flame who has been absent and estranged, proved eminently adaptable to the context in which Keillor used it.[13] As opening number for the entire 13-year run, it provided a invitation not from a lover to a beloved as much as from a companionable host and paterfamilias welcoming listeners into the warmth of an imaginary family circle, addressing them affectionately and asking, "Where in the world have you been so long?," telling them they have been sorely missed during the intervening week. A verse added and occasionally used by Keillor addressed the show's links with old-time radio:

> I've heard it said for oh so long
> Live radio is dead and gone

I've heard it so often I guess it's true
But here we are, and there are you.[14]

Not quite 32 on the occasion of the first show, Keillor may have
been a bit young to make a convincing father figure, though even in
his thirties he often lamented how his years were weighing on him,
mainly in a spirit of humorous self-deprecation. Still the role of genial
host/father is evident in the show's first year, though the impression
of his venerability is diminished by two of the guests featured on the
first live broadcast: Bob DeHaven, a veteran old-time radio host-
announcer, and Ernie Garvin, an early commercial jingle and song
writer. DeHaven and Garvin perform, in a sense, the ritual "laying on
of hands," ordaining Keillor into the service of live radio. DeHaven
had been host of WCCO-AM's "Good Neighbor Time," the last
regularly scheduled live music show in the Twin Cities. It was he
who "read the school closings and never read mine," said Keillor. In
their banter, DeHaven addresses Keillor as Gary (the name used only
by intimates and by Keillor when referring to himself as a youth),
thereby reinforcing the sense that an investiture of some sort was
taking place. Keillor's new job, said DeHaven, was "making
something out of nothing," reviving a lost art, without which radio
has been stunted and hurt. Keillor in turn recalled how as a boy he
skipped his swimming lessons to go to the studio performances of
"'Good Neighbor Time" and continued listening to DeHaven when
he was a parking lot attendant at the university.[15]

On subsequent shows Keillor would occasionally address the
audience as "children," but in the company of a man who called him
Gary, and given the almost makeshift character of this initial broadcast, his role as folksy Companion and Amateur superseded that of
Fatherly Host. His companionability is evident in the broadness of
the Stearns County accent (in a higher pitch than he would later
use). His affectation of informal, rustic, and seemingly artless speech
was in fact quite deliberate. Recalling the first show, he wrote,
"Nervous about emceeing, . . . I wrote out every word I would
say – from 'Good afternoon, ladies and gentlemen . . . ' to 'Thank
you very much.'"[16] His determination to control the effect his show
created was consistent with his stringent standards as editor of the
Ivory Tower and his characteristic concern for detail and dedication
to the nuances of style in his writing for publication. Thus his talk,

like his later monologues, was carefully written out beforehand; yet it is clear from his colloquial delivery that he did not read from a script but worked from memory, spontaneously adapting what he recalled to the dynamics of the moment and the response of the live audience.

In 1983 he gave a description of the regimen he settled into for preparing the oral monologues:

> I usually will just write a first draft, which for me is about four or five double spaced pages, and I will try to make that draft something that a person could actually stand on a stage and say, but once you get on stage with it, it doesn't always work out that way, so I just find it to be a simple process of editing to write a rough first draft, look at it a couple of times, then go on stage and do something that is more or less based on the draft. It's hard, too, to write for voice. I think playwriting is probably the hardest writing there is.[17]

Many if not most of his listeners over the years would be fooled by his simulation of spontaneous, improvisational talk. His mastery of "studied artlessness" and pose as Amateur again recalls the platform manner of Twain, who had imitated not only the yarnspinners he observed in the mining camps during his western years but professionals like Artemus Ward. Indeed, a description of Twain's delivery, with allowances for differences in dialect, provides fitting commentary on this first and many subsequent Keillor talks: "A good mimic, assuming the role of the stammering amateur, he could delight an audience with an imitation of confusion. . . . His way of speaking . . . was so nonchalant, so remote from stylized elocution or resounding oratory that audiences believed he spoke extempore. As if taking part in a living room conversation, he drawled lazily along like a clever improviser inventing a monologue on the spur of the moment" (Fatout, xxiii). The air of informality and community is maintained and reinforced when Keillor converses with the audience and when, near the end, he asks them to join in singing the old Roy Rogers theme song, "Happy Trails to You."

Perfection on "PHC" involved planning for a certain quantum of imperfection, because Keillor apprehended from the outset that a few mistakes paradoxically intensified the audience's perception of the show's naturalness. Yet studied artlessness, though a consistent "PHC" principle, cannot account for the poor technical quality of this and other early shows. There are considerable periods of dead air, voices speaking off-mike, and unpleasant feedback – many more flaws than needed to eradicate a perception of excessive slickness. Moreover, Keillor's pose of Amateur is surely heightened by genuine jitters.

Even so, after he sang "Hello Love," he called attention to his vulnerability and used it in a short speech – there was no "News" monologue – to ingratiate himself to the audience: "How did that sound?" he asked. Self-consciousness and uncertainty were the part of the message as well as the ethos as he talked about how doing a live show was "such a long way from where I started out in radio at KUOM," where he could sit in the studio playing long, classical records and "didn't have to worry about the audience not liking the music." Turning up the irony, he warned the audience that "in a live show like this we get into a lot of cheesy music – folk music and country music. . . . And we don't know if it's any good because there's no criticism. Like polka music – there's no music critic down in New Ulm writing reviews of polka music down there." That he was joking became increasingly evident as he hyperbolized about the oddities that this show might include, such as lectures on macramé, a talk by the mayor, or Tibetan nose-flute music. That most of his self-deprecation is meant to be discounted as mock–humble pie is also evident from the presence of DeHaven, who was introduced in this same brief speech. DeHaven, the epitome of the professional radio announcer, is after all the guest of Keillor, who, no matter how he may protest his ill-preparedness and inexperience, has just told how he has been in radio since his college days; that he should be host to such an icon underscores the comic incongruity generated by his pose as Amateur, essentially a "pose of inferiority."[18] This opening talk deepens the sense of intimacy and one-to-one communication between the companionable host and the listener – one of the principal functions later served by Lake Wobegon monologues.

The Rise of Powdermilk Biscuits

The most obvious continuity between Keillor's morning show (which he had left in November 1973 but resumed July 1976) was the inclusion of mock-commercials and public-service announcements for Lake Wobegon establishments. The first live broadcast includes spots for Powdermilk Biscuits, Art's Baits, and two for Jack's, plus the "Presentation of [the] Doud Vocal Award." Wilma Haskins Doud is said to be the founder of the Lake Wobegon Academy of Song, on whose behalf an award for vocal is presented to Vern Sutton. Art's Baits, right across the bay from Jack's in Lake Wobegon, is offered for sale, since sewage has killed the fish, and boats in the marina are offered as homes free from property tax as the water is so low (this establishment remained by the lake but was known as Art's Baits and Night O'Rest Tourist Cabins).

The Powdermilk Biscuit Company was most likely conceived as a parodic poke at the Pillsbury Corporation, headquartered in the Twin Cities. Slogans for the product in an early spot included "Win one for the biscuit," "Man does not live by bread alone," and finally, " 'Nothin' says lovin' like something from the oven' – no, that's not quite it" ("PHC," 3 September 1977). Though the show was not being broadcast nationally at this point, listeners would not have had to be Minnesotans to recognize the last slogan as a Pillsbury jingle. A quasi-annual event on the early "PHC" was the Powdermilk Biscuit Mouth-Off, which featured contestants making music via "dental percussion" or other unusual techniques; this event involved a more "inside" joke that played off the annual Pillsbury Bake-Off (Lee, 193n37). Powdermilk Biscuits (or PMBs) became the preeminent sponsor on the show, overshadowing Jack's enterprises, which had flourished even before there was a Lake Wobegon. The PMB spots contributed more to the lore of Lake Wobegon than any of the other mock-commercials partly because there were so many of them; yet the nature of the product and the ways Keillor found to promote it provided a special impetus to the parallel evolution of the mono-logue. For just as the monologues moved beyond jokes and toward longer, more realistic, and even sentimental stories, so the PMB spots evolved until they also accommodated a sort of homely wisdom delivered with the deadpan earnestness of a Shy Person – a pose that was crucial to the development of the most successful narrative poses in the later monologues.

The biscuit commercials make mighty tall claims for such an humble product, and the taller the claim for the powers of the bis-cuit the sharper the parody of the familiar commercial premise that relief is just a purchase away. Since the PMBs were said to "help shy persons get up and do what needs to be done," it was not much of a stretch for Keillor to begin playing the part of Shy Person himself: "Our show tonight is brought to you by Powdermilk Biscuits, heavens they're tasty. They're the biscuits that make it possible for shy people to do a radio show. Yes, Powdermilk Biscuits give you the courage to do those things that you shouldda done probably a long time ago" ("PHC," 28 November 1975). The Shy Person is a role that fits Keillor only as a caricature, but it is one he played with more than enough plausibility to make shyness his trademark in the media and popular opinion.

Adding the Shy Person to his roles as Announcer, Companion, and Fatherly Host did more than help forestall boring the house by multiplying his range of expressible attitudes; it complicated and deepened the on-stage character of Garrison Keillor by allowing him to don different masks in sequence and, more importantly, by teaching him how to subsume several diverse poses within a single, complex persona. The resultant composite character could be a source of humor – since, as Judith Lee points out, a Shy Announcer is an anomaly and inherently funny (Lee, 60) – or he could deploy poses in such a way that evoked wistfulness or even sorrow. In any case, the PMB spots allowed Keillor to experiment with multiple poses, adding greater complexity until he was ultimately capable of conveying a wide range of attitudes, all of which emanated as plausible aspects of a complex on-stage ethos.

Eiron and *Alazon*

In the Powdermilk spot on the first live show, Keillor, in his pose as professional Announcer, interviews Bill and Judy, who mimic country bumpkins. They tell how they left trails of biscuit crumbs on the sidewalks to find their way home in the big city. One day Bill followed Judy's trail, and the two lonely countryfolk came together. The spot has some structural kinship to the frame tale used by nineteenth-century humorists in their efforts to adapt oral yarns to print, as in T. B. Thorpe's classic tale in the tradition of the Old Southwest, "The Big Bear of Arkansas" (1841), or Twain's "The Notorious Jumping Frog of Calaveras County" (1865). In both of these stories the formal language of "gentleman" narrator sets off the ungrammatical and colorful dialect of the inner narrator.

This comic pairing was familiar to the Greeks, to whom the gentleman character was known as an *alazon*, a presumptuous fool who says more than he knows; the unsophisticated character was an *eiron*, a wise fool whose rustic manner conceals his wit. Keillor gave his opening-night talk in the pose of the vulnerable, amateurish announcer – a posture of assumed inferiority (an *eiron*'s posture). For the PMB spot, however, he shifted to a posture of assumed superiority – a slick professional announcer (an *alazon*'s posture), which contrasted humorously with the exaggerated rusticity of Bill and Judy. The switch is accepted easily by the audience since Keillor's on-stage character is not perceived to be identical with either pose. Both the Amateur and the Announcer are simple masks, donned for the moment but then exchanged in new circumstances. A pose, in this sense, is more ephemeral than the writer or performer's persona. And while both pose and persona are masks, the former are less elaborate, more readily exchanged; yet neither pose nor persona can be assumed to represent the personality fully. Such minor role reversals were commonplace in the written and oral burlesques of the literary comedians, who typically signed their works and performed under pseudonyms and thus were always "playing a part" (Blair, 115).

On his morning show Keillor as Announcer had for years played the *alazon* to Jack's *eiron*. Jack was an *eiron* of a churlish and obstreperous sort, a con man or a trickster character whose ever-burgeoning, continuously changing businesses bear comparison with the entrepreneurial dealings of William Faulkner's Flem Snopes. Jack's spots remained a "PHC" fixture, although there were fewer of them after the first few years; still, his empire grew to include Jack's School of Thought, Dry Goods Emporium, School of Music, Warm Car Service, Scraps for Dogs, and many other ventures.[19] Yet the genre Keillor used more consistently to perpetuate his first Wobegonian was the rustic letter, a form well-known in the tradition of American humor since the popular success of the Jack Downing letters by the Down East humorist and newspaper editor Seba Smith (1792-1868). Downing was a small-town *eiron* from Downingville, Maine, whose naive and presumably "straight" letters home about goings on in the big city (Portland) provided a satiric or humorous subtext to the appreciative reader. The letters from Jack, sometimes read by Keillor or by a musician or guest, often directly attack and subvert the values of the host-announcer and the nature of his show. In a letter read on the air by Adam Granger, the jazz-loving Jack complains about all the "gospel songs and weepy country-Western ballads" and the "maudlin, meandering about Mom and apple pie" on the part of the host; he added a P.S.: "Tell Mr. Hello Love to get his beard trimmed" ("PHC," 12 May 1979). After the show had gone national and toured the East Coast, Jack wrote, "Every ten years or so the Eastern press rediscovers the Midwest. And suddenly we get a truckload of editorials about honesty and simplicity in the heartland and all the rest of it. I've lived here for fifty-five years and that stuff makes me sick" ("PHC," 14 November 1981).

Though presented in a different genre, Jack's comic juxtaposition with Keillor as Announcer works analogously to the contrastive pairing of Keillor with rustic lovers Bill and Judy in the PMB spot on the first live show. Yet whereas Keillor wrote rustic letters from Jack right down to the end and beyond the end of "PHC," Keillor soon altered the structure of the PMB spots and began to play both the *eiron* and the *alazon* himself.[20] In similar fashion, he would come to narrate the monologues not as a citified Announcer who might tell about or quote rustic Wobegonians but as a once and sometimes Wobegonian himself, who speaks out of a comic identity complicated by internal division. The Shy Person who found Powdermilk Biscuits a great help in coping with his job as radio announcer also manages to subsume at least two additional poses commonly associated with the character who narrated the late monologues: the Crackerbarrel Philosopher and the Preacher.[21]

The duality of the narrator's pose is audible in an 8 June 1979 PMB spot published on *A Prairie Home Companion Anniversary Album* (1980). He begins using the Standard English syntax, grammar, and pronunciation of the Announcer, enabled to be a professional by the powers of the product: "In the end and down deep it is Powdermilk Biscuits that really make it possible for us to stand out here on a stage with all these people staring straight at us." The Announcer shows off his perfect enunciation as he rips through a recital of all the drugs and stimulants people rely on these days, and as he nears the middle of the pitch Keillor slows down and segues into his Stearns County dialect, and musicians whoop and call out responses as congregants might to a revival preacher: "But I'll tell you there is one thing that does the trick for us and that is

Powdermilk Biscuits, made from that good whole wheat raised in the rich bottomlands of the Wobegon River Valley ['Amen!']. Yes sir. I'm talkin' biscuits now ['That's right, keep talkin'!']. Raised by those Norwegian bachelor farmers so you know they're not only good for you, they're also pure, mostly."

The rhythm and diction become colloquial, and the mask of the *alazon*/Announcer is exchanged for that of the *eiron*/Preacher. The pose of the Preacher, often a noisy and farcical burlesque of the stock revivalist, was common in PMB spots, which frequently included biblical quotations. This camp meeting flavor was in keeping with the abundance of gospel and country music on "PHC" and fit with the early ambition to re-create old-fashioned radio. While Keillor satirizes the radio preachers and gospel performers in *WLT: A Radio Romance*, the country Preacher on "PHC" could come across as a lovable *eiron*, whose words sound foolish while they ring true. The mellower Pastor David Ingqvist and the stern but lovable Father Emil were favorite characters in the later monologues, which also included ultraliberals like Father Todd and "grass-eaters" like Brother Bob or old Pastor Tommerdahl.

Doing a PMB spot 18 September 1982, instead of playing the Shy Person, Keillor used the pose of the Crackerbarrel Philosopher (with an admixture of Preacher). *Reader's Digest* had released a condensed version of the Bible, and Keillor called this an instance of an event that is difficult to satirize since it is so ridiculous that it defies exaggeration: "About all a person can do is just stand there and say, 'This is ridiculous!' Which isn't a lot. But it is something. And it takes strength even to do that little bit." The strength, of course, is enhanced by PMBs. His talk conveyed a touch of genuine righteous indignation, and he verged on sounding more like a moralizing commentator than a humorist. The pose of Preacher was risky in this way and was generally handled gingerly – no sooner taken up than ironized or denied – but unmistakable, nevertheless, in some PMB spots and many monologues.

The complexity of the ethos Keillor evolved is evident in a PMB spot in which the Announcer is a Shy Person with enough perspective and sufficient confidence and proficiency to explain the fragile psychological nature of the shy. He recalls how it was for him growing up shy:

I'm back on the playground during recess and there are two captains and they are choosing up sides. And I'm looking at them and I'm thinking, "Choose me. Pick me. Me, here – diss skinny kid with the thick glasses. Choose me." But I know that they won't. . . . So you see what shy people do is that they anticipate this moment of pain and so they say, "Oh I don't really need to, I don't want to," before you get around to the choosing up. . . . Somebody says to a shy person, "Why don't you – " "Oh I don't really need to – I don't really feel like it." . . . There are shy people who'll come down [to watch "PHC"] – they'll find their seats and see the other people sitting there and they'll say, "Would you mind if I just sat here real quietly for the next couple hours?" And then they say, "Oh no, I don't really need to; I'll just go home and listen to it on the radio." And we have to chase 'em out into the lobby and say, "No, they *want* you in that row. They voted on it. You were voted row monitor." Oh dear. Life is too short. ("PHC," 15 January 1983)

The composite character who offers this testimonial incorporates aspects of the Shy Person, Announcer, Companion, and Crackerbarrel Philosopher, playing each as needed. He starts as a Shy Person sharing a painful anecdote from his youth (another version of which is given in the "School" chapter of *Lake Wobegon Days*), and in the telling he mimics himself as a Young Shy Person and also the voices of the team captains. He makes a transition in the voice of the Shy Announcer and then imitates assorted shy persons and himself as Companion and Fatherly Host of the show, calling out assurances to the shy. He ends in the pose of the Crackerbarrel Philosopher or Preacher, who has clearly transcended the hangups of the Shy Person and whose final remarks turn the spot into a parable on the folly of excessive anxiety. Using several poses and a half-dozen differentiated voices, evoking emotions from pity to hilarity to reflection, the spot is a compact tour de force of the storytelling art.

News That Was Never News

In addition to mock-commercials, the morning-show format always included regular news broadcasts, and early on Keillor began to give news about Lake Wobegon to parody this other staple genre of radio. The idea of broadcasting fictional news items on a program that also included real news broadcasts made for an implicitly humorous juxtaposition, and the incongruity between the grave and momentous in real news broadcasts and the banal and trivial events of life in the rustic backwater redoubled the comic effect. The more mundane and inconsequential the news from Lake Wobegon, the better it was for the purpose of evoking this sort of comedy. The origin of the monologues in the episodic form remained discernible throughout "PHC," although in the latter years the news format was frequently little more than vestigial. Yet even after Keillor had begun telling some fuller, more unified narratives, many monologues before 1979 or so remained mere episodic lists, such as this truncated example:

> Tomorrow . . . the Whippets will play their final game of the season against the St. Albans *Allgemeinschaft* at the Wally "Old Hard Hands" Bunsen Memorial Stadium. . . .
>
> Monday . . . a big day at the Sons of Knute Lodge . . . The big ritual of the storage of the lawn chairs. . . .
>
> [At] Our Lady of Perpetual Responsibility Church . . . Father Emil will deliver a reflection on the life of St. Margaret whose sainthood was proven by the fact that she could always do the dishes in boiling hot water and always dusted the tops of things above eye level and she always ironed the sheets.
>
> [And finally] the Church of the Foursquare Gospel of Revealed Truth invites all those who desire baptism to join them at Art's Baits and Nite O'Rest Motel off the dock at noon tomorrow. . . .
>
> It's out in Lake Wobegon, where all the women are strong, all the men are good looking, and all the children are above average. ("PHC," 3 September 1977)

The limitations of such a form impeded the realistic development of the material and the evocation of sentiment or pathos, since the form precludes the sustained description and character development necessary to deeply engage the audience. With his emphasis on the ludicrous nature of the town and the triviality of what passes there for news, the humorist invites the audience to laugh conspiratorially with him from a position of assumed superiority. The joke in this instance is still largely at the expense of the little town, and those inside the joke can almost gloat as they enjoy their elevation above its stagnant, small-pond ways.

The simple machinery of this standing joke implicit in the concept of Lake Wobegon is evident in another humorous routine of the same period based on a similar pattern. When Keillor resumed his early-morning broadcasts with "A Prairie Home Morning Show" in 1976, he and his co-host, Tom Keith (who joined him in the role of

Jim Ed Poole after originally serving only as the show's engineer),
would regularly read aloud from the police reports published in the
Northfield [Minnesota] News. With mock-solemnity and sonority,
voicing over soft music, they would read the actual news items:
"10:30 P.M. – a dog was barking; 11:00, a door was left unlocked;
strange noises were reported." The comedians enlisted the listeners'
complicity with them against the people who reported, published,
and consumed such items; even if they lived in Northfield themselves, the listeners likely enjoyed a laugh at the inconsequentiality
of such news, which becomes even funnier as items are repeated.

The "mechanical inelasticity" of the police report invites
recourse to laughter of the sort described by Henri Bergson, who
said that "something mechanical encrusted upon the living" was
fundamental to the comic effect.[22] And this principle of anticipated
anticlimax made subsequent readings from the *Northfield News* more
enjoyable than the first, as on the first occasion the listener needed
to recognize the nature of the joke and had merely to enjoy it on
subsequent readings. Thus up to some ultimate and indefinite point
of saturation the backwardness of Lake Wobegon could remain
humorous and seemed even funnier as the number of those in on
the joke expanded and the stock of retrograde characters, customs,
and events increased. Similarly, the repetition of formulas and
patterns in the telling about Lake Wobegon remained part of its
essential comicality. Tag lines such as "the little town that time forgot
that the decades cannot improve" and the formulaic opening and
closing of the late monologues remained unchanged after a period of
experimentation partly because they provided a ready-made shape
and easy cloture and partly because the redundancy afforded a sense
of recognition and familiarity. Those hearing the tag the first time
could savor its comic ambiguity while listeners already familiar with it
enjoyed the sense of belonging in the circle of those in on the joke.

Such dynamics are the common stuff of joke-telling and standup
comedy, and Keillor never completely abandoned use of the superior poses, often employing the Professional Announcer in mock-
commercials for such fictional enterprises as The Fearmonger's
Shoppe and Bertha's Kitty Boutique. Such material recalls the burlesque patterns and verbal humor of the literary comedians, but the
evolved form of Lake Wobegon monologues is much more consonant
with the nostalgic realism of the local-color humorists and with the

even hoarier traditions of the tall tale. The monologue after 1980 retained remnants of the episodic chronicle, but when fully evolved it often took the form of a seemingly realistic, autobiographical narrative, calculated to induce not merely laughter but a range of emotional effects including tears. The news spots did not simply develop from episodic recitations of discrete items to occasionally linked anecdotes to plotted narratives; they evolved suddenly from chronicle to elaborately plotted, first-person-narrated tall tale, followed by a period of reconnoitering and experimentation with a variety of forms before the Lake Wobegon monologue achieved its typical structure and tone.

A Corner Lot in Lake Wobegon

Asked by Roy Blount, Jr., when he started "the long monologue," Keillor said that the first was "around 1976 maybe" (Blount, 14). Precise dating can be difficult, since Keillor almost never dated his manuscripts, but the actual air date of the first "long monologue" is almost certainly 13 December 1975. The working rundown indicates "Keillor: Lake Wobegon story (voice & little harp)" for just after 6 P.M. on a 90-minute show that began at 5:30. Keillor often played the autoharp on early shows, and as on this occasion he strummed it bardlike as he spoke (a practice he later abandoned, along with his cowboy hat, granny glasses, and beard). The story as recorded is a little over 15 minutes long, narrated at a rapid pace, in keeping with its action-packed plot; at its end Keillor indicates Lake Wobegon as his hometown, perhaps for the first time on "PHC." He said to Lee in 1989 that his turn to storytelling "seemed like a long leap," and he summarized this particular tale, though he did not recall the exact date:[23]

> The story was a real departure. . . . I did tell it. The story was written; it was a real manuscript, more polished than monologues to come. It was a story in which the Bunsens were there; there was a family feud of some kind. It was kind of dumb story, backing the car down the driveway. . . .
>
> It was nothing distinguished. But it was such a departure that my boss [Bill Kling] spoke to me about it and asked me if I was going to do more of this. He gave us absolute freedom doing the show, but he felt this was a change. I told him yes, I absolutely was going to do this. I felt that I had turned a corner. (Lee, 34)

Perhaps Keillor subconsciously recalled the title or titles, as two versions of the tale in manuscript are "A Corner Lot" and "Corner Lot Outside Town." The manuscript for this story is unusual in several ways. Many of the manuscripts for early spots and stories are typed out on paper torn off wire-service machines or on MER or MPR letterhead; some are handwritten, many are coffee-stained, and hardly ever do any bear name, date, or title. This manuscript not only has a title but two different titles for two of four versions, 23 pages in all, in four versions or drafts of seven, one, six, and nine pages, all of which are typed double-spaced on clean white paper; the two titled versions carry a typed signature at the end. Even in physical appearance the manuscript copy has more polish than most, longer than the four to five pages Keillor said were his average, and the multiple versions provide evidence of his struggle as he tried to "turn a corner."

In his rambling talk the previous week Keillor had embroidered for eight minutes his pose as Amateur Announcer. This was the first live broadcast following a five-stop tour that took him from Fargo, North Dakota, to Sioux Falls, Iowa, and he began by saying he was glad to be back but very nervous. He had always been "high strung," from before he was born, in fact, when his mother startled herself by shouting "good gracious." He learned at broadcasting school how to sound bored on the air even if you were excited; the final exam required a play-by-play account of the extraction of a wisdom tooth of your choice and he finally passed "on a lower bicuspid." He was speaking broad Minnesotan and assuming an inferior pose, but it was a transparently phony simplicity, a joker's pose, not suitable for the Sojourner from Lake Wobegon. Now that he's downtown, he continued, the State Capitol on one hill and Cathedral on the other are watching to see if his jokes go or not: "You fail down here and it's back to Fargo, where we were a few weeks ago. . . . I suppose I'd have to go back to Freeport to really feel like myself." After a string of such mock-confessional stretchers, he took a hand mike and, David Letterman–like, waded into the audience to "have a little contest," offering PMBs for good answers ("PHC," 6 December 1975). One week later he stood on the same stage and unwound a coherent story, which he not only narrated in the first person but in which he presented himself as a native son in exile.

In Lee's view, the later monologues' main distinguishing features are Keillor's inferior pose of a Wobegonian insider in place of "the Announcer's superior voice"; with this new pose we get a "realistic sense of ongoing life," partly effected by keying events in the story to the passage of time in the lives of the teller and audience and partly by using familiar characters whose lives seem to gain depth and complexity as details are added in subsequent stories. The transition was primarily effected, according to Lee, via an intermediate stage of narrative development as seen in the series of letters home from Barbara Ann Bunsen, which Keillor read as the monologue between the summer of 1976 and the winter of 1981. Introducing the letters, Keillor could continue to pose as the Announcer who ironized from on high about lowly Wobegon. Yet reading the letters in the first person voice of Barbara Ann, a native Wobegonian in exile, he adopts the insider's point of view, a shift that allows him a range of tones and effects unavailable to outsiders. After several years of experimenting with the monologue form, and especially after learning to appreciate the greater range of emotional effects afforded by the insider's perspective in the Bunsen letters, Keillor abandoned the epistolary mode and started telling stories in which he was himself an Exile from and a Witness to the town's intimate goings-on (Lee, 70-76). According to Lee, Keillor first presented himself as a Lake Wobegon insider in 1981, when he "adopted Lake Wobegon as his hometown" (Lee, 66, 70, 76).

Lee's account is convincing in its insistence on the importance of Keillor's switch to the insider's more sympathetic point of view, and in most other regards it seems sound as well. Still, however convoluted the transition, Keillor and Kling had reason to see the 13 December 1975 story as a dramatic turn, for even though there is only sham wistfulness in the narrator's attitude toward the town, he is a first-person Witness and Exile, a native of the town. Moreover, the story demonstrates that the recipients of Barbara Ann Bunsen's letters – her parents, Clarence and Arlene – were not invented subsequently to sustain and expand the illusion of Lake Wobegon's real existence (cf. Lee, 73). The Bunsens are leading actors, and it appears that Keillor first named them during the composition of the corner lot material, which predates the first letter of Barbara Ann by about half a year or more. In one untitled draft the family name of "Peters" is crossed out and "Bunsen" inserted; first names "Virgil" and "Bessie" are replaced by "Clarence" and "Arlene"; the new names are used in the other versions. None of the versions mention Barbara Ann.

Keillor's opening lines in the version of the story he told on the air are very close to the formulaic opening he consistently used some six years later: "This part of our program is brought to you by Jack's Auto Repair in Lake Wobegon and I'll tell you it has been quite a week in Lake Wobegon," he began on air. In one of the four manuscript versions he actually began with the later conventional wording – "Well it has been a quiet week in Lake Wobegon" – but did not speak the line perhaps because the action is anything but quiet.

It is Duane Bunsen's vain desire to glimpse himself in the rear-view mirror as he exhales smoke through the nostrils that causes him to crash the family Buick into the living room of his Uncle Clint and Aunt Irene Bunsen. This mishap reignites a smouldering feud involving the three Holm sisters – one of whom is Irene, Mrs. Clint Bunsen, and another is Arlene, Duane's mother, Mrs. Clarence Bunsen. Comic confusions and misunderstandings goad Clint to drive the Buick out of his living room and ram it into Clarence and Arlene's sunporch. Arlene then takes the wheel and smashes the car again into her brother-in-law and sister's place. The neighbors swarm out to take sides in the feud, and countless old scores are remembered as the people "went nuts out there," lighting bonfires in the roads and running the car back and forth, smashing at both houses. The Bunsens, having had their fill, made up their differences, "but the neighbors wouldn't listen to reason. 'One more, just one more,' they said, 'and we'll *have* it,' meaning Clarence's kitchen or Clint's family room, and someone brought a truckload of sand to improve the traction on the slope."[24]

Finally the Holm sisters, Arlene and Irene Bunsen, hugged and made up after 15 years of not speaking, and their public reconciliation inspired the crowd to start "confessing all the sins they had done in the grip of winter fever." As the smoke from their night of mayhem started to settle, they began to discuss their need for "a sheriff and a government and police powers," which Lake Wobegon lacks, since it was never incorporated. It was never incorporated because it is not on the map, and in this connection Keillor tells, probably for the first time, how Lake Wobegon was omitted from the map of Minnesota.[25]

Before the Civil War when Minnesota was not yet a state, "a man named Berg was put in charge of surveying county and township lines so that sections could be staked out and land could be claimed. . . . Berg's method was unusual, though it made pretty good sense. He divided the bunch into four teams, each led by a man who spoke English, and dispatched the teams to the four corners of the state, instructing them to survey in towards the center, where they could join maps in November." The crews were drunken and unreliable, and the maps of the four surveyed sections overlapped; to solve the problem the overlap was folded under, leaving Lake Wobegon "underneath Stearns County."

When a government commission studied the problem in 1926 they took no action because if they did "Moorhead would be in North Dakota, Minneapolis would be in St. Paul, and Duluth would be under fifteen foot of water . . . , so Lake Wobegon has remained a legal non-entity and people have learned to live with it and never complained about it except to ask the Highway Department to put up a proper sign on the Interstate (all we have had for many years is an arrow marked '6 miles'). Until this week, people seemed to feel it was wrong to ask for more" ("Lot").

The gross impossibilities are salted down with homely and realistic details, and in the classic deadpan manner Keillor moves toward the conclusion by slipping in his personal stake in the town's pursuit of legal status: "I am preparing to move to St. Paul and am putting up for sale the corner lot I inherited from my father, cheap, $150. I have no legal papers, as you can well understand, but can supply accurate descriptions to any interested party. You can't miss it, it's right on the corner Lake Wobegon is on, and I do thank you for your kind attention" ("Lot"). The words of the oral conclusion are almost the same, oozing with disarming affability that on reflection redoubles our suspicion that we are being diddled. The story perfectly exemplifies a definition of the tall tale as "a fictional story which is told in the form of personal narrative or anecdote, which challenges the listener's credulity with comic outlandishness."[26]

A Gifted Liar

From the first jokes about Jack's Auto Repair there was always a "tall" element to the Lake Wobegon material. The early Jack's spots and other talk about Lake Wobegon had an inverted tallness since the town they represented was unbelievably backward. But as the town grew from the 224 souls of "Corner Lot Outside Town" in 1975 to a population of 942 10 years later (*LWD*, 1), the narrator was more likely to celebrate its homely virtues than ridicule its deficiencies. The stories became realistic enough that the American Automobile Association saw fit to identify the town as an "imaginary community" in its regional guidebook for tourists who hoped to visit.[27]

According to MPR staffers, an astonishing number of listeners believed in the truthfulness of the tales. Yet the failure of so many listeners to realize that they were being taken in was not for want of warnings. Even the Shy Person of the PMB spots was an obvious Yarnspinner's pose: "Here I stand as usual without anything to show you," he said to an East Los Angeles audience after an involved explanation of why he had no actual biscuits to show them. He went on,

> I tell you it's not the worst position to be in. Stand up here on a stage as we do every Saturday night to remember things that I'm not really sure actually happened. All of it taking place in a little town that is real so long as you don't go looking for it, and all of it brought to you by a product that you can't even buy around here. . . . It's imagination that got us into this problem anyway and I believe it can get us out. Powdermilk Biscuits! ("PHC," 20 August 1983)[28]

The narrator self-deprecatingly confesses that he is a liar, but as a Crackerbarrel Philosopher he says that such lies are productive and powerful. Such explicit moralizing was less frequent in the monologues than in PMB spots, but a sense of the paradoxical, even religious earnestness, of the on-stage character of the teller was typical of the middle and late tales. He was a liar, but an amiable one whose self-revelation lent credibility to his insinuation that, as Huck Finn said of Mark Twain, "there was things which he stretched, but mainly he told the truth." Though millions took this character for Keillor himself, the narrator of these monologues and some spots is more accurately identified as the Storyteller who created Lake

Wobegon in his imagination and sent Garrison Keillor down there to gather experiences.

By 1982 James Traub could say of the narrative tone in the monologue, "The sense of superiority that makes campiness possible is entirely foreign to Keillor" (117). Such an assessment would have been far from accurate if made prior to 1979. Yet the shift away from the superior poses of the Announcer was already under way in the "Corner Lot" narratives, since the narrator presents himself as an Exile. Burdened with his insider's knowledge of the town's history and its citizens – "barn-shootings, nocturnal hair-cutting, road-blocking, howling (Bernie's pastime on cold winter nights), acts of spell-casting and grave-dancing, common lowdown vandalism . . . and malicious gossip, years of it, and even bad thoughts such as covetousness and carnal desires" ("Lot") – the narrator may be a diddler, but he also poses as the reluctant émigré, looking over his shoulder like Lot's wife at a comedically developed rural Sodom.

Once Keillor was committed to a weekly monologue of considerable length, the inclusion and gradual expansion of the realistic and even the sentimental was practically inevitable. If he was going to tell anecdotes and stories about Lake Wobegon week after week, he needed to vary not only the characters and action but the tone as well. Realistic characters inevitably face conflicts, and as they do the humor must be salted with pathos. And since he was performing face-to-face before a live audience, what worked and what did not was immediately and vividly apparent to Keillor. Adjustments in tone, the augmentations of particular moods and themes, could be intuitive and spontaneous in the dynamic give-and-take of the performance. The accumulation of such on-stage modulations in response to audience feedback must have played a large part in determining the steady movement away from camp, insouciance, and irony and toward realism, sentiment, and sincerity as the decade end neared. "The ethical responsibility of a writer is to himself, his own perception of the truth more than to the audience," Keillor has said, differentiating between the demands of writing for print and for performance. But the performer "has a real obligation to the audience and not to appeal to a higher authority, you see. In the business that I'm in on-stage, if people don't laugh, it's not funny. It may be theoretically funny or high class, but if they don't like it, it's not any good. And the performer who complains about being misunderstood or unappreciated somehow has missed the point" (Interview, 10 August 1990).

Still, in the "Corner Lot" monologue Keillor's fast-paced delivery has achieved neither the sonority nor the conversationality and range of expressiveness – from booming whoops to slow whispers and sighs – of the monologues of the mid-1980s. Yet his pose as native Wobegonian, as mock-rueful and mock-wistful Exile and Witness, together with the length, coherence, and polish of this first "long monologue," does mark it as a dramatic turn. Though in subsequent months Keillor would pick up threads of the "Corner Lot" story and use them in subsequent narratives, advancing the action further in "real time," the form of the monologue was still fluid. The Sojourner from Lake Wobegon who would offer nuggets of crackerbarrel wisdom or wax warm and poetic about the ephemeral, homely beauty of life in the town he left behind was not yet in evidence.

Visitor's Day in Lake Wobegon

During winter and spring of 1976 Keillor did not continue telling long, first-person narratives about Lake Wobegon, but he made frequent use of episodic news chronicles. One variation on the news formula he used intermittently for more than a year began with the announcement that "Sunday is Visitor's Day in Lake Wobegon and you're all invited to come and see what it's like." Following this invitation, he would talk about events visitors might expect, such as a meeting of the Lawn Club, complete with a speaker on sod and prizes for the best lawn ornaments; a family meeting of the Hootens, open to the public since "everybody knows about it anyway" ("PHC," 10 April 1976); or the showing of "Meet the Bunsens," film highlights of the family over the years, including Duane's first Christmas and Clarence's thirty-fourth birthday "when he received the camera" ("PHC," 18 July 1976).

Some of the items were much longer than others, however, and many dealt with characters and events from previous broadcasts in such a way that the illusion of life proceeding in Lake Wobegon in real time gained depth and complexity. One "Public Service Announcement" sponsored by Jack's Auto was in effect a nine-minute tall tale about how the town dump in Lake Wobegon came to be situated on top of a high hill, blowing papers and fumes along the streets, whereas earlier there had been a huge trash mound in the lake that the Walker Art Center in Minneapolis tried to purchase as a work of art ("PHC," 7 February 1976). The Announcer who presents such messages is still more alien than exile; yet while most items within the news, public-service-announcement, and Visitor's-Day formulas are still basically brief rube jokes with a regional flavor, some were long enough to qualify as short-short stories, usually tall.

One of the longer Visitor's Day announcements continued the story of Duane Bunsen, recapping briefly how he had wrecked the car "while he was watching himself inhaling and exhaling in the rearview mirror while he was backing down the driveway" ("PHC," 8 May 1976). Over the years Keillor used the basic situation of a young man whose vanity causes an automobile accident or near-accident at least five times, and its germ lay in the author's own experience.[29] As in the "Corner Lot" narratives, Duane is 16 and wrecked the Buick on his way to pick up his girlfriend, whom he had hoped to impress with the cigarettes he sneaked. The girlfriend is now identified as DeeDee Olson, an "older woman" of 19, whose lipstick-stained cigarette butts have been found in the family car (miraculously, it has been repaired). The "big news is that Duane Bunsen is in love," and he and DeeDee find common cause in debunking their parents and hometown. She contends that Lake Wobegon "is shallow," and under her influence "Duane is starting to say that about Clarence and Arlene, that they don't talk enough and when they do talk, they only say dumb things." His parents are "fighting back" by forging a philosophy of life to set beside the one being fashioned by Duane: "Life is basically happy but you can find tragedy if you go looking for it," they contend. "Duane thinks that is dumb, but at least they are talking and he has agreed not to smoke for one more year and Clarence will give him $100."[30]

The Bunsens are developed with more realism than in the earlier tall tale, and this sequel adumbrates many stories about families with rebellious teenagers, including one the Sojourner tells about the times he would go out parking with his high school girlfriend and they would "make devastating remarks" about their parents ("PHC," 21 November 1981). The tale can also be seen as a reworking of his 1966 *Ivory Tower* story "Frankie," in which the teenage protagonist also had a wreck in a Buick on the way to see his girlfriend. Keillor moved his character Frankie from almost comic naïveté to a modicum of enlightenment, but the story is only incidentally humorous. No longer writing for the collegiate literati and 10 years farther from his own adolescence, Keillor had achieved a perspective from which he could exploit teenage agony for laughs and simultaneously convey realistic action in such a way that the teenage characters maintained their integrity.

The Letters of Barbara Ann Bunsen

The saga of the Bunsens expanded in a five-year-long series of rustic letters home written by Duane's older sister, Barbara Ann. Keillor as Announcer would introduce the letters and contextualize them, usually by recapping her history to date, since the series developed as a consecutive, picaresque tale, beginning with her departure from the small town for the big city. There were 70 or more of these letters read between the summer of 1976 and March 1981. After the last letter Barbara Ann never figured so prominently among the cast of Lake Wobegon familiars, but even in the last "PHC" season she made occasional appearances. In a story reprinted in *Leaving Home* as "Thanksgiving" (told 29 November 1986), Clarence fears she and her husband, Bill, are divorcing but learns instead they are expecting a child; he awaits news of the birth in the tale told 11 April 1987 and was still said to be waiting in the last "PHC" monologue, 13 June 1987.

It is not surprising that the letters were never identified as monologues in "PHC" rundowns, since that rubric was not consistently used until 1984. Yet not only were they designated as "spots" in the rundowns, but the surviving manuscripts of the letters were filed (in Keillor's American Radio Company offices in New York as of July 1991) along with the hundreds of scripts for PMB and Jack's spots instead of being collected in the several voluminous looseleaf binders specially designated for monologues. The news chronicles, many of which were delivered before the first Bunsen letters and some of which were delivered on alternate weeks, are collected in the monologue binders. Although the letters were omitted from this de facto canon, taken together they are closer in many ways to the familiar, first-person Lake Wobegon stories of the 1980s than they are to the episodic chronicles. They are also closer, despite their epistolary form, to the late monologues than they are to the rustic letters from Jack. Their omission from the binders says more about the gradual emergence of the monologue's preeminence and the informality of recordkeeping in the early days of "PHC" than it does about the particular character of these letters.

At first glance, the Bunsen letters seem just another application of the same burlesque pattern used in the letters from Jack. The dynamic interplay between Barbara Ann and the Announcer seems to replicate the contrastive pairing of Jack with Keillor as Announcer. The familiar juxtaposition of *eiron/alazon* is especially marked in the earlier letters, where the distance between her simplicity and the Announcer's sophistication is greatest; in these she seems little more than a stock type of the naive country-girl-come-to-the-city. But Barbara Ann is young and open to experience, and as the series lengthens and she encounters various conflicts, she deepens and her views and predicaments demand more sympathy and less irony.

The distance between Announcer/Fatherly Host and character soon decreased, and the series provided another medium in which the on-stage doubleness of Keillor's pose, as seen earlier in the PMB spots, moved toward fusion and the emergence of the complex Sojourner character. There was no such movement over the life of the longer-lasting series of letters from Jack, primarily because Jack's character was static. Before there was "PHC," after all, there was Jack, a middle-aged character, fixed in his ways. The humor of his letters continued to depend heavily on the clash between the crotchety *eiron* and the host as effete *alazon*. Furthermore, his letters were too infrequent to generate a rich sense of his personality, much less his changes over time. Jack personified the humble origins and early values of the show (looking back to the days in Collegeville), and his letters were used to provide a stable point of comparison against which the change could be measured and assessed. Barbara Ann's story, on the other hand, was open-ended, and by allowing her adventures to unfold serially and by taking a young woman's point of view, Keillor found a fresh perspective and even a way to transpose his own experiences into the third person. More than a decade later when he was exploring new forms and subjects during the first season of "American Radio Company of the Air," he would adopt the point of view of "a young woman from Manhattan," the protagonist of his serialized musical drama, "The Story of Gloria," featuring Ivy Austin as Gloria.

Before she wrote a letter home, Barbara Ann's departure from Lake Wobegon was probably announced as a news item, since the archives hold a handwritten list that includes the following note: "Barbara Ann Bunsen goes to Mpls to (Clint & Irene's) get a job and apt. attends the Mpls School of Modelling and Waiting."[31] Perhaps at this point Keillor thought to make Duane her cousin rather than her younger brother, since Barbara Ann's parents are Clarence and Arlene, who are the recipients of her letters. Barbara Ann, not mentioned as a member of the Bunsen family in the first long monologue, was possibly introduced as a character sometime in summer 1976, since in August Keillor led into a letter by saying that it had been "a few weeks that Barbara Ann Bunsen left Lake Wobegon and has been living down in the Twin Cities with her roommate Carol Sue and two other roommates in a two bedroom apartment over by Lake Calhoun" ("PHC," 21 August 1976).

What might be the first in the series begins "Dear Mom & Dad," followed by her customary reassurance that "everything is just fine" and continuing with an account of the breakdown of the Buick and other adventures she and Duane endured on the road. She was chagrined that the person who stopped to assist them was Wally Pilcher, a local swain who longs to make Barbara Ann his farm wife. She discusses Duane's resentment of all the attention recently showered on her but ingenuously plays for sympathy when she discusses how, in the big city, "you just feel you hardly exist at all. . . . I will never get used to this as long as I live." She used her standard "Hugs & kisses" in her complimentary close, and this letter, like most, ends with a postscript: "Tell Duane that – well, don't. It's all right."[32]

Barbara Ann feels lost, a lamb among wolves, not at all unlike the heroine of Samuel Richardson's *Pamela; or, Virtue Rewarded. In a Series of Familiar Letters from a Beautiful Young Damsel, to Her Parents* (1741), often said to be the first novel to realistically treat the psychological development of its protagonist. Pamela is also a naive country girl who writes home about her worries and ordeals not from the city but from the daunting and unfamiliar environment of the aristocratic household of the lecherous Mr. B. But despite her innocence and inexperience in the ways of the world, Barbara Ann, like Pamela before her, proves to be a fast learner possessed of a formidable spirit and an independent mind. By late August she announced her plans to enroll in the University of Minnesota and study liberal arts: "I know that Dad will be upset, but there is nothing to worry about. I don't intend to be a communist or anything" ("PHC," 21 August 1976).

Soon Barbara Ann was writing home about her classes, teachers, new boyfriends, and her job as parking lot attendant near the Mississippi River. Keillor himself took a parking lot job as a freshman and recalls worrying that in going to the university he was being unfaithful to the values of his family and disloyal to his social class (interview, 10 August 1990). While it is difficult to demonstrate, since the manuscripts of the letters do not typically include the Announcer's framing comments (and most of the master tapes are currently unplayable), the Announcer seems to sympathize and identify with Barbara Ann increasingly as the series continues.

Four months or so into the series, by the time she was to go home for Thanksgiving vacation, Barbara Ann was a woman with real interest, not just a rustic come to town. The narrator begins by noting that there is no letter this week since she is home and having a "wonderful Thanksgiving at the Bunsens." He proceeds with a curiously intimate, four-minute "news" story about the visit: Arlene doubled the amount of brandy in one of the dishes when she should have halved it, but it tasted so good, she emptied the bottle onto it. Barbara Ann got a lot of attention as she is the first Bunsen to go to college and people asked her about what she's learning: "She tried to explain that it isn't easy to do that when you're learning sort of basic general concepts type of ideas, you know, I mean like theories and undercurrents and social thought, I mean it's not like state capitals or the multiplication table," Keillor says, slipping into the voice of the character herself ("PHC," 26 November 1976).

In *Lake Wobegon Days* Gary Keillor has the same difficulty when, home from the university for Christmas, he is asked by old Mr. Thorvaldson what he is learning in his freshman humanities course: "Well, it covers a lot of ground, I don't think I could explain it in a couple of minutes," he says. "That's okay," the old man replies, "I got all day" (20). But the Thanksgiving monologue not only anticipates many later stories about similar visits by the exiles; it also recalls the wistful, first-person reminiscence about holidays at the Keillor homeplace as told in the Thanksgiving special show of 1973.

Even before Thanksgiving, two of Barbara Ann's roommates got homesick and returned to Lake Wobegon, including Carol Sue, who had talked the rest of the girls into coming to Minneapolis in the first place. But Barbara Ann thrives in the Twin Cities and in spring thanks her parents for seeking summer jobs at home for her, but diplomatically she tells them that leaving home was too hard to do more than once. Besides, she thinks it would be embarrassing "to keep running into kids I went to school with who don't have anything in common with me anymore but we would both have to pretend that we do."[33] She stays in the Cities and works at the "Freeway 494 People's Co-op," writing home about the squabbles between the "brown rice and wheat germ" types and those who want to sell "stuff like Hamburger Helper" (a situation that calls to mind Keillor's 1973 story, "The People's Shopper").

By the spring of 1978 Barbara Ann has dropped out of the university and into the counterculture, having married a man identified only as Bill; the couple live on farm near La Crosse, Wisconsin, raising walnuts and llamas and trying to renovate their ramshackle house. Soon down to the last dollar, she wrote, "And yet we have an enormous woodpile. We have a warm tight house and a big bed with each other in it. We have the six-volume set of Charles Dickens. . . . And we have the $100 check that you sent with your last letter."[34] But with the advent of the "me" decade, as the bonfires of the vanities were kindled all over America, they abandon the farm and in September of 1980, Barbara Ann writes: "It is all a rather sudden end to our alternative living experiment on the farm, but I was getting curious about exactly what it was that the farm was an alternative to, and when I got the course catalogue from the University, it was like getting a seed catalogue in the dead of winter."[35]

Keillor made use of Barbara Ann's letters to exploit the narrative potential of Lake Wobegon which he had sensed at least as early as the "Corner Lot" story. Taken together, they almost comprise a humorous, epistolary bildungsroman as Barbara Ann passes from country girl to city dweller; she has also become something of a crackerbarrel philosopher herself, a credible commentator on the end of an era. Bill finds work as a real-estate salesman, and Barbara Ann goes back to school. As Bill prospers and becomes a yuppie, however, Barbara Ann drops out of the university again, sardonically quipping that her husband had gone "from son of the soil to Daddy Warbucks in six months. . . . I liked him better when he was barefoot and pregnant."[36] In what may be the last letter of the series, Bill has become a successful businessman, but Barbara Ann is sick with the flu and does not know what she wants to do with her life.[37]

The Sojourner

Keillor stood apart from his character as he introduced and commented on her letters, and as Announcer he was free to wink over the top of the text and ironize. Through writing the letters and impersonating Barbara Ann as he read them aloud, however, he discovered new tonal and thematic possibilities for stories about Lake Wobegon. All that remained between the letters and the late monologues was for him to stand in the place of Barbara Ann while retaining some of the possibilities of the Announcer's perspective. This he accomplished in playing the composite character of the Sojourner from Lake Wobegon. The Sojourner can pose as the Announcer if need be, but more often he comes across as a slow-talking Shy Person, a Witness to the world of Lake Wobegon, now an Exile, who can surprise himself by sharing tales that reveal homespun truths. In doing so he stands as Crackerbarrel Philosopher or even an inspirational Preacher at times. Given the character of the Sojourner, there was no structural need for a condescending Announcer to set off the naïveté of a rustic Barbara Ann or the ways of the town. The Sojourner could condescend on occasion for easy laughs, but he could just as readily identify with what was now consistently his home town, and this character could replace ridicule with regret. To the narrator of "A Corner Lot," when the cartographers folded Lake Wobegon "underneath Stearns County" they buried only a comic backwater; but from the perspective of the Sojourner they also folded under an Arcadia set in the county of Mist.

Even during the period of the Bunsen letters Keillor was already giving news features, which though in the third person and often only four minutes long, made use of the standard opening and closing formula of the late monologues. (Keillor later used the formula to frame stories such as "The Royal Family" ["PHC," 13 November 1982, reprinted in *Leaving Home*], which he has said was "not really a Lake Wobegon story.")[38] At least one of the 1981 talks conforms to none of the patterns previously discussed. "Christmas Story Re-told" ("PHC," 19 December 1981) is a paraphrase of the scriptural accounts, narrated in the Stearns County dialect of the Sojourner, whose dimensions as Crackerbarrel Philosopher and Preacher predominate.

By 1982 it was clear that not only had the character of the narrator changed, but the town itself was substantially transformed. In the month previous to Keillor's announcement that he was leaving his morning program to work on a book about Lake Wobegon, he wrote an unusual epistolary monologue, a letter from a boyhood friend in Lake Wobegon who was now a middle-aged classics professor. Jim tells a tale of mid-life crisis – how he lost his job when the college cut back his department, and how he almost lost his marriage by starting an affair. He stopped short of adultery after an epiphany in which he realized that since "we all depend on each other . . . his sins would be no more secret than an earthquake." In closing, he asks Keillor to tell the folks in Lake Wobegon, whom he has not seen in 20 years, that he is "all right," making it clear that he looks to the town as a moral cynosure.[39] Lake Wobegon had come a long way since the night its citizens lit fires in the streets and demolished the Bunsens' Buick.

A monologue about "the return of the exiles" ("PHC," 27 November 1982, published as "Thanksgiving" on the "Fall" cassette of *News from Lake Wobegon*) is representative of the mature monologues on which most of *Lake Wobegon Days* is based. While Lake Wobegon is still comically provincial, its moral ascendency over the Cities is clearly evident, as the Thanksgiving pilgrimage demonstrates: "The exiles – the grown-up children – return . . . children who moved away and learned how to complicate their lives in all sorts of new and interesting ways, return to a town so much the same, it's hard to believe you're not twelve years old."[40] It is still "the little town that time forgot," but by this point the formulaic close has begun to connote not stagnation but perdurability.

The monologue bears some superficial resemblance to a news chronicle – in that the narrator skips from one scene to another – but the episodes do not function as discrete jokes or news items: they work together in a unified paean to the town. Just as he had described Arlene Bunsen's cooking problems on Thanksgiving in 1976, here he tells how Viginia Ingqvist winds up serving turkey in bowls. Barbara Ann and her husband have returned, and the Sojourner's narrative is a conjuration of family warmth and an invocation of national symbolism, as well as a celebration of regional culture. Its mood is surprisingly close to Keillor's 1973 autobiographical reminiscence of Thanksgivings past, where grandfather Keillor told stories, and yet it is strikingly close to the Thanksgiving passage at the end of the "Fall" chapter of *Lake Wobegon Days*:

> Everything in the kitchen was the same except the mixer was moved to the counter by the stove. Barbara Ann found, to her not very great surprise, that she knew it by heart; she got the colander out and rinsed strawberries; the meat platter was on top of the fridge, the gravy boat down behind the cereal, the sieve was nesting in the mixing bowls. She got out the big bowl, moved the mixer back to its old home by the toaster, and was about to mash the potatoes when, on an impulse, she opened the small cupboard high over the sink. There were the little china Pilgrims, their log cabin, two pine trees, and one surviving Indian who looked like Uncle Stan. The smoke was broken off the cabin chimney where she had dropped it while setting the table eighteen years ago. (*LWD*, 215)

> Well, Barbara Ann dried the dishes, her mother washed. They got to doing the dishes and her mother started to sing. . . . "Tell me why the ivy twines. . . ." And as they sang and did the dishes, Barbara Ann was surprised to know that she still knew where everything went. The platter went up on top of the refrigerator. The sieve nested in the mixing bowls down to the left of the sink. The spatula went in the little drawer by the stove and the wooden spoons went in the drawer with the silverware. And the gravy boat went up behind the cereal boxes. And the little centerpiece, the little plaster Pilgrims standing by their plaster cabin with the plaster pine tree and the plaster smoke coming out of the chimney – is wiped off with a damp cloth and put away in the china cabinet until next year. ("PHC," 27 November 1982)

In the oral version Barbara Ann discovers she remembers where everything goes as she is putting things away, not as she is preparing the meal as in the printed version, but the reversal makes little difference. And although in the printed version Barbara Ann and her mother do not sing "Tell Me Why" over the dishes, in the "Spring" chapter of *Lake Wobegon Days* the same song is sung as Gary Keillor does the dishes with his sister: "She sings a song we always sing together when we do dishes, but I don't feel like singing it, so she sings it with my mother" (*LWD*, 300).

Chapter Four

A Real Writer

I write in the morning and I write at night,
I've written with Thurber and Perelman and White;
They mostly wrote better than I and I mean it,
But I am still livin' and that is convenient.

("Whoopi Ti-Yi-Yo," *Lake Wobegon Loyalty Days*)

Keillor's ethos as the Sojourner from Lake Wobegon was so natural and convincing that many readers and listeners accepted the stories that featured Gary Keillor as protagonist as genuine self-disclosures by the author. Though sometimes the teller crowed about his talents for lying and intentionally disclosed the ironic distance that separated the person without from the persona within the tale, very often the Sojourner, Gary, and Garrison seemed all subsumed in one. A 1989 article in a journal for college composition teachers even promoted the use of Keillor's written and oral Lake Wobegon tales as ideal models for helping students write personal narratives about their own lives and experiences. Though the author identified the genre of Keillor's narratives as stories, he emphasized their qualities of vividness and sincerity, which made them felicitous models for writers of nonfictional narratives.[1]

While it is true that many of the actions in Keillor's Lake Wobegon tales were based on personal experience, these narratives were conceived and constructed first and foremost as fiction, and their aim was to entertain rather to reveal the self or accurately describe feelings, places, or events. And even though there is no reason that such fictions cannot serve well enough as models for sincere personal narratives, it is ironic that the composition teacher did not mention any of Keillor's non–Lake Wobegon writing, which included many bona fide nonfiction, first-person narratives such as his 1974 *New Yorker* profile of the "Grand Ole Opry." Between 1970 and 1987 Keillor published at least 28 signed essays or editorials, a few of which were essentially personal narratives and almost all of which were in the first person. Nor did the teacher mention any of the several first-person, non–Lake Wobegon stories and sketches that are either openly autobiographical ("Drowning 1954" and "After a Fall") or at least obliquely autobiographical ("Found Paradise" and "The Drunkard's Sunday"). The narrators in these pieces are not exactly the same from one work to the next; even so, many of these voices sound very much like one another, and some are quite like that of the Sojourner.

But prior to the end of "PHC" Keillor published another 42 short stories, sketches, and burlesques that have nothing directly to do with Lake Wobegon. It is perfectly understandable that the teacher did not mention any of these pieces, for while many may have first-person narrators who sound like one or another of the voices Keillor used in his mock-commercials and radio dramas on "PHC," and while quite a few of them include details, jokes, or comic premises that found their way into the radio show, none is told in the familiar registers of the Sojourner. Nevertheless, the college teacher's exclusive focus on the Lake Wobegon stories effectively demonstrates how Keillor's remarkable acclaim as the Sojourner tended to overshadow and obscure his achievements as a writer of a wide range of other fiction and nonfiction in a variety of genres for an audience that did not think of him first and foremost as a radio performer and storyteller. Indeed, the singularity of the Sojourner's voice reveals itself as all the more remarkable when heard against the background of the legion of characters and narrative personae that populate his writing from before, during, and after the years over which his most famous narrative persona evolved. The non–Lake Wobegon humor ranges widely from colloquial, first-person narratives that could have been placed within the formula opening and close and served as monologues on "PHC," to writerly pieces that depend almost as much on visual techniques and literary wordplay as on oral narrative flow.

G.K. the DJ

During 1969-70 in the very early morning Keillor spun his records and began talking about Jack's Auto Repair, and at night he rattled the keys of his old black Underwood writing for the *New Yorker* and filling the wastebaskets with crumpled paper. He enjoyed his "DJ days," but at the end of his shift on the air he felt a tremendous letdown, since there was nothing left to show for his work: "I wanted to do something that would last a little while after I had finished doing it" (*DJ*, 1-2). By the time he wrote those words in early 1977 his ambivalence toward radio had become part of his stock in trade, so much so that the very title of his first slim volume of collected works is doubly ironic. For not only would MPR never refer to its announcers as "deejays" but "Garrison Keillor" was first promulgated as a *pen* name, not as a stage or radio signature. His prefatory essay, "To the Reader," has more than a little of the still-evolving Sojourner, mildly rueful and self-deprecatory, as he tells how the collection of 20 pieces came into being because the membership director of MPR wanted a "product" to offer to the supporters of that most ephemeral medium, radio: "Perhaps it helps to offer them a tangible item, even one so modest as this," he wrote, "as a sort of nightcrawler" (*DJ*, 12).

G.K. the DJ was never sold commercially and was published in a magazine format with paper covers illustrated by a drawing of pensive Keillor in a cowboy hat and round-rimmed glasses, his bearded chin resting on a closed hand. Except for the preface and two poems, all of the pieces were reprints: five selected from 22 stories that had appeared in the *New Yorker*, 11 from the 15 humorous features and op-ed pieces he had written for the *Minneapolis Tribune*, and one of his four pieces from MER/MPR's *Preview*.

The prestige value of Keillor's being a *New Yorker* writer was certainly important in the decision to publish the collection. But another principle that guided the selection was the salience of each piece to the immediate audience – the MPR listening public. The poems, "Ode to the Street System of Southwest Minneapolis" and "Our Counties," which had been read on the air and in live performances prior to "PHC," put regional and local place names into clever doggerel verse. And while relatively few of Keillor's *New Yorker* stories make extensive use of regional material, of the five collected here only "Local Family Keeps Son Happy" makes no obvious recourse to material of special regional interest. "My North Dakota Railroad Days," for example, is a tall tale that relies heavily on the abundant jokelore associated with the interstate rivalry between North Dakota and Minnesota. "Found Paradise" (reprinted as "Happy to Be Here" in *Happy to Be Here*) purportedly draws on a Midwestern writer's journal, after the manner of Thoreau, of his attempt "to wring something like ecstasy out of what is an ordinary Minnesota farm" (*HBH*, 267). In the story the narrator proves that, unlike Thoreau, he has very little detailed knowledge of the flora and fauna around him; in one of his first attempts to write "plain country prose" he recounts how he stopped to say to an old farmer looking over his crop, " 'That's certainly doing well.' Then realized I didn't know what 'that' was. Also, it looked burnt" (*HBH*, 269).

Though "Found Paradise" echoes passages from *Walden* as it parodies the pretentiousness of latter-day Thoreauvianism, it also offers a self-deprecatory portrait of Keillor in his Freeport farm period (1970), when he "planted a garden and wrote stories to support my wife and year-old son" (*WASM*, 214). In an essay originally published as a *Newsweek* cover story in 1988 about the values of the Fourth of July, Keillor mentioned a detail that links the narrator of "Found Paradise" to himself. He recalled that he rented his country house from a farmer named Norbert whose fields were in "corn and oats. (I believed it was oats, but on the odd chance it might be wheat or barley, I didn't mention anything to Norbert about it being oats)" (*WASM*, 214). "Drowning 1954" is such a realistic backward look at the author's boyhood in Brooklyn Park and Minneapolis that it could be read as nonfiction. Even "On the Road, Almost" has some "inside" local significance: the title alludes to Minnesota-born Bob Dylan's "On the Road Again" (recorded in 1965), and *New Yorker* readers who also listened to 29-year-old Keillor's morning show might have seen the first-person narrator, also 29 and a radio disk jockey, as a caricature of the sad, rich, and misunderstood deejay Keillor might have become in commercial radio: "A radio personality with his own show in a major market," whose rhapsodic lament about the burdens of being on top reveals how styles, rhythms, and verbal formulas of the pop records he spins day and night have taken over who he is (*DJ*, 33).

Whether he wanted to abandon radio completely in favor of a career as author may still have been in doubt at this stage of Keillor's career, as he may have been revealing indirectly in "On the Road, Almost." He had recently left KSJN for the second time and with the first article in a series that ran through 1974 in the *Minneapolis*

Tribune, Keillor was identified only as "a freelance writer living in St. Paul."[2] Actually, the editor who had asked him to write for the paper said that he had gotten the idea that "this fellow might be able to write good little pieces for the op-ed pages on Sunday" (Fedo, 64-65) after listening to the morning show before Keillor left the station in the fall of 1973 (though it seems likely that the editor had also heard of Keillor's publishing in the *New Yorker*). The series, which appeared between 14 January and 15 December 1974, was undertaken before Keillor had resolved to begin "PHC" and concluded a half year after the show's first live broadcast 6 July – a year of remarkable activity, especially considering that during that time Keillor also researched and wrote his "Opry" profile and published two short stories in the *New Yorker*.

The Editorialist

All 12 nonfiction pieces in *G.K. the DJ* are not only locally targeted but are narrated by a presumably maskless Garrison Keillor – a man not wholly unlike the Sojourner, though more given to comic persiflage, parody, and political partisanship than to understatement and genial asides. In most of these pieces, however, Keillor's satirical wit predominates, and he sounds most often like the antic Announcer from the morning radio show. Still, there are several pieces in which this narrator comes down solidly for horse sense in preference to expert "feasibility studies," for "Aunt Myrtles and Uncle Harrys in the stucco bungalows with hand-trimmed lawns" as opposed to "the Craigs and Cynthias with the four kids and the eternal revolving illuminated mortgage" (*DJ*, 9) – a cultural dialectic he perpetuated later in the juxtaposition of "The Dales" and Lake Wobegon.[3] All in all, while most of these pieces are topical and never appeared in subsequent commercial collections (by contrast, all five stories reappeared in *Happy to Be Here*), as a group they provide a virtual index to recurrent subjects of his humor and targets of his satires and burlesques.

The most characteristic and longest-standing subject in Keillor's work – Minnesota as a place and distinctive culture – is richly represented here. In "42nd in Hot Sauce" Keillor offers a travesty of the journalistic penchant for statistics and boosterism, targeting the stereotypical blandness of the state – just as he would continue to do in the early 1980s in his "PHC" spots for "Ajua! the Swedish Hot Sauce." Keillor's whimsical statistics reveal predictably, that in Minnesota "Food is typically bland: ground-beef patties, mashed potatoes, green beans and jello, for example. We are 38th in the use of garlic, 42nd in hot sauce," and that "Minneapolis . . . uses less irony in the month of January than any major city except Philadelphia" (*DJ*, 5).

Keillor's stance, however, is not invariably one of superiority, and in "We Shall Not Be Curbed" he exchanges the pose of the know-it-all pundit for that of the populist, Crackerbarrel Philosopher, who prefers the ragged avenues of relatively rustic St. Paul to the curbed and numbered streets of more ruthlessly urban Minneapolis – a pairing that draws on the rivalry between the Twin Cities and conforms to the archetypal "PHC" opposition of country and town. In political pieces Keillor tends to target conservatives, as in his burlesque of Watergate circumlocutions in "Testimony" and in "The Vanishing Republican," in which he sheds crocodile tears over a supposedly endangered species, the Republican electoral candidate.[4] Keillor's identification with working-class values is also evident in "Pecunia Pro Arte" and "What Do You Do? (How Much Do You Earn?)" as he exposes the "Philistinism" inherent in the hegemony of commercial and upper-class elites over artists, who he says come primarily from the working class.[5]

In "Me and Myrtle and Harry" and "Uncle Don's Grounder" Keillor takes on urban renewal and city planning schemes."[6] In the latter he indicts the moral vacuity of bureaucratic reasoning as evidenced by the buildings government officials choose to tear down and the kinds of things they think worthy of preserving. Specifically, he laments the demolition of the old Minneapolis YWCA (which he restored in *WLT: A Radio Romance*, locating Frank White's apartment just across the street) and the Chamber of Commerce literature placed in the new building's cornerstone. Alternatively, he offers as truly worth preserving the sorts of effluvia that furnish his nostalgic monologues: "high school annuals, souvenirs of Split Rock Lighthouse, attendance pins, term papers, locks of hair, Twins scorecards, old ties, old prescriptions, old whatchamacallits" (*DJ*, 7). The value of his most cherished souvenir, an old T-shirt he was wearing when he made a fabulous play in a family softball game, is tangible only in memory and in stories, through the telling of which "every year it gets better" (*DJ*, 7).

Keillor's love of softball and baseball, as evidenced in "Uncle Don's Grounder," continued to show up in later nonfiction (such as his 1979 op-ed piece "If Begonias Bloom, Can Baseball Be Far Behind?") and on radio in his hundreds of stories or anecdotes about the Lake Wobegon Whippets. His memories of family games and experiences with an MPR slow-pitch softball team during the late 1970s probably supplied the germ for "Attitude" and "How Are the Legs, Sam?," two of four fictional treatments of baseball or softball reprinted in *Happy to Be Here*.

Keillor's pastorally nuanced, biblically grounded, populist attacks on the supposed material improvements to be wrought by private developers and government technocrats derive from his aversion to the American pursuit of continual, useful, and quantifiable progress in every sphere, including the private and personal. In "On Getting in Touch with Yourself," a piece that leads off with an attack on a Methodist church's advertisement for "Human Relations Training Labs" (in subject matter and structure it resembles his 1964 indictment of the Campus Crusade for Christ in "God by Magic"), he takes on "the self-improvement industry" and the rampant narcissism that provides a bottomless appetite for books on transactional analysis, positive thinking, encounter groups, and popular psychiatry (*DJ*, 6). His testimony about his own experiments with such schemes reveals core values of Keillor and Keillor-as-Sojourner, as he admits to having been a "an eminently dislikable person – secretive and solitary, ineffective with others and unskilled at communication." Dissatisfied, he tried self-improvement, but gave it up since he realized that it led him nowhere save deeper into narcissism. He concluded the piece with a proclamation characteristic of the man and his most famous persona – "I now believe that we live by miracles, not improvements" – followed up with a Protestant confession that "our hearts are hard, the world is merciless, but God intends His mercy to soften us in miraculous ways," and a petition that God "save us from sanctimoniousness about ourselves and open our hearts. May he forgive me this irreverent column about people who, earnestly, humorlessly, are learning to express more openly their inability to express and feel more deeply their lack of feeling" (*DJ*, 6).

The only subject and source for humor that rivals the preeminence of Minnesota in Keillor's work is language itself. In some of his stories, even in the early 1970s, he takes an experimentalist's delight in the kaleidoscopic possibilities and intricacies of language, making words themselves the subject and substance of his art. More typically, his short humorous sketches exploit the eccentricities or abuses of language as these are exposed via one form or other of burlesque or parody. This fascination with language is evident in many of his editorial pieces, which deal with abuses of language ranging from linguistic foolishness or "sheer humbug" to the conscious use of language to deceive. In "Thinking Metric" he travesties the government's efforts to streamline the nation's terminology for weights, measures, and distances, concluding that while the metric system may afford more logical and consistent terminology, our understanding of distance and other such abstractions is, finally, experiential and not amenable to logic.[7] St. Paul will always be "not far" or "just east" of Minneapolis "whether Congress likes it or not. You can't legislate language. It's too complicated" (*DJ*, 18).

In another piece Keillor mocks the president of the University of Minnesota for his inflated discourse, as in the overused phrase "excellence in education," when "goodness in education" is all that can in verbal honesty be claimed.[8] In "Testimony" he mimics the circumlocutions of President Nixon's co-conspirators in the Watergate coverup to satirize the insincerity of politicians, and he lampoons the doublespeak of grantsmanship in "Pecunia Pro Arte" and the hype of real-estate developers in "Me and Myrtle and Harry." He is not righteously indignant in any of these pieces, but in several his scorn is genuine and he lampoons particular jargons not only because they provide him comic grist, but out of a moral conviction that certain professions seem to proliferate highly developed forms of lying in the interest of gaining commercial advantage. And in the case of bureaucratic and political jargon, Keillor would probably agree with Orwell's remark that "political language . . . is designed to make lies sound truthful and murder respectable, and to give an appearance of solidity to pure wind."[9]

Cracking the *New Yorker*

Keillor valued the writing he did for print above what he wrote to be spoken over the air. His ambition since high school days of being a "real writer" had been bound up with being published by the *New Yorker*, a dream he carried forward at the University of Minnesota, as his sophisticate's pose in "The Broadsides" columns of *Ivory Tower* and his many Perelmanesque pieces there demonstrate. His failure to land a job as a "Talk of the Town" reporter in 1966 had probably only increased the value of the *New Yorker*'s approval, which finally came after he had taken the radio job with KSJR to put bread on the table of his small family.

Early in the morning over KSJR his listeners knew him for his countercultural eclecticism and exuberant whimsy; late at night at the typewriter he was a very serious fellow. While many of his radio scripts undoubtedly derived from sketches he started for the *New Yorker* and vice versa, writing for radio was quicker and more spontaneous because it had to be. But it was also faster and looser because there was no comparable basis for the intense anxiety of influence he felt writing for a magazine that published E. B. White, "the person I would like to be like . . . the most meticulous writer who ever was" (Letofsky). He recalled slaving away at his sketches, poring over the magazine "to get ideas on how to write another story they would want. It did me no good and I knew that but just to be busy and be neurotic and try to have a plan about it and go at things straight" (Letofsky). "I went through a great many drafts," he said, "and I studied every sentence, and it was work that I enjoyed doing, but it was also . . . very difficult" (Traub, 112). He says in "To the Reader" that, as the crumpled drafts accumulated in his wastebasket, he "kept hearing a dismal voice, saying 'Once again, you are wasting your life' " (*DJ*, 2).

Keillor told Roy Blount, Jr., that he did not think his radio work influenced the way he wrote for the page, but he did feel that the status he accrued as a *New Yorker* writer afforded him greater leeway to violate the taboos of public radio: "I wasn't just some Wahoo," he said, although he believed "I would have done a better show if I *had* been a Wahoo." Whether his radio shows would have been better had he been "some loose, wild, self-educated person from the out back who came to town and whooped and hollered and sang and

talked loose, wild talk" will never be known (Blount, 16). Nevertheless, Keillor's belief that they might have been better brings into
focus the clear separation of realms he felt between his work as the
Wahoo disk jockey and as a promising young author.

Keillor's two first credits in the *New Yorker*, "Local Family Keeps
Son Happy" (19 September 1970) and "Snack Firm Maps New Chip
Push" (10 October 1970), were submitted together, probably
accompanied by other equally brief sketches. "When *The New Yorker*
accepted a story of mine," he wrote, "I didn't feel happiness so
much as relief. Their letter was so kind and full of praise, and I sat
down on the porch steps [of his house in St. Cloud] and drew a
deep breath" (*DJ*, 2). This bit of encouragement was probably
instrumental in his decision to quit KSJR in Collegeville in 1971 for
nine months to concentrate on his *real* writing, but by October he
was back with KSJN in St. Paul, touted in the station magazine as a
New Yorker writer.

The letter of acceptance was from Roger Angell, the *New
Yorker's* baseball writer, general contributor, and editor since 1956,
who remained Keillor's editor at the magazine since accepting his
first sketches off the slush pile in 1970. Of Keillor, Angell said in
1989, "When he first turned up, he was closer [stylistically] to E. B.
White than anybody I'd ever seen. . . . I had never heard of Garrison;
his stories weren't addressed to me. I opened up the envelope and
they cracked me up."[10] Angell was in a position to know about the
stylistic similarity to White as his mother, Katherine Sergeant White
(1892-1977), herself an editor and writer on the *New Yorker* from its
inception in 1925, had married E. B. White in 1929 when Roger was
nine years old. Keillor's fantasy of writing exclusively for the *New
Yorker* soon came almost literally true, since the magazine arranged
with him to have "first right of refusal on his short fiction since the
early seventies" (Lee, 142). (His series of regular contributions to the
Minneapolis Tribune ended in December 1974, a consequence of
the *New Yorker's* more prestigious and more lucrative agreement
[Fedo, 65]). By 1989 the *New Yorker* was using Keillor's reputation
to promote itself. They ran a corner flap that said "Fiction by GARRI-
SON KEILLOR" on their newsstand copies heralding "The Chuck
Show" in July, and in spring and summer issues they ran ads for
subscriptions featuring a picture of Keillor and text about his long-
standing romance with the magazine.[11]

Happy to Be Here

Though Keillor had worked much longer and harder to make his mark as an author than he had as a radio performer, when his first book by a major publisher came out in his fortieth year, relatively few of the two-to-three million radio fans were more than dimly aware of the quantity and quality of his writing that had little or nothing to do with his radio shows. Yet for a decade prior to May 1980 (when regular satellite transmissions of "A Prairie Home Companion" began) his writing had already been reaching a national, albeit narrower, audience via the *New Yorker*. His first piece in 1970 was followed by 27 more articles, stories, and comic sketches before his radio show could be received live outside the region served by MPR.

The power of the live national radio broadcasts to develop and command an audience relative to that of his publications proved to be on a different order of magnitude. Even with a decade's head start in such a prestigious magazine, by the time 29 of his pieces (26 from the *New Yorker*, one from the *Atlantic*, and two others previously unpublished) were collected in *Happy to Be Here* (1982), the book was fated to be reviewed as a sideshow, with "PHC" as the main event.[12] Most reviewers led off with a backgrounder on "A Prairie Home Companion" and the shy storyteller from Lake Wobegon, only gradually working their way around to the book, giving the impression almost that he had written it in his odd hours, as if writing for publication was his hobby, which, ironically, is exactly how he had thought of the radio show at its inception.

The book served as a vindication of sorts to those who were impressed by the *New Yorker*'s reputation for quality and who might have felt a bit uneasy with their affection for Keillor's folksy oral tales. Seeing a solid, hardcover collection in print soothed some esthetic consciences, just as a would-be sophisticate who was a closet fan of a country fiddle player might take comfort in the knowledge that his favorite used to record with the New York Philharmonic. "Anybody who's listened carefully [to "PHC"]," wrote one reviewer, "knows that this isn't just a rustic intuitively spinning yarns but a writer, a real writer."[13]

In the Introduction to *Happy to Be Here* Keillor told once more of his first discovery of the *New Yorker* and of his admiration for its

"great infield of Thurber, Liebling, Perelman and White," and he
added an often-cited credo on the value of humorous writing:

> They were my heroes: four older gentlemen, one blind, one fat, one delicate,
> and one a chicken rancher, and in my mind they took the field against the big
> mazumbos of American Literature, and I cheered for them. I cheer for them
> now . . . and still think . . . that it is more worthy in the eyes of God and better
> for us as a people if a writer make three pages sharp and funny about the lives
> of geese than to make three hundred flat and flabby about God or the Ameri-
> can people. (*HBH*, 11)

While no nonfiction pieces are represented in *Happy to Be Here*,
all of the basic themes that Keillor wrote about in his 1974 series of
editorials turn up in one or more of its selections. In nine or so of
the stories, including all of those dealing with fictional Minneapolis
radio station WLT, local color about the Upper Midwest is crucial to
the effect of the tale. (His four WLT stories – "The Slim Graves
Show," "Friendly Neighbor," "WLT [The Edgar Era]," and "The Tip-
Top Club" – provided the basis for *WLT: A Radio Romance* and are
discussed in Chapter 8 in that context.) His fascination with language
is, predictably enough, even more pronounced in his fiction. In
some of these pieces his interest in words as words approaches that
of experimental or postmodernist writers. But the majority of them
have just as much in common with the works of the literary comedians, those late nineteenth-century humorists renowned for their verbal comedy (puns, funny spellings, malapropisms, etc.) and fondness
for the forms of the mock–oral tale and the burlesque (including
parody and other subtypes of the genre).

More than half of the selections in *Happy to Be Here* burlesque
genres of writing, such as the newspaper feature, the market letter,
the memo, science fiction, the action comic book, the detective
story, social science prose, rock music criticism, advertisement and
public relations copy, the rhetoric of "rights" advocacy groups.
Keillor also parodies particular literary styles, such as that of Richard
Brautigan in "Ten Stories for Mr. Richard Brautigan," and particular
works, such as Nancy Friday's *My Mother/Myself* (1977) in "My
Stepmother, Myself." That Keillor not only wrote but performed
what he wrote on stage also links him to the tradition of the literary
comedians. Indeed, throughout the long run of "PHC" and also on
"ARC" he drew on and adapted his published fiction for comic

sketches. Still, owing to the historical distance between Keillor and his nineteenth-century antecedents, the modes, manners, and subjects of his short stories and sketches carry more immediately recognizable similarities to the work of the famous *New Yorker* humorists he named as his "heroes" – White, Thurber, Perelman, Liebling.

"Local Family Keeps Son Happy"

Keillor's first two pieces in the *New Yorker* are fairly representative of the burlesques that make up the greater part of *Happy to Be Here*, though with fewer than 400 words each they are shorter than most of the others. As in the mock–oral tales of the literary comedians, the first-person narrator in each is not to be confused with the author. Actually, as Lee has noted, very few of Keillor's pieces are really mock–oral tales since what we read is typically presented as the written text rather than the represented speech of the first-person narrator (though in some pieces, including "On the Road, Almost" and "My North Dakota Railroad Days," Keillor does mimic the unique *speech* of an individual). Nevertheless, the structure remains essentially the same as in the classic mock–oral tale, though few of these stories make use of a frame device. The author remains silent, allowing the narrators to reveal their comic ineptitude directly to the reader/audience.

The implied author and narrator of "Local Family Keeps Son Happy" is a newspaper writer, and that of "Snack Firm Maps New Chip Push" apparently writes business reports or market letters. But while the distance between Keillor and his most familiar *eiron*, the Sojourner, steadily diminished over time, following the pattern familiar in the gradual fusion of the character Mark Twain with the author/performer Samuel Clemens, the superiority to and ironic distance between Keillor and these narrative personae is considerable. During his editorship of the *Ivory Tower* in the mid-1960s Keillor had published a number of burlesques (such as "The Vulgarians") and had targeted newspaper genres and styles in satirical articles (such as "Off to the Smut Wars"). But the biting satire that was common enough in Keillor's raids on newspapers and other targets in the *Ivory Tower* is almost entirely absent these pieces. In the genteel tradition of the *New Yorker*, the satire tends to focus on how something is said as much as it does on what or why.

If readers encountered "Local Family Keeps Son Happy" in the pages of an urban daily, they might take it as a poorly written and rather lame attempt at sensationalism, a mix of what Alan Neuharth, founder of *USA Today*, called "the journalism of joy" with the more exploitative aims of the gossip rags. On the slick pages of the *New Yorker*, however, we take it as a satirical swipe at such dubious journalism in general, and at the "lifestyles" genre in particular. The language and structure of the story are utterly conventional and shopworn and cast in such boilerplate prose that the actions and statements of the people seem wildly incongruous. The premise is set forth in a lead that amateurishly attempts to catch the reader's attention with a rhetorical question: "What happens when parents buy a woman for their sixteen-year-old son? Even in this 'swinging' age, such an arrangement would seem to violate most commonly held moral standards. Not so, say Mr. and Mrs. Robert Shepard, of 1417 Swallow Lane" (*HBH*, 228). The fundamental outrageousness of the reported action strains against the flatness of the prose, its clichéd presentation of the newsworthy, and the reporter's absurdly objective treatment of the Shepards' new "arrangement."

The teenage son, Robert, "seemed restless and unhappy," says his mother. To keep him out of harm's way the parents "obtained . . . a twenty-four-year old prostitute from the County Detention Farm." Everyone is satisfied: " 'Our boy has matured greatly in the few short weeks since Dorothy came to work for us,' says Mr. Shepard, forty-eight, who is an electronics engineer. 'He is more poised and relaxed.' " The prostitute, too, has presumably adjusted well to her new surroundings, as the reporter rounds out the story of her domestication by noting that "in addition to her other duties, Dorothy also cooks breakfast. One of her specialties is 'fancy eggs,' " and concludes by tacking on the recipe (*HBH*, 228-29). Not only the style of the implied author is being mocked, however; the piece also digs at the ethical relativity of writer and subjects, who all appear unduly proud of their simple economic solution to the family's structural and moral difficulty.[14]

"Snack Firm Maps New Chip Push," which appeared a few issues after "Local Family," parodies another unnamed author, whose eccentric, telegraphic style of writing is one of the targets. At the outset, the piece might seem to aim at the Nixon administration and its handling of the Vietnam War, as its opening paragraph uses real names and lampoons the notorious alliterative rhetoric of Vice President Spiro Agnew (who once condemned the administration's enemies as "nattering nabobs of negativism"):

> Unrest lessens, says Attorney General Mitchell; rest increases. Survey shows Viet struggle major cause of turmoil, but New Moderation policy curbs protest. . . . Simpering, self-appointed smarty-pants targets of Agnew blast, but Vice-President says most young people reject illogical tiptoe-through-the-tulips tactics, instead are "turned on" by realistic attempts to solve problems, truth.[15]

But the writer is not interested in social and political conditions except insofar as these define the market conditions and determine the sales outlook for the snack industry: "Unrest turns youth toward liquids, especially dairy products, and away from crunchy morsels, figures show." The central concern of this analyst is on appraising the sales prospects of "Buffalo Chips," a new product that, as its name indicates, will not sell itself with its intrinsic appeal but will have to be precisely targeted to young consumers and pitched remorselessly.

While "Snack Chips" was not collected, it is representative of other indirect satires included in *Happy to Be Here*. While Keillor throws darts at Richard Nixon or Ronald Reagan (as in "U.S. Still on Top, Says Rest of World" and "The New Washington: An Inside Story") and snipes at the venality of marketing strategies and hubris of urban developers (as in "Your Wedding and You" and "Re the Tower Project"), he eschews biting political satire and frontal assaults against moral outrages in favor of clever parody. It is true that *New Yorker* humorists like Thurber and White had supplied ample precedent for parodies of the genres and dialects of the increasingly technocratic and commercial society – for example, they collaborated in *Is Sex Necessary?* (1929) to parody the then-novel genre of psychological self-help books – but Keillor's penchant for extravagant parody and verbal humor was probably intensified by the work of the experimentalists in the 1960s and 1970s. In any case, both "Local Family" and "Snack Chips" and many of his other *New Yorker* pieces share characteristics of postmodernist fiction.

Words as Words

The words of the Lake Wobegon stories, as critic Jerome Klinkowitz says of traditional fiction in general, "draw little attention to themselves as they work as transparent windows upon the world their stories represent."[16] As we listen to a Lake Wobegon monologue about how David and Judy Ingqvist have quarreled over their Florida vacation plans, we imagine them in our mind's eye, seeing them in the pauses between the spoken words. The words enabling us to "see" the Ingqvists are not objects of interest in themselves but are transparent agents that have only an instrumental importance in creating the illusion of the domestic love narrative that is unrolling on the waves of sound from the teller. The words *as words* efface themselves in the service of the reader's involvement in the flow of narrative, in service of which they lose their own insistent and unique character as signs.

The words of some experimental or postmodernist fiction writers, on the other hand, not typically written to be read aloud but to be scanned visually, may be offered as objects of attention in their own right, like the objects in a nonrepresentational painting or a collage. They are not as "transparent" as the words in traditional stories but are more "'self-apparent' . . . more opaque, forcing the reader to attend to the form of transmission (where the story's action now takes place)" (Klinkowitz, ix). They resist dissolution in the service of some "larger" picture beyond themselves, some already existent cultural pattern toward which words might point. They present themselves as elements of experience to be dealt with directly, not as tokens to be immediately exchanged for the illusionary tableau of the narrative they disappear into to compose.

In Keillor's first two credits in the *New Yorker* and in quite a few other pieces published there, early and late, the traditional storyteller's aims of evoking a shared, communal illusion are displaced by the writer's fascination with words as words. In some of these Keillor's work shows similarities with one of the best-known experimentalist writers of the past 30 years, fellow *New Yorker* regular Donald Barthelme (1931-89). Barthelme's first story in the *New Yorker* appeared in 1963, seven years before Keillor's first, and he continued to publish there regularly through the 1970s. Barthelme's works were surely among those Keillor studied while attempting to first crack that magazine, and he no doubt continued to read more of them after he, too, started publishing there.

In characterizing the distinctive qualities of Barthelme's stories, Larry McCaffery mentions their "resistance to paraphrasable interpretations, their surreal landscapes, unusual characters, and fragmented, seemingly chaotic style." He also mentions "the inward, metafictional quality of his writing, the way he uses his fiction to explore the nature of storytelling and the resources left to language and the fiction-maker." Moreover, his thematic concerns are related to his "metafictional concerns": "the difficulties of expressing a total vision of oneself in a fragmenting universe, the failure of most of our social and linguistic systems, the difficulties of making contact or sustaining relationships with others."[17]

Since Keillor's stories usually aim at evoking laughter rather than at probing the limits of the medium or attempting to disrupt the conventional forms of art and communication, he is not best described as an experimentalist. Even so, many of his pieces do draw on themes and techniques common to experimental fiction of the sort exemplified in Barthelme's stories, such as those collected in *Come Back, Dr. Caligari* (1964), *Unspeakable Practices, Unnatural Acts* (1968), and *City Life* (1970). "Local Family Keeps Son Happy" preceded Barthelme's short story "A Film" by one week. Two issues later Keillor's second credit, "Snack Firm Marks New Chip Push," appeared. The Barthelme story, like the two by Keillor, is also essentially a parody that preys on and disrupts the conventionalities of conventional genres, making visible linguistic structures long since become transparent by virtue of familiarity. Thus it can be argued that even in his first appearance in the *New Yorker*, Keillor dealt with such typical Barthelme themes as "the failure of most of our social and linguistic systems" and "the difficulties of making contact or sustaining relationships with others." "Snack Chips," with its peculiar, truncated style and ostensible concern with the impact of real political events on the fortunes of hypothetical snackfood companies, shares several features with Barthelme's "A Film." One critic has said that this story "juxtaposes the significant with the insignificant" and concerns the making of a film that has been interrupted by "a real life drama," thus blurring "all distinctions between art and reality, real or simulated emotion, and evil and innocence."[18]

First among the distinctions of Barthelme's career, if McCaffery is right, has been his role as "our society's most consistently brilliant critic of the language process itself and of the symbol-making activity" (100). Keillor's own concern with language, his eye for style and ear for dialect, is apparent throughout the burlesques that make up the greater portion of *Happy to Be Here*. Keillor's project is hardly so philosophically pregnant or tendentious as that of Barthelme, but in "Nana Hami Ba Reba," which travesties the genre of science fiction, "the prime target of the parody is language itself" (Lee, 134).

"Nana Hami Ba Reba"

The nonsensical words of the title "Nana Hami Ba Reba" are supposed to form a meaningful sentence in a language named Metro (created by the metrification of English). The heavy use of nonsense words allows Keillor to engage in *bricolage* – to assemble opaque words that point beyond themselves only obscurely, if at all, as when a Metro phrase, "kaba anoka," incorporates the name of the town where Keillor went to high school. The first-person narrator, identified as Curt, works in Long Range Linguistics in the administration of the C.E., or Preemy Gaga – Metro for President of a comic-dystopic United States. The C.E. won election on a campaign that centered on a metrification plank, the brainchild of Curt: "'We need a break-through,' I output. 'People are down on America. We need to change their minds.' I thought metric could stop the drop and start the upturn" (*HBH*, 180). The "metrification plank" recalls the topic of Keillor's 1974 editorial "Thinking Metric," in which he opposed the government's imposition of the metric system, arguing that language is too complicated to be legislated. Originally published in February 1980, the story incidentally satirizes the first election campaign of President Ronald Reagan. But the satiric energy is not concentrated on Reaganism or the metric system; its targets are so generalized that it can be read as an exploration of the displacement of the natural – including natural language – with technological and bureaucratic substitutes.

Special homage is paid to George Orwell: "It was then almost 1984 (O.T. [Old Time])," says Curt about the time of the election campaign, "four digits that, owing to George Arliss's book, were embedded in the national mind as the date of totalitarian onset" (*HBH*, 180). In Orwell's *Nineteen Eighty-four* (1948) Winston Smith had worked at rewriting history and struggled against the toils of Newspeak. Curt's work on Metro seems similar as he is engaged in manipulating symbols to alter the public reality: "I got a low-lying job in Linguistics verbalizing nouns, etc. 'Language lags. Make updates. New it,' the C.E. sentenced. (Or, in Metro, 'Swakfon na wah to neba. Dit. Moto')" (*HBH*, 181). But Curt's heart is not in his job, and he cannot or will not master Metro completely enough for the C.E.:

> He had always been impatient with those who could not keep up. After years of speaking English, some of us were accustomed to looking up strange words in Western's, but Metro had no Western's, of course, because it changed so rapidly. And the C.E.'s daily update chips gave no English equivalent for new modes and phrases. "Metro cannot *be* equaled," he often stated. "It does not translate, it separates. Think Metro on its own terms. Don't relate it – *resonate*." (*HBH*, 181)

At the conclusion the C.E. "retros" Curt "to a time in the past that I was then unable to have remembered." Though the story does not center on character, the narrator, Curt, is represented as a bemused, alienated, perplexed man, full of unresolved anxieties, who is ultimately punished for his failings by being mysteriously exiled.

A similar situation obtains in Barthelme's "Me and Miss Mandible" (1961, reprinted in *Come Back, Dr. Caligari* in 1964). This story is offered as the diary of Joseph, a 35-year-old married veteran, a former insurance adjuster, who has found himself mysteriously back in the sixth grade. Joseph decides that he must have misread the signs that governed his life; he was "plucked from my unexamined life among other pleasant, desperate, money-making young Americans, thrown backward in space and time" to be reeducated and possibly punished:

> I . . . read the company motto ("Here to Help in Time of Need") as a description of the duty of the adjuster, drastically mislocating the company's concerns. I believed that because I had obtained a wife who was made up of wife-signs (beauty, charm, softness, perfume, cookery) I had found love. . . . But I say . . . that signs are signs, and some of them are lies. This is the great discovery of my time here.[19]

Although this story takes place "after" Joseph's transportation through space and time, while most of Keillor's shows the events preceding the time of Curt's transportation, both stories deal significantly with the nature of language and the elusive nature of signs in general. Curt and Joseph have both tried to do what was expected of them, to be solid members of their group, patriotic citizens, and reliable followers of their leaders. But the solid ground of family, job, and country reveals itself as an insubstantial network of arbitrary and ever shifting signs, and it seems their very steadfastness and loyal, literalistic devotion proved to be their downfall. They were doomed logocentrists who believed in stable meanings of the words they lived by, slow to discover that the words were only signs that referred endlessly only to other signs.

Dueling Dialects

One parodic technique Keillor often uses involves the combination of two incongruous styles or genres in one text in such a way that each subverts the other. In "Around the Horne," for example, nothing is quite what it seems at first glance. The title of the piece is a pun on the name of a newspaper sports columnist, Bill Horne, who, according to a note, is sick and replaced for the day by the first-person narrator and author, Ed Farr. Farr is the comic butt as well as first-person narrator, since his own words reveal that he is not only a nonprofessional sportswriter but an unprofessional journalist. He announces that it would be easy to criticize the local baseball team or the manager for their losing season but that, instead of doing that, he will offer "constructive criticism," based on his insider's knowledge as the team's new manager. Thus he claims what journalists would see as bias as his advantage and lays the blame for a losing season on the fans. Instead of showing the proper support, the fans booed mistakes and became bitter, he claims, sending the team the message, "You are not O.K. You are bums" (81).

Keillor's main subject, his terminology, and even the organization and style of the rest of the piece conform to that of pop-psychology and self-improvement books such as Thomas A. Harris's best-seller *I'm O.K., You're O.K.: A Practical Guide to Transactional Analysis* (1969). Unlike the typical sportswriter, Farr discusses his players as if they were clinical subjects and describes new training routines that owe more to trendy therapeutic regimens than baseball fundamentals.

The awkward necessity that compelled MPR to continually ask for money yet avoid sounding either like mendicants or mercenaries often drove Keillor to distraction. Fund-raising and grant-grubbing provoked him to write such editorials as "Pecunia Pro Arte" and inspired the humorous poems he wrote for several years to be read over the air during Pledge Week at MPR, each of them using the station's phone number in the refrain.[20] This cup-rattling dimension of the arts provided the germ for two of the stories, including the lead, in *Happy to Be Here.*

In "Jack Schmidt, Arts Administrator" and its sequel, "Jack Schmidt on the Burning Sands," Keillor crosses the hard-boiled detective story with the bureaucratic jargon of arts management as he allows a former private eye to narrate his adventures in the grants game. The first sentence of the earlier tale sets the tone: "It was one of those sweltering days toward the end of the fiscal year when Minneapolis smells of melting asphalt and foundation money is as tight as a rusted nut" (*HBH*, 17). Jack's tough talk collides uproariously with his newly acquired grant-ese so that the style of the page-turner exposes the pomposity of the grant proposal. He succeeds where more deferential arts managers fail because when the funder reads one of Jack's grant applications, "he knows that you are counting on the cash, that you fully expect to get it, and that if you are denied you are capable of putting his fingers in a toaster" (*HBH*, 22).

"Shy Rights"

One of Keillor's short masterpieces of the burlesque, "Shy Rights: Why Not Pretty Soon?," parodies not so much the rhetoric of any particular "rights" advocacy group but the capriciousness of such rhetoric and its liabilities to self-contradiction and downright senselessness. The shy narrator's text is derived from a letter he wrote to President Carter "demanding that his administration take action to end discrimination against shy persons" (*HBH*, 217). Truly shy, he never mailed the letter. Similar jokes abound, most of them based on comic paradoxes or oxymorons such as those inherent in the notion

of the "militant shy" who "advocate doing 'less than nothing'"
(*HBH*, 220). Shy Pride is celebrated in "many private moments when
we keep our thoughts to ourselves, such as . . . 'Be proud – shut up,'
and 'Shy is beautiful, for the most part'" (*HBH*, 218). The denial of
shy rights is difficult to prove "not only because the shy person will
not speak up when discriminated against, but also because the shy
person almost always *anticipates* being denied these rights and
doesn't ask for them in the first place. (In fact, most shys will politely
decline a right when it is offered to them)" (*HBH*, 219).

On "PHC" Keillor had become famous as a Shy Announcer, and
most of his spots for Powdermilk Biscuits treated the problems of
"shy persons" with considerable sympathy. His inordinate deference
and sensitivity to the plight of the shy was, in fact, part of the joke.
The narrator of "Shy Rights," however, unlike Keillor as the Shy Person, is a comic butt who does not arouse much sympathy from the
reader. Like most of the narrators in Keillor's published burlesques,
he is a shallow character since the comedy in such pieces is not generated from psychological depths but plays across the verbal surface.
Many of the jokes built into the story found correlatives at one time
or other on the air – as many of Keillor's published stories have
done double duty, usually in truncated form in spots or rewritten as
"radio drama" on the air. But the "PHC" Shy Person was a character
of considerable depth, a lovable *eiron* who appeared week after
week; the selfsame jokes from his lips had resonance that could
never be generated by the flat figures who only appeared in a single
short story.

Autobiographical Stories

Keillor resists the easy generalization that there is a sharp divide
between the stories he wrote for the *New Yorker* and the residually
oral, primarily realistic and emotional fiction of the Lake Wobegon
monologues. Certainly it is true that stories such as "Don: The True
Story of a Young Person," one of the few stories in *Happy to Be Here*
narrated in the third person, could be transposed to the first person
and put into a Lake Wobegon frame, where it would sound very
much like many another of the Sojourner's tales about misunderstood teenagers and their parents.[21] Using "Who We Were and What

We Meant by It" (a 1984 *New Yorker* story reprinted in *We Are Still Married*) as an example, Keillor insisted that his *New Yorker* stories could be refashioned as Lake Wobegon monologues. When asked if burlesques such as "Nana Hami Ba Reba" could also be so transposed, however, he implied that the answer was no, characterizing that story as "purely literary play and not most satisfying" (Interview, 10 August 1990). On the same occasion he also said that the two openly autobiographical stories in *Happy to Be Here*, "Drowning 1954" and "After a Fall," could both be spoken as monologues with very little change, and indicated that he valued these stories more highly than his metafictional or experimental pieces.[22]

The only other non–Lake Wobegon story published prior to 1987 in which an "I" narrator is identified as Keillor himself is "If Robert Frost Had an Apple" (uncollected, published in 1983). In this story, however, Keillor plays an *eiron* yarnspinner, and almost every word is at right angles to the truth. The story opens with Keillor boasting about his word processor (he had recently begun using a CPT with eight-inch floppy disks) and how he impresses "typewriter-type writers" with its amazing capabilities. When they ask if he is not afraid that he might lose some manuscript with one push of a button, he dismissively snorts, "Ha!" and launches into the episodic middle.

The tall tale inside the frame features extravagant lies about his friendship with E. B. White and how Keillor was with him in 1946 when White's epic novel was wiped out by the impulses from a home-made phonograph. One whopper leads to another as he tells of the word-processing disasters suffered by Robert Frost, F. Scott Fitzgerald, Ernest Hemingway and other American greats. Keillor confesses in the conclusion that he is undaunted by the setbacks technology placed in the way of those artists and tosses out a grain of truth by telling that he is "pushing ahead with my own big book [he was working on *Lake Wobegon Days*], a *very* big book" (84), even though recently an alien space ship in a computer game he was playing "swooped in and captured a whole bunch of stuff I had written over the past few months."[23]

"If Robert Frost Had an Apple" masquerades as a memoir, but the first-person narrator discloses next to nothing about the author's real life and feelings. But the same cannot be said of the two other stories in which Keillor looks back on his own experience. He told an interviewer that most of the stories in *Happy to Be Here* began in "extravagance": "Some of them started way off in left field, and it was only through quite a long process that they became anything" (Schumacher, 35). But "After a Fall" and "Drowning 1954" came to him almost as if they were impelled. "Every writer has," he said, "those streaks of intuitive, finished writing, where the piece simply comes to you and teeters on the edge in your mind, and you sit down and very carefully put it down on paper. It's like washing very fine china: you're afraid you're going to break this story as you write it down, but you don't. It goes right down on paper" (Schumacher, 35). In these two stories, Keillor as the "I" narrator sounds like the Sojourner and the Garrison Keillor who narrated "Jason's Birth" and the prefaces and introductions to his books. The style is colloquial and unpretentious but still meticulous, and the self-deprecatory humor ripples over an undercurrent of melancholy to create an effect that recalls some of the personal essays of E. B. White.

God Writes Comedy

In "After a Fall" Keillor characterizes himself as "a tall man who fell now sitting down to write his memoirs" (*HBH*, 256). His tallness paradoxically links him with the perplexed Little Man figure, since people as tall as Keillor have trouble keeping upright and a long way to go down when they lose their precarious footing. Tall fellows "are the funniest to see fall, because we try so hard not to" (*HBH*, 253). His "memoir" opens with an account of a fall down the front steps just two hours previous. A "muscular young woman" jogging by stopped and helped him up – an act of charity that deepened his sense of ineptitude, ridiculousness, and impotence. He goes on to tell in detail about three other infamous falls and provides a chronological list of many others.

While the events of "If Robert Frost Had an Apple" were obvious prevarications, this litany of lapses seems heartfelt. Many readers familiar with "PHC" would have heard him tell in other contexts about his head-first leap into a concrete ceiling, which he also mentioned in a chronology of "PHC": "'Death Leap' by GK (Rochester, [Minnesota] April 20 [1977]) who hit head on low ceiling while jumping onto stage & dropped to knees."[24] Despite the comic embroidery and exaggeration, the self-characterization and the narrated events carry conviction, and the jocose tone deepens to include notes of pathos in the last principal anecdote, which treats the remembrance of one of his most embarrassing falls in the past. That the title alludes to Genesis becomes obvious as Keillor introduces this final anecdote about the time he fell in the company of Donna, a college friend:

> Both of us had grown up in fundamentalist Christian homes. . . . We both felt constricted by our upbringings and were intent on liberating ourselves and becoming more free and open and natural. So it seemed natural and inevitable one night to wind up at her house with some of her friends there and her parents gone and to take off our clothes and have a sauna. (*HBH*, 258)

Clad in the dress of Eden the teenagers recapitulate a slapstick version of the Fall after a hand-held shower "jumped out at us like a snake and thrashed around," spewing ice-cold water on the Eves and Adams, sending them slipping, falling, and grabbing for their fig leaves.

The pratfalls of the naked teenagers are all the funnier because they are so guilt-ridden. But the narrator's theological perspective some 20 years later seems to emphasize grace over guilt, because in the coda he shifts away from the belly laughter of the climactic scene to the quieter humor of the Crackerbarrel Preacher. In this guise he apostrophizes Donna to tell her that "God didn't turn on the cold water to punish us for taking off our clothes – Tom did. . . . Let's try to forget it." So many falls in life are fortunate not from sheer luck but because, ultimately, "God writes a lot of comedy, Donna; the trouble is, He's stuck with so many bad actors who don't know how to play funny" (*HBH*, 259-60).[25] He implies that when as a young father he dropped a storm window from a falling ladder and almost hit his two-year-old son, God protected them both from harm.

Even though "After a Fall" in both style and substance seems to present a Keillor playing only himself, this "memoir" bears similarities in subject, style, and theme to E. B. White's "Afternoon of an American Boy" (1947). White, too, called his piece a "memoir" and recounts his own years as a bashful and backward teenager who was afraid to ask a girl out for a soda and who never went to a high school dance because he was such a terrible dancer. Just as in Keillor's tale, an embarrassing encounter between a young man and woman is transmuted through telling a story that exorcises the shame and transmutes the guilt to comedy.

White's mock-confession begins by mentioning that he grew up on the same block in Mount Vernon, New York, with J. Parnell Thomas, "who grew up to become chairman of the House Committee on Un-American Activities."[26] In the year White first published the piece, HUAC was investigating the film industry, and the refusals of 10 witnesses to answer questions led to their imprisonment and attendant notoriety as the "Hollywood Ten." What made Thomas special to White in his teen years had to do exclusively with his sister, Eileen. Totally smitten, White decided to ask Eileen Thomas to a tea dance in New York City: "The plan shaped up in my mind as an expedition of unparalleled worldliness" (White, 20). It was a plan doomed from the start by his anxieties, inexperience, and the fact that he did not know how to dance. Of course White was not raised a fundamentalist, so there is no fear of a vengeful God to exorcise. There is, however, the brother who became chairman of the infamous HUAC of the Senator Joseph R. McCarthy era. And in the coda the narrator ironically confesses how for 35 years he has "often felt guilty about my afternoon at the Plaza," and when Thomas was investigating writers and grilling them about possible ties with the Communist party he would imagine himself on the stand. Thomas would confront him, and after some preliminary questions, probe deeper, asking if he recalled "an afternoon . . . when you took my sister to the Plaza Hotel under the grossly misleading and false pretext that you knew how to dance?" (White, 22).

The Wages of Sin

"Drowning 1954" in some ways promises to show Keillor's literary kinship with Mark Twain rather than with E. B. White. This account of Keillor as a young boy trying his best to please God and his mother, after all, bears a surface resemblance to Twain's burlesques of Sunday-school tales such as the "Story of the Bad Little Boy" (1865). In the Sunday school books, Twain tells us, the boys are usually named James and have a pious mother who suffers from consumption and who "would be glad to lie down in the grave and be at rest but for the strong love she bore her boy, and the anxiety she felt that the world might be harsh and cold toward him when she was gone." Twain's boy is named Jim, however, and does every sort of wickedness that should, but does not, drive him to confess to his mother "and beg her forgiveness, and be blessed by her with tears of pride and thankfulness in her eyes." In fact, Jim leads a "charmed life," and though he goes boating on Sunday, he does not drown; indeed, he sins constantly, and he winds up "universally respected, and belongs to the legislature."[27]

Just as Twain explodes the Calvinist economy and its lessons about the wages of sin, in "Drowning 1954" Keillor seems at first to be setting out similar charges along the foundations of his fundamentalist upbringing. Instead of faithfully attending his swimming lessons at the Minneapolis YMCA (undertaken at the insistence of his mother after his cousin drowned), the young Keillor would sneak away. Deathly afraid of the water, he hated being "naked among strangers" and under the command of an arrogant swimming instructor. Like James in the Sunday-school books, he reviles himself for deceiving his mother by taking the bus to Minneapolis for his lessons but slinking away to the WCCO radio studios to watch the shows featuring Bob DeHaven and Cedric Adams, wishing he were like them but fearing that he would end up among the derelicts he passed on Hennepin Avenue:

> My life was set on its tragic course by a sinful error in youth. This was the dark theme of the fundamentalist Christian tracts in our home: one misstep would lead you down into the life of the infidel. One misstep! A lie, perhaps, or disobedience to your mother. . . . I marvelled that my fear of water should be greater than my fear of Hell. (*HBH*, 274-75)

His fear that a single misstep would lead him to a bum's life followed by eternity in Hell, intensified by the tracts, is so disproportionate as to seem ludicrous. Yet Keillor does not follow all the way with Twain to blast the theological and moral grounds of his childhood fears to smithereens. Many readers, however, may feel that this is in fact what he is trying to do with the last paragraph, where he tells how he has a young son who is just as vulnerable to fears and bullying as he once was at the YMCA pool with its "imperial swimming instructor."

Keillor told an interviewer how when he reads this story aloud the audience "almost cheers" at the point when he addresses the swimming instructors of the world to warn, "The Big Snapper knows

who you are, you bastards, and in a little while he is going to come
after you with a fury you will not believe" (*HBH*, 276). But audience
laughter at this point, Keillor says, surprises him since the final passage in his view is merely a fantasy of revenge, just "empty threats":
"And it doesn't have any effect," he says (Smith, 14).

Keillor has said that the story is about the cost of deceit. The
young Keillor's fears – that he will be damned for lying to his mother
and later deceiving her by pretending that he *had* learned to
swim – are overwrought and proper targets of ridicule. But the story
in his view, has a solid core of melancholy: "It's a story about deceit
and weakness and you pay the price for deceit. In the story, the
price that he pays is that he steals from himself the pleasure of the
accomplishment once he learns how to do it [swim]." Moreover, this
is a lesson that the young son of the narrator will have to learn for
himself, and nothing a father can do can protect him from suffering
such lessons.

The narrator watching his boy sleep feels reduced to childish
helplessness again, and, empathizing with the pain his son will pass
through, he reacts like a child again, hurling imprecations against the
bullies of the world and plain old death. These are "empty threats"
because such pain, according to the faith of Keillor's parents, is
native to the human condition. The children suffer what their ancestors suffered. As he wrote in his introduction to *Leaving Home*
(1987), "Everything they went through: the loneliness, the sadness,
the grief, and the tears – it will all come to us, just as it came to them
when we were little and had to reach up to get hold of their hand"
(*LH*, xix).

Although most of the pieces in *Happy to Be Here* are satirical to
one degree or another, Keillor commented apropos of "Drowning
1954" that his paragraph of invective against the bullies of the world,
like satire itself, "doesn't really count for anything. It's just like children yelling, 'I hate you, I hate you.' . . . And it doesn't have any
effect, not against bullies and people in power. The older you get,
the more you see what you would like to write powerful satire
against, and the less impulse you have to do it, because you know
what an empty gesture it would be" (Smith, 14). Thus while Keillor
seems to lay a satiric charge under the theology of the Christian
tracts in the manner of Twain, the bang at the end has a hollow ring.
"It's hard to write directly about death," Keillor says, "because we

don't know that much about that, not having died. But I think the anticipation of death is everywhere. Any writing that does not have the anticipation of death in it is kind of foolish, you see, and I don't think that comedy is foolishness. It's very moral" (Smith, 14).

Such a sentiment has a good deal in common with E. B. White's statement in "Some Remarks on Humor" (1941) that "there is a deep vein of melancholy running through everyone's life and that the humorist, perhaps more sensible of it than some others, compensates for it actively and positively. . . . They pour out their sorrows profitably, in a form that is not quite fiction nor quite fact either. Beneath the sparkling surface of these dilemmas flows the strong tide of human woe" (White, 174).

"Drowning 1954," like so many of White's famous pieces, is "not quite fiction nor quite fact either," and its final scene of a father watching his seven-year-old son sleeping and thinking over the dreaded swimming lessons of his own youth corresponds to the conclusion of White's "Once More to the Lake" (1941). In White's autobiographical narrative about his childhood vacations with his family at a lake in Maine, there is the same theme of eternal recurrence, the narrator entertaining the illusion that his son was himself and he was his father and that in the enchanted spell of the lake "there had been no years." But in an epiphanic moment at the conclusion the father's sense of peace and time's suspension is crossed and made poignant as he watches his son take his swimming suit from the line outside the cottage: "Languidly, and with no thought of going in, I watched him, his hard little body, skinny and bare, saw him wince slightly as he pulled up around his vitals the small, soggy, icy garment. As he buckled the swollen belt, suddenly my groin felt the chill of death."[28] White's nostalgia for the past, mingled with his humor and his sense of mortality, his elegiac pastoralism – all these qualities as much as the similarity of subject and theme – find counterparts not only in "Drowning 1954" and "After a Fall" but in many Lake Wobegon stories. Many of Keillor's burlesques and literary jeux d'esprit are funnier than his relatively few passionate, personal tales. But these few rank high among the tales that he values most. Moreover, with their intermingling strands of fiction and fact, their alternating incidence of pathos and slapstick, these stories share the qualities of the oral tales for which Keillor has been most widely acclaimed.

Chapter Five

The Complex Pastoralism
of *Lake Wobegon Days*

And he arose, and came to his father. But when he was yet a great way off, his father saw him, and had compassion and ran, and fell on his neck, and kissed him. (Luke 15: 20)

In the Paul Davis illustration on the 4 November 1985 cover of *Time* magazine, Keillor gazes into the middle distance, his expression radiating quiet pride and conviction, as an idealized lake and town floats across and somehow through his face and glasses. Deng Xiaoping, the leader of the People's Republic of China, peeks impishly from an upper corner, dwarfed by this luminous apotheosis of "Author and Radio Bard Garrison Keillor." "The centerpiece of 'A Prairie Home Companion,'" *Time* said, "is a very long monologue, or out-of-body experience, in which Keillor, his low, breathy voice achieving sonorities like those of a train whistle in the distance at midnight, gives the news from a tiny, some say imaginary, Minnesota farm hamlet. . . . The same sturdy but hard-to-find settlement is the subject of Keillor's new book, *Lake Wobegon Days*, . . . a pack of beguiling lies that has been on the *New York Times* best-seller list for ten weeks and, with some 700,000 copies in print, is the publishing sleeper of the year."[1] The book stayed on the *Times* list for 44 weeks in hardcover, 21 weeks in paperback, and as of January 1992 there were an estimated four million copies in print.[2] The book was a main selection of the Book-of-the-Month Club and the *Lake Wobegon Days* set of four audiocassettes (1986) won a Grammy for best spoken-word recording of 1987 – an award that accentuated the hybrid virtue of his talent as writer and oral storyteller.

In the early 1980s Keillor was often called a "cult hero" in accounts of the growing popularity of "PHC." Yet with the *Time* cover story and the dozens of less prominent reviews and feature stories the book precipitated in the print media, Keillor's celebrity-hood, if not his reputation as a major American author, was assured. *Time* mentioned his writing for the *New Yorker* and his book *Happy to Be Here* but said that it was "the Lake Wobegon imaginings" that warranted comparisons with James Thurber, E. B. White, and Mark Twain. The *Time* story concentrated on Keillor's achievement on "PHC" and did not make a serious attempt at a literary judgment of *Lake Wobegon Days*, and while it noted that the book had some bitter passages, a reader could come away expecting the book to somehow reproduce in print what the monologues achieved over the air (Skow, 73). That this was, strictly speaking, impossible, Keillor probably understood as soon as he seriously set to work. That success in reproducing in a book the warm, pastoral, elegiac strains that *Time* compared to the sound of a "lonesome whistle blowing" could derail his literary ambitions was something he also understood.

The problem was not simply that his rich vein of lore about Lake Wobegon consisted of spots, songs, and self-contained short pieces and that a book, if it was to cohere, demanded a different and larger structure. This problem of genre and unity was compounded by the need to transform or replace words written for Keillor's oral performance with material that would work well in print. Beyond these problems of form and style there was a third, thematic or tonal problem clouding the literary prospects of a long work about Lake Wobegon. Any humorous book in our culture risks automatic dismissal from serious regard by virtue of being humorous. But a humorous book that was convicted of being sentimental or nostalgic, deriving from material generated on a show that had been heralded as a revival of old-time radio, could handily be dismissed as a throwback, an anachronistic return to the forms and methods of earlier local-color writing, an appeal to America's bottomless appetite for escapist kitsch.

The concept of Lake Wobegon from its earliest invocations on Keillor's morning radio show was rooted in the myth of pastoral, a broad and ancient body of beliefs and attitudes that has found expression in the literature of the Western world since the Greeks.[3] The pastoral myth can be defined as a wide set of themes and motifs, including the notion of a Golden Age set in some historical past or in some wholly imaginary or utopian past or future and involving a simple human society living close to nature. Keillor's use of the pastoral was always comic, and although in the early days the comedy was chiefly ironic, it developed elegiac strains, which Northrop Frye associates with the mode of romantic comedy. Frye also notes that both the "theme of escape from society" in such comedy and the "close association with animal and vegetable nature" (common in elegy) correspond with biblical imagery, especially as that imagery is used to embody the theme of salvation.[4]

That many readers found *Lake Wobegon Days* tonally and thematically ambivalent derives in no small measure from Keillor's failure to find a fully successful literary means of resolving the tension between the elegiac and the ironic strains that weave through this comic pastoral. Yet while the novel is tonally ambivalent and structurally imperfect, among the corpus of Keillor's published works it may someday be accorded something like the place currently held by *Huckleberry Finn* among the body of Mark Twain's many volumes – that is, *Lake Wobegon Days* may come to be seen as Keillor's own imperfect crowning jewel, a book that more than makes up for its uneven facets and structural weaknesses with its compelling evocation of moods, powerful themes, and many astonishingly successful episodes.

Though in 1982 he left his morning radio intent on making a novel out of the Lake Wobegon material that had been accumulating since 1969, the most important stage in its composition preceded his conscious attempts to fashion it into a shapely whole. In stark contrast to his *New Yorker* pieces, which he wrote slowly and worked over "with tweezers," the decade's worth of coffee-stained scripts that comprise the first draft of *Lake Wobegon Days* – undated, unsigned, and written discontinuously to an uncompromising weekly deadline – evolved gradually and without any overall plan in mind. Even though Keillor was always writing episodes and creating characters to suit the demands of particular occasions, the Lake Wobegon stories, taken together, comprise one continuous narrative.

Over the first 10 years of "PHC" there unfolded, if not Keillor's novel, then his comic epic, and by 1982 (the year he published *Happy to Be Here*) he was ready to edit, refine, and turn his attention to the literary priorities of unity and coherence. Still, it is the singularity of the narrative voice and the richness of the Lake Wobegon lore that give the book most of its considerable power; and it bears reemphasizing that these essential features developed simultaneous to Keillor's creation of dozens of other fictive voices and settings – most of them quite distant from the voice of the Sojourner and the town of Lake Wobegon.

Although the Sojourner character and voice are not simply that of the man speaking, this voice was not consciously scripted in the normal sense. The character and the voice, as has been shown, evolved dialectically, in many successive imaginings after hundreds of evenings "trying it out on the dog." Keillor had evidently worked at expanding his *New Yorker* stories about radio station WLT into a novel at least as early as 1976 (Letofsky), and the manuscript he eventually produced around 1981 was rejected by Harper & Row, which at the same time rejected Keillor's alternative proposal to write a book based on his "PHC" monologues (their loss was Viking's gain).[5] Around the same time, or perhaps a little earlier, Keillor filled a cardboard box with the manuscript pages of a work he evidently conceived of as a novel from its inception. In his Introduction to *Happy to Be Here*, at least, he tells an anecdote about this "shelf novel" that he worked on in St. Paul sometime after 1974 and before 1981. As he describes it, it does not resemble the WLT manuscript; moreover, he says he "threw the novel into the back of a truck along with some other trash" and forgot about it (*HBH*, 11). If indeed this counts as a third failure at writing a novel prior to 1982 (counting also the WLT manuscript and the idea of a Lake Wobegon novel rejected by Harper & Row around 1981), then it is supremely ironic that in his Introduction to his first collection of short fiction he should be confessing his abject failure as a novelist just as he was about to start freeing from a mountain of scripts the novel that may eventually be seen as his most significant and enduring, if not his most elegantly wrought and artistically polished, literary work.

"Nostalgia Is My Sin"

"The sense that the show draws its strength from the past is inescapable," James Traub wrote in his 1982 *Esquire* profile of Keillor, which concluded by identifying Keillor's voice as one that "rescues something from the past to give comfort to hundreds of thousands of strangers. . . . It speaks of home. . . . 'A Prairie Home Companion' is something different; it is something warm" (Traub,

114, 117). Even the friendliest reviewers of "PHC" had long been talking of the show's homespun values and its redolence of an earlier era; when *U.S. News & World Report* did a cover story titled "The Great Nostalgia Kick" in March 1982, there was mention of "PHC" as a reincarnation of a radio variety show from the good old days. Humor scholar Jesse Bier had generalized in 1976 that contemporary American humorists had not measured up to their predecessors, and he wondered rhetorically if the present age was not "confessing itself a vacuum of talent and ideas" and instead of finding new forms was simply repeating "the heydays of the past."[7] A decade later Bier applied such a thesis specifically to the Lake Wobegon material: "During World War I and into the twenties as America was becoming urbanized, small towns were passing and were the object of nostalgic regard. Keillor's gone back to that – not that *we* have – but we want to migrate back. There are demographic figures that show there are people who want to reverse the urbanization of America. They want to go back to something that's more comprehensible, and he appeals to them" (quoted in Fedo, 138).

On the tenth anniversary of "PHC," nearly two years after Keillor had told of the return of Barbara Ann Bunsen to a town that had started to sound like a pastoral retreat, he acknowledged his drift away from the ironic mode of the earlier "PHC": "I think the current monologues are much different than they were even just two or three years ago. They're much more adventurous. It's a difficult thing to carry off when comedy veers in the direction of sentiment."[8] After telling how in his university days he had satirized his own family and community's values "in the same way Sinclair Lewis satirized them, as leading empty, shallow lives," he talked about how he was (in 1985) no longer a satirist: "I used to be one. But I've become something else, something odd that I don't understand. It seems to be that on the radio show I took a turn back there somewhere and I got out of the comedy business and veered off away from satire and started being more interested in sentiment and, to some extent, bathos. I became much less a cool performer and more emotional" (Beyette, V2). During the first season of "American Radio Company" in the spring of 1990, Keillor distinguished between the monologues he was currently telling and those on "PHC," noting that "they're not so elegiac or pastoral now."[9]

Although the stages of this evolution – at least for "PHC" – are evident enough, and although Keillor would occasionally admit that "PHC" indulged in sentiment and even nostalgia, he more frequently resisted such terms to characterize the show. "I'm not talking about the simple and pure rural life, because this never was," he told the *New York Times* in 1982. "It does the people of Lake Wobegon a disservice to present them in simple nostalgic terms."[10] And in interviews following the publication of *Lake Wobegon Days* he was particularly resistant to the notion that his material was nostalgic: "I'm surprised when people use the term *nostalgic*, referring to the book or Lake Wobegon, and suggest that what I describe is a life that is no longer lived. . . . People who think that towns such as Lake Wobegon no longer exist lead lives of such isolation that I can only pity them."[11]

Keillor had attempted to write a book that was substantially different from his monologues, and he needed to defend the book from an unquestionably pejorative label. Yet many reviewers failed to distinguish between the essentially social and emotional comedy of the oral monologues and the more satirical, sometimes darker, and finally ambivalent movement of the book: "Devotees of 'A Prairie Home Companion' . . . will feel right at home," said an Associated Press reviewer of the book.[12] Even academic communications specialists, sensitive to the differences of the acts of reading/writing as opposed to listening/performing, effectively ignored the importance of those differences. In " 'A Prairie Home Companion' and the Fabrication of Community," the authors seeking to "specify the appeal of 'Prairie Home' " centered "primarily upon those Lake Wobegon monologues that have appeared in the book *Lake Wobegon Days* and also have been broadcast on the program." However effective for studying Keillor's appeal to an audience of both readers and listeners, such a strategy obviates consideration of the significant differences between the book and monologues.[13]

Keillor has noted that the "PHC" audience as he conceived of it was "*not* an arts audience" and that his movement away from satire had much to do with what he perceived about their nature: "The audience that would have enjoyed sharper satiric humor, I think, was an audience more like me – but also a fickle audience. The longevity of the show . . . is really due to the sort of audience that finds storytelling appealing. An audience that has had more experiences, older people, but at the same time is more innocent, and can sit, unlike me, and be appealed to directly, by the guy on the stage" (Blount, 14). Keillor was probably torn between writing a book that would appeal to his wide and variegated radio audience and one that would appeal more exclusively to the literary tastes of the much narrower group within that audience who preferred his *New Yorker* pieces to the emotional stories he told on the air. The judgments of the smaller "arts audience" would weigh more heavily in the determination of Keillor's literary reputation, but his responsiveness to the expectations of his wider public complicated his search for equipoise between the elegiac and the ironic.

The resultant structural complexity of *Lake Wobegon Days* – not to mention its peculiarity or unevenness – must account for the failure of so many reviewers and readers to distinguish the aims and effects of the book from those of the monologues. In conversation in 1990, Keillor was willing to agree that the "PHC" monologues, taken together, could be characterized as crackerbarrel humor, but he recalled a specifically literary motive in adapting them for the book: "*Lake Wobegon Days* is a sort of compromise book. It's taking stories that I thought were better than my performance of them and so that suggested to me that they wanted to be in printed form" (Interview, 10 August 1990). A "compromise book" is not necessarily a *compromised* book, but Keillor's use of the word does seem to indicate that he regards it as a partial success. Such, at any rate, is the estimate of Lee, who judged it a literary experiment that fell short of its goals (Lee, 175). A number of reviewers anticipated her assessment, including Richard Eder, who said that "the effort to transform the 20-minute monologues of his radio program into a more sustained written form doesn't work entirely."[14]

A few months before *Lake Wobegon Days* was published, Keillor characterized the book equivocally as "a collection of pieces which are trying to make themselves into a novel," and when asked if it was "a series of short stories stitched together" or written in a "traditional novel form," he answered that it was

> not a traditional novel. It's episodic, cyclical. It begins in summertime, goes through the fall and the winter and the spring, and it returns to summer. But that's its only sense of time. I go from one thing in the fall of 1959 to something in the fall of '32, and they lie on top of each other. That's my feeling about history in a small town or among families: It has to do with the time of

year. Everything, every story, comes around again. And the course of the year is always tied to the growing season or the liturgical season or a particular seasonal smell or kind of feeling. (Hemingson, 22)

The seasonal pattern resembles that of Thoreau's *Walden* (1854), which also conflates the experience of several years in real time into a single, literary cycle of seasons (Lee, 94). While *Walden* is an important influence on Keillor generally and perhaps directly influenced his arrangement of *Lake Wobegon Days*, the similarity may be largely coincidental. The *News from Lake Wobegon* (1983) anthology of monologues, after all, consisted of four audiocassettes, each named for one of the seasons. The cyclical ordering provided an obvious and fitting way to present tales written and originally performed in close correspondence to seasonal rhythms. It was not used, and would not have sufficed, as the sole structural principle in the book; in addition to adding substantial new material, the monologues from "PHC" have been severely truncated, mixed, extensively rewritten, recontextualized, and supplemented by new material not written for oral performance.

The problem of how to structure and unify the book, however, was subordinate to and in some ways a consequence of Keillor's long-standing ambivalence toward Lake Wobegon. Was Lake Wobegon – as he presented it on the show or in his book – primarily a satire on the simpleminded idealization of the American small-town and rural values, or was it essentially a further contribution to the sentimental local-color tradition? Keillor's need to resolve the tension between his ironic and the elegiac strains was not just a challenge he encountered when he set out to write the book but one he faced every week over the life of "PHC." While the original parodic conception of Lake Wobegon was never abandoned, the material expanded over the years in the direction of the idyll. Eventually, as Keillor elaborated and complicated his stock of poses and representations, he managed to have it both ways, and the town seemed alternately (and sometimes simultaneously) a rural backwater and a pastoral haven. In addition to his various poses, Keillor made use of a number of tactics to subvert or contain sentimentality; some of these he could employ in the book as well as on the air, but some were medium-specific. Overall, live performance by its very nature offered more resources and more room for maneuver.

It is a commonplace of media theorists going at least as far back as Plato that the spoken word has powerful and more versatile communication resources at its disposal than the written word. The latter literally have no voice but are silent and must be decoded and interpreted by the reader without the multiple cues of variation in tone, volume, pace, emphasis, and paralinguistic elements (such as grunts or sighs) supplied by a speaker.[15] Bereft of the storyteller's support, especially in the eyes of an inexperienced reader, the written text may seem a much diminished thing. In *Phaedrus* Plato compared the written word to a bastard child who, unable to answer questions or defend itself, is always in need of the help and protection of its father, the spoken word. Contemporary theorists have convincingly argued that the ambiguity and perpetual deferral of meaning characteristic of the written word pertains to all language, whether written or spoken, and that writing owns distinctive powers unavailable to speech. Yet it remains the case that writing lacks the sensory fullness of speech and that the two media have different potential.

Winged Words

Because he was a skilled performer who could take advantage of the dramatic potential of the oral medium, Keillor could move rapidly between moods, going from irony to reverential awe within several minutes. To do the same in print was much more difficult, even if the aim was merely to transpose an oral tale into a written short story – and the challenge was greater in composing *Lake Wobegon Days*, since Keillor said he was trying to write a novel. Sentimentality and nostalgia could be countered in the fluid and dynamic context of the radio performance much more easily than within the relatively static structure of a book. The overall impression left by the show, after all, was created by the cumulative effect of all the music, spots, and other features in which the monologue was embedded. Swept up in a communal experience, in the participatory movement of the actual performance, the live audience had an altered tolerance for material that, encountered in print by isolated readers, would have seemed redundant and excessively mannered or rich.[16] Furthermore, the sentimentality of a monologue could be subverted by the ironic commentary of a letter from Jack or balanced by an interval of "good, dirty dance music" of the Butch Thompson Trio.

Although "PHC" was a "variety show," it did develop a recognizable structure that, despite being flexible and variable, took on what some considered a ritualistic cast. As such, the distinct nature of the different parts, their relationship to one another, were mutually involved in the determination of the esthetic effect, or the meaning and feeling of the show as a whole. A historian of religion observed that "the entire structure of 'A Prairie Home Companion' . . . resembles a Protestant church service." The standard opening theme, "Hello Love," functioned as an introit or call to worship; the musical numbers, even when they were not gospel or other overtly religious music, functioned as prelude, postlude, and other musical elements of worship. The audience joined frequently in "congregational singing"; the messages and greetings read by Keillor served for the parish announcements and banns; the Powdermilk Biscuit was the Eucharistic bread; and of course the monologue was the centerpiece, just as the sermon is the focus of the Protestant service.[17]

Within the course of an hour or two, with the help of the spoken word, music, and overarching structure of the ritual, a typical Christian service ranges from moods appropriate to the confession of sins and penitence to acceptance of redemption and joyous celebration. That Keillor was aware of such religious resonances is unquestionable; writing of "PHC" in 1980, he said, "Our show down deep in its heart is a gospel show."[18] In 1988 he told Alison Lurie that, out on the stage, "the audience will [often] lead you towards that vanishing point where your own personality and your own ego disappears, where you cease to worry about yourself and what you are about to say. You have the feeling that is described in the New Testament where people stood up and gave witness and were told that God would give them the words. I don't think I've ever come to that point sitting in front of a typewriter."[19] Many of the monologues were sermonic, and even though Keillor would on occasion deny the fact, he would also say, "All comedy is preaching, but it can't show its hand."[20]

The Tomb of the Unknown Shepherd

As he said of the structure of *Lake Wobegon Days*, its cyclical order corresponds not only to the seasonal revolutions but to "the liturgical season." If he had wished to do so, Keillor could have approximated in print much of the sermonic character of the monologues, but he could do little to recapitulate the rhythms and feelings of the whole ritual performance in which they were embedded. Yet some of his methods for resisting the powerful pull of sentiment on "PHC" were quite amenable to adaptation and even augmentation in the book. One of his earliest and most effective means for maintaining this balance was his use of the theme *Et in Arcadia Ego*, "Death is even in Arcadia."[21]

Keillor's recognition that nostalgia was easy but fatal was a corollary of his thorough understanding of the pastoral tradition in which he worked and, more specifically, of the abuses or dangers that commonly attended it. While the pastoral ideal – termed variously as *agrarianism, rural values*, or *the myth of the garden* – has been and continues to be a powerful force in American culture, as Leo Marx argues, the ideal has a "pernicious side." Unsubtly entertained or crudely popularized, the pastoral can take the form of "primitivism," a neurotic refusal to recognize that the benefits of industrialized civilization are not "the spontaneous fruits of an Edenic tree" but the result of organized human endeavor and art. The indulgence in such "sentimental pastoralism" – characterized by irrational affirmation of the natural as opposed to the artificial, the untouched or pristine wilderness as opposed to the cultivated or urbanized landscape – encourages infantilism, anarchy, and "diffuse nostalgia."[22]

The same "theme of withdrawal from society into an idealized landscape" that marks the sentimental pastoral is, however, also central to the "complex pastoralism" found in Jefferson, Cooper, Thoreau, Melville, Whitman, Twain, Faulkner, Cather, Hemingway, and Frost. In the works of such sophisticated artists and thinkers, there is no simpleminded indulgence in a wholly affirmative, escapist idealization of the withdrawal. The ideal is complicated and crossed, or, as Marx puts it, a "counterforce" is introduced in opposition to the idyll. The counterforce might take the form of a dispossessed shepherd in the classic eclogues of Virgil or appear as a locomotive erupting into the stillness of the woods, as in Thoreau's *Walden* and the notebooks of Hawthorne. The latter instance provides the metaphor in Marx's title – the machine in the garden – an image he identifies as being of the same general type as expressed in the motto *Et in Arcadia Ego*, as used by certain European painters of the seventeenth century. Most notably, the motto provides the title for a pastoral landscape of Nicholas Poussin (1594?-1665) in which three shepherds contemplate its words, "*Et in Arcadia [E]go*," carved on a sarcophagus that perhaps contains the remains of a deceased companion. A skull on top of the tomb communicates the message for any who miss the import of the inscription.

Keillor makes consistent and deliberate use of the "death in Arcadia" theme as counterforce against the sentimental pull of the pastoral in his representation of Lake Wobegon and in other comic works not concerned with that little town, such as "The Drunkard's Sunday" and "Drowning 1954." In a series of letters from various imaginary fans and critics of his morning show in 1972, Keillor parodied the mail his controversial show received in the radio station magazine, *Preview*. In one, a fan wrote, "I was much struck by your account of the friend who went back to the old home neighborhood and found his former home replaced." He went on to talk about his own sentimental journey in search of his roots in a small town, only to find that "the meadow with a lovely brook where I once had rendezvous with a lovely farm girl" had become a sand pit and "even the *brook* was gone." The letter immediately following, supposedly from a staff member of the *Minnesota Earth Journal*, says, "Most of the time we know when you're kidding or not kidding, but sometimes we're not sure if we 'get' all your jokes. Ah well, as the Latins used to say, *Et in Arcadia Ego*."[23]

The name Lake Wobegon, with its lugubrious connotations, is antipastoral, and the name of the radio show on which Keillor first talked about the town is itself a cryptic memento mori. The word *companion* he adopted from late-nineteenth- and early-twentieth-century magazine titles, such as the *Woman's Home Companion*. The phrase "prairie home" was borrowed from a Lutheran cemetery. Driving through Moorhead, Minnesota, he saw a billboard advertising a "horrendous new Byzantine prairie mausoleum, which seemed to promise people there was no such thing as death, they were just going to take a nap for a while. The cemetery itself . . . [was] an old

Norwegian cemetery with a cast-iron gate that said Prairie Home. I thought, 'How right, how simple, how true.' . . . The original idea was that radio was your companion as we head toward our ultimate prairie home."[24] The name of the Lake Wobegon cemetery is the Prairie Home Cemetery (*LWD*, 119).

In some of the monologues the elegiac evocation of loss moves toward a comic resolution enabled by the biblical theme of the sovereignty of God and the promise of salvation. Yet in adapting such monologues to the demands of the novel, Keillor has diminished the specifically religious affirmations that may have counterbalanced accounts of impending discord or death. A case in point is the section in "Summer" concerning the Lundberg family and the marital spat of Marlys and Harold Diener (*LWD*, 144-48). The Dieners' argument is aggravated by what Marlys sees as her unfair lot as wife, burdened with child care and household work, expected to be sexually compliant and, above all, obedient to her husband. Harold's invocation of scriptural authority for his belief in wifely obedience had led to his throwing a Bible through the bedroom window when Marlys tried to show a passage that instructed that husbands should love their wives. The differences between this material as it appears in "Summer" from the 13 February 1982 monologue not only provide an example of how scriptural and sermonic dimensions are cut back but also show how the more leisurely, often double- or triple-stranded monologues are tightened, abbreviated, and reworked to fit the structural constraints of the novel.

While many of the episodes that make up "Summer" are narrated in the first person by the Sojourner, many are transposed into the third person, including the tales about the Lundbergs and the marital spat. In the oral version the integrative function of the first-person narrator was much stronger, and he linked a set of anecdotes about the night-prowling Lundberg family to that of the couple (who were named Harley and Naomi Barley) and tied the two strands together in a moral-packing peroration delivered in the pose of the Preacher/Philosopher.[25] In the book Keillor perfunctorily links the two tales, along with several others, by gathering key characters in the Chatterbox Café and shifting the narrative focus from one group of eaters to the next. In both versions the marital fight is put into a comic perspective by placing in the foreground the governing trope of "domestic drama." The husband shouts out his "exit line," preparing to storm out of the house before the stunned audience of wife and children, but his grand moment is crippled by a blast of wintry air when he opens the door. Going to his room to find warmer clothes, he becomes just another guy looking through his dresser drawers for underwear; the kids drift away, the scene changes to life as usual. In the book the trope of drama is not continued or used to link this tale to that of the nocturnal, prowling Lundbergs, and the two episodes seem to do little more than provide vivid particularity to the depiction of eccentric domestic life.

In the oral version, however, they converge in a rhetorical structure in which they serve as tandem illustrations for a meditation on the theme that life is essentially a comedy. After telling how the Lundbergs do not encounter real beasts or fall off high buildings in his own stories, as they might in the hands of many contemporary writers, the Sojourner says that their life is not tragic because "God is the writer in their case, and God writes a lot of comedy. . . . And one of the problems is that God has such bad actors to work with."[26] He uses the trope of drama to return to the marital pair, saying they "are just bad actors. . . . And life isn't a tragedy." Under the aspect of eternity, their fight is comic, since, as he tells us, it took place beneath a needlepoint plaque of a passage from Psalm 36: " 'How excellent is thy loving kindness, O God! Therefore the children of men put their trust under the shadow of Thy wings. . . . For with thee is the fountain of life: in Thy light shall we see light.' Now that's the basis of comedy!" ("PHC," 13 February 1982). No passages in *Lake Wobegon Days* are as resoundingly affirmative as this, nor are any so thoroughly sermonic. The symmetrical, self-contained rhetorical structure of the oral version would have seemed out of place in the episodic "Summer," and such a pattern depended on the intrusive presence of the Preacher/Philosopher, a pose that Keillor diminished almost to the vanishing point in the book.

Circles and Lines

In addition to deleting many of the most affirmative notes struck by the original monologues, Keillor used a number of strategies to transform the typically emotional monologues into material for a novel that was more suitably astringent. The episodic development within a cyclical scheme of order, which at once embodies the theme that "everything . . . comes around again," is supplemented by four significant strands of chronological narrative: an anecdotal narrative history of the town; a fictionalized autobiography of Gary Keillor; the partial biography of Johnny Tollefson; and the account of a life that is presented by the anonymous author of "95 Theses 95." The latter two lives complement and counterpoint the story of Gary, and several critics have interpreted these two characters as avatars of Keillor. The cyclical life of the town, as Keillor imaginatively visited it season after season in episodes on the air, revolves endlessly, but in the novel the circular, atemporal life of the town is crossed by these finite lines of history and biography, which death allows only a certain length. The reinforcement of consecutive narrative elements already present in the monologues with additional lines of continuous development not only helped unify the novel but provided a structural means of counteracting the residual sentiment of the Lake Wobegon pastoral.

The first chapter, "Home," begins with a disembodied, "camera-eye" view, providing a panoramic tour of the town: "It would make quite a picture if you had the right lens, which nobody in this town has got" (*LWD*, 3). A first-person-plural voice soon takes over and tells representative anecdotes. The town still inspires the same immediate conviction that struck an early explorer looking for the source of the Mississippi: "*It doesn't start here!*" (*LWD*, 3). This is a town where "the buildings are quite proud of their false fronts" and where a citizen can be proud of owning a 1966 Chevy with only 42,000 miles on it: "He has lived here all his life, time hardly exists for him, and when he looks at this street and when he sees his wife, he sees them brand-new, like this car" (*LWD*, 5). The dominant tone is ironic: "Left to our own devices, we Wobegonians go straight for the small potatoes" (*LWD*, 7). Eventually, the narrative switches into a first-person-singular voice, the literary equivalent of the Sojourner, known as Gary Keillor before he left Lake Wobegon at 18.

Although more than half of "Home" is given over to first-person autobiographical vignettes in the life of Gary, the initial panoramic perspective does not encourage a reading of his story for itself and its uniqueness but as a representative specimen of the sort of lives lived in this place. In "Home" Gary's life story is highly condensed, and while it is given in chronological order it is so epigrammatic that it works well as a representative instance without causing a wobble in the book's cyclical scheme. Yet as his story accumulates in episodes and anecdotes scattered through the book, its linear trajectory – deemphasized by its dispersal and jumping backward and forward in time – strains against the cyclical structure and its associated theme of recurrence. The disjunction between the continuous/linear and the episodic/circular ordering demands careful narrative alignment and control, which is not maintained with perfect success throughout the story. The biographical and historical elements provide a narrative armature that helps bind together many episodes that otherwise would have in common only their seasonal or thematic associations; sometimes, however, the sense of inexorable motion through time of the linear patterns, with its implicit undertone of mortality and change, seems inconsistent with the cyclical principle and its associations of perdurability and changelessness.

The linear and the cyclical patterns align well through the first six of the 12 chapters, since there is an almost equal proportion of each type. The historical chapters (the second and third chapters, "New Albion" and "Forebears") comprise one-quarter of the book, and Gary's autobiography (in chapters 1, 5, and 6: "Home," "Protestant," and "Summer") takes up about another quarter. But in the latter half of the book – in chapters such as "School," "Fall," "Winter," and "Spring" – the weight shifts decidedly toward the cyclical, and the sense of narrative momentum falters. The inclusion in the second half of Johnny Tollefson's story and the long complaint of the "95 Theses 95" moderate this imbalance; yet the stories of these two characters, even taken together with continuing anecdotes from Gary Keillor's autobiography, are not quite enough to restore equilibrium.

History

The medium of print and the flexibility of the novel as a form allowed Keillor to write passages that could not easily have been spoken in any of the poses used on the air. "I thought I could put in the historical part," Keillor told an interviewer, "that you could never do on radio. The parodies of 19th-century correspondence, the memo-

rial prose. . . You couldn't do this in the frame of a radio narrative . . . it wouldn't sound right."[27] Thus he was freed to invent the
journal of Unitarian missionary Prudence Alcott and to indulge in the
transcendental diction of Henry Francis Watt's poem "Phileopolis: A
Western Rhapsody," an antipastoral vision that idealizes an urban
future: "Turn from this weedy, tepid slough / . . . To richer soil of my
belief: / Phileopolis" (*LWD*, 29). "New Albion" not only parodies
nineteenth-century diaries, letters, poetry, documents, speeches, and
historical narratives but uses "eye-humor," such as when Keillor
offers a student's fragmentary outline of the address delivered by
Watt at the dedication of the ill-fated New Albion College:

> a. Gratitude. Much accmp. Much rmns.
>   1. Orpheus. Made nature sing.
>   2.
> B. How puny comp. to Words of God. Moon,
>   stars &c. (*LWD*, 47)

The burlesques of rhetorical fustian and tumid poetics, the use of
cacography and other visual-humor techniques, characterized the
humor of the literary comedians, who used them for much the same
purpose as Keillor: to make war on sentimentality (Blair, 123). The
many footnotes in "New Albion" and throughout the book not only
provide more visual humor but often introduce additional burlesques of scholarly or otherwise pretentious prose.

   Keillor's direct assault on sentimental idealizations of the frontier via the Phunny Phellow techniques that emphasize verbal and
visual comedy is supplemented by lavish use of the stretcher. In
addition to tall explanations, such as the tale he serves up in answer
to the question, "Why isn't my town on the map?" (*LWD*, 90), the
raucousness and even bloodiness of some of his episodes occasionally exceed those of the humorists of the old Southwest. As Lee has
observed, his bear story in "New Albion" is so tall (with *two*
unhuntable bears) that it one-ups its literary precursors, Thorpe's
"The Big Bear of Arkansas" and William Faulkner's "The Bear," and
effectively "parodies the genre" (Lee, 100).

   The parodies, tall tales, and humorous characters that fill "New
Albion" and "Forbears" are set into a reasonably accurate outline of
Minnesota history, complete with references to names, dates, and
historical events. Examples of how the larger contours of his histori-

cal sketch also conform to the record include his portrayal of the successive stages of settlement, with the early settlers being primarily American-born, followed later by Norwegians and Germans; his treatment of push- and pull-factors affecting immigration, including the importance of "America letters"; his account of inter-ethnic rivalry and the importance of language and cultural maintenance through institutions such as the ethnic church, press, and fraternal organizations such as the Sons of Knute (modeled on the Sons of Norway, founded in Minneapolis in 1896).

"New Albion," with its chronicle of the initial stage of settlement by the New Englanders, is largely made up of material specifically written for the novel and not previously used in oral monologues. While Keillor had for years been saying that the town was founded by Unitarian missionaries bent on going west and converting "the Indians to Christianity by the means of interpretive dance" (*LWD*, 25), the ethnic origin of most of his characters was Norwegian or German. Bruce Michelson suggests that this chapter, with its mockery of the earnest New Englanders' attempts to establish their Phileopolis-on-the-prairie, amounts to a subversion of the traditional myth of the Founding Fathers. "The chapter," he says, "is a declaration of independence for the Midwest, and for every region and people who have been exhorted to take their culture, their identity and their heritage from the chromos of The First Thanksgiving, the first thousand pages of the *Norton Anthology*, . . . or any other official source."[28]

Keillor's treatment of the land-taking, while often hilarious, convincingly explores the cultural and psychological "cost of settlement," an emphasis he shares with the treatments of this theme in Willa Cather's *My Antonia* (1918) and Ole Edvart Rölvaag's *Giants in the Earth* (1927). There are more than enough suicides, murders, and pitiful deaths to match or exceed the dire toll paid by the settlers in Cather's Nebraska, and "as far as frontier catastrophes go, Keillor's chronicle of the early settlements puts Rölvaag's to shame" (Michelson, 26). In a two-page subsection in a series dealing with various "firsts" – first schools, physicians – Keillor describes the earliest murders or suicides in a series that begins humorously but becomes increasingly grim, including a case in which two daughters plot with their lovers to have the rest of their family shot down at supper so they might inherit their house. The last paragraph tells of

"a newborn child found in a privy," the discovery of the decom-
posed body of a young woman, and the body of a man who had
been "stabbed and left to die in a ditch" (LWD, 59-61). Such dark
passages set off the lighter tones, but there is surely another purpose
at work, again in keeping with Cather and Rölvaag: that of getting it
right, of reminding subsequent generations of the difficulties of those
who went before.

The toughness of the lives of Keillor's Norwegians, their stal-
wartness in the face of poverty and the pain of their divided
hearts – is ironically juxtaposed to the effeteness of their urban
descendants, and nowhere more sharply than in "Fall." Some of the
Ingqvists flew to Minnesota for Thanksgiving in a blizzard, where
they cower in a downtown hotel; while they sleep, the road crews
remove the snow and salt the streets, and a few hours later the
Ingqvists revive and drive off happily to surprise the grandparents in
Lake Wobegon, even though they had previously telephoned to say
they could not make it. Between the passage that recounts their fear
and depression over the storm and their later descent on the unsus-
pecting Wobegonians, Keillor inserted an anecdote about an
Ingqvist's great-grandfather, Sveeggen. In 1887, at the age of 12,
Sveeggen "was lost in a blizzard between the barn and the house"
and got his bearings only because the house caught fire; certain of its
location, he was able to run into the barn (breaking his nose, but
surviving to continue his line) (LWD, 207). This juxtaposition not
only functions to insinuate comically the notion of cyclical decline
but foreshadows the novel's final scene, which alludes to similar
encounters with the Troll-like treachery of the Midwestern snows as
depicted in Giants in the Earth (and many other novels set in the
region).

Keillor satirizes the romanticization of ancestors and the foolish
pride in who came first with an anecdote about the founder of the
Daughters of the Pioneers – an exile who returned from Honolulu.
Her suspicion that one of her own forebears was one of the earliest
settlers was corroborated by research; it also turned out, however,
that the ancestor in question, Magnus Oleson, stole a horse,
deserted from the Union Army, and believed that Abraham Lincoln
was "a butcher and a barbarian" (LWD, 67). He married three times,
and his surviving children saw to it that his portrait hangs in homes
of descendants from Chicago to Michoacan, Mexico: "Anyone who

looks hard at him gets a good hard look back telling you to buck up, be strong, believe in God, and be about your business" (*LWD*, 79). The stern old face must raise a question for his descendants – a question Keillor articulated years later in a monologue about a visit to Ellis Island, where he saw a striking picture of immigrants and apostrophized them: "If you knew that your descendants were going to be such *foreigners*, that you would hardly recognize them; if you knew how this story turned out, would you still stand in line, or would you get back on the boat and go back where you came from?"[29]

Prodigal Sons and Daughters

It is tempting to speculate as to whether the novel might have seemed more coherent had there been further development to Gary Keillor's story in the world beyond Lake Wobegon. There was precedent for sustained development in his picaresque saga of Barbara Ann Bunsen, in which he followed the course of her life from the summer of 1976 to the winter of 1981. In her single appearance in the novel, Barbara Ann comes home for Thanksgiving from the Cities, accompanied by her husband; this episode curves into the theme of recurrence as she mothers her father, mailing him information on health and exercise and watching what he eats (*LWD*, 204, 216).

Barbara Ann's story as originally told in her letters paralleled her creator's own, but it dealt almost entirely with what happened *after* she left Lake Wobegon. The parallelism remains implicit, but the focus in Gary's autobiography is on his life *before* leaving home. There are only a few pages devoted to Gary's wayward years between 18 when he left and 43, his age at the time of narration. But while this period is addressed briefly in "Home," it remains largely a blank, unless the reader is willing to supplement it with the narrative of Garrison in the Preface. Restricted to the bounds of the novel-proper, the reader is left to guess how Gary, who from the age of 14 or so "ran a constant low fever waiting for my ride to come and take me away to something finer" (*LWD*, 15) and who in college "didn't care where I was from so long as it was someplace else" (*LWD*, 19), managed to become this narrator, a figure quite distant from any of his represented avatars.

During the period he was actively working on the novel, Keillor experimented with a comic version of the parable of the Prodigal Son ("PHC," 15 October 1983) and later published it as a one-act play. Keillor's retelling follows the original pattern of the younger son's moody rebellion, riotous living, helpless failure, and remorseful return to his father's joyous welcome and the elder brother's consternation. He departs from the paradigm, however, by concluding not with the father's astonished reproof to the jealous elder brother – "But your brother was dead and he's alive again! He was lost and now he's found!" – but with even more complaining from the elder brother.[30]

The Sojourner, for all his ironizing, ridicule, and self-deprecation, is a mature, successful, and emotionally stable adult who can with considerable equanimity chronicle and even rise to celebrate the town despite its faults, which he remembers but is strong enough to forgive. His story of Gary corresponds to the paradigm of the Prodigal Son in its beginning and end, but its middle is for the most part undramatized. He has returned, if not to stay put, then for repeated visits and with sustained interest, and even a sense of nostalgia, quickened by a middle-aged sense of the inexorability of time: "Now all the giants are gone; everyone's about my own size or smaller," he says, and concludes his condensed autobiography in "Home" citing Shakespeare's sonnet Number 73, which expresses how a sense of mortality intensifies affection: "This thou perceiv'st, which makes thy love more strong, / To love that well which thou must leave ere long" (*LWD*, 23).

Family Romance

The undramatized middle in this Prodigal's case is clearly not about riotous living and waste, culminating in abject failure and remorseful return. On the contrary, the Sojourner's various allusions to his radio show provide evidence of considerable success in the wider world. Other clues about the middle are offered in the several episodes that chronicle the story of Johnny Tollefson. While this Prodigal's narrative also has a fragmentary middle and lacks any account of a return, Johnny's early rebellion evidently takes the same path – that of authorship – that Gary followed in achieving the independent identity and authority that enable him to return to Lake Wobegon on his own terms. Johnny's acute embarrassment over being identified with his family, hilariously recounted in an earlier tale about his trip to register at St. Cloud State University, parallels Gary's shame when his family walks out of a St. Cloud restaurant (because they are too poor and because alcohol is being served there): "Why can't we be like regular people?" Gary asks (*LWD*, 110).[31]

Both Johnny and Gary are tall and skinny, and the two are further identified by their similar fantasies about changing places with Tony, the teenage son in the detective novel series featuring the sophisticated and cosmopolitan Flambeau family: "Tony was treated like an adult, and he got to live life to the full. He wasn't always being told to wait" (*LWD*, 163). At one point Gary imagines his mother calling his father "Chonny" – Johnny pronounced with an accent – in a passage that details another fantasy wherein his parents became "more interesting" by way of being Italian, the voluble and passionate Keillorinis (*LWD*, 20).[32] According to Freud, fantasies of this type are "known as a child's 'family romance,' in which the son reacts to a change in his emotional relation to his parents and in particular to his father." As the child begins to compare his parents to others and experiences slights, disappointments, and rivalry with siblings, "the child begins to detach himself from his parents and to adopt a critical attitude towards the father." At the level of myth, the family romance takes the form of the hero who is raised in obscurity by humble folk, but whose real parents are royal.[33]

The particular hostility toward the father is made explicit in the final Johnny Tollefson episode in "Revival," which reports that one of two poems he published (both under pen names) was titled "Death Dad." "Our home isn't like that at all," says his outraged mother; "Where did you get those ideas?" (*LWD*, 307). Gary, too, from an early age wrote under a pen name, as readers can infer from the text, though Keillor's rechristening of himself as Garrison is not represented in the novel.

In "News" the Sojourner recalls telling the local editor that he was writing a novel about Lake Wobegon (*LWD*, 259), and at several places in the chapter he alludes to his nationwide travels, presumably "in the radio show business," as his Aunt Flo puts it in her account of his visit printed in the *Herald-Star* (*LWD*, 273). In addition to these details that match what readers know about Keillor, the narrator also throws in an outrageous fable about how his "real mother was in the carnival, she was the fat lady and the tightrope walker," and she left him with the cotton-candy man, who laid him on a doorstep, giving him a pencil to play with. Exploiting the comic incongruity of such an imposture amidst the "news" is not the only function this passage serves, however, since it can be read as a parody of a youngster's family romance. While it offers no reliable news whatsoever, the fable ascribes his destiny as an author to an uncanny or at least a self-begotten origin: the pencil, the token of his destiny as author, does not come from his parents.

Readers may know from sources outside the text that Keillor's parents disapproved of his early interest in writing, but such knowledge is inferable from what the Sojourner tells about his family's beliefs as members of the Sanctified Brethren in "Protestant": "The Brethren did not hold with ambition of worldly success. . . . College was not necessary, nor was a well-paying job." They hold up the host of a locally popular radio show as an negative example of "what happens to people who get too big" (*LWD*, 118).

Telling several parallel narratives rather than concentrating on the story of a Gary or some single protagonist prevents the linear structures from obscuring the cyclical plan and the theme of recurrence. The lives of Barbara Ann, Johnny, Gary, and the author of "95 Theses 95" are intended as specimens of the larger life of the town, and it is the representative life, not the life of a particular protagonist, that is the central subject of the novel. There are, of course, many other specimen lives offered in the text with no fuller development than that given to Barbara Ann's story in the single episode in which she appears. Stepping back from the particularity of each linear narrative and looking at all of them as aspects in the larger design of this complex pastoral, the individual anecdotes represent stages on anyone's life journey, and Lake Wobegon begins to yield its regional character and flavor, becoming anyplace or, more exactly, home.

Four-year-old Gary's innocent and fervent conviction that Adams Hill in Lake Wobegon is the actual site of Eden and God's creation of the world runs afoul of his sister's rivalry and her eight-year-old child's skepticism: she forces him to renounce his belief or chew dirt (*LWD*, 10). Adams Hill is the pastoral scene of the idealized child-

hood, what Cardiff Hill was to Tom and Huck in *The Adventures of
Tom Sawyer* (1876): "Cardiff Hill, beyond the village and above it,
was green with vegetation, and it lay just far enough away to seem a
Delectable Land, dreamy, reposeful, and inviting."[34] At about the
same age as Huckleberry Finn when he ran away from St. Petersburg,
Gary argued with 12-year-old Jim that the drowning of their friend
Paulie was part of God's plan. But Jim insisted it was just an accident,
and the two wrestle the question back and forth: "Jim believed that
God sort of generally watched over the world but didn't try to over-
see every single detail. He said that, for example, when you're born,
you could be born American *or* Chinese or Russian or African,
depending. In heaven are millions of souls lined up waiting to be
born, and when it's your turn, you go down the chute like a gumball
to whoever put the penny in the slot" (*LWD*, 11-12).[35]

An even 100 years earlier a novel was published in which an
older Jim, riding downstream a few hundred miles on the same river
in which Paulie drowned, sided more with Gary in a similar discussion with Huck: "We had the sky, up there, all speckled with stars,
and we used to lay on our backs and look up at them, and discuss
about whether they was made, or only just happened – Jim he
allowed they was made, but I allowed they happened; I judged it
would have took too long to *make* so many."[36] Striking parallels as
this and others – including those between Tom Sawyer's gang and
Gary's various rituals; Huck's chafing under the stern Calvinism of
Miss Watson and Gary's chafing under the Sanctified Brethren
– probably owe more to the common sources of complex
pastoralism in the American tradition than to the earlier book's influence on the later (although a few years later Keillor quoted Huck
talking about "laying on our backs looking up at the stars").[37]

Neither *Huckleberry Finn* nor *Lake Wobegon Days* allows the
episodes of pastoral bliss to go unchallenged for long. The idyll on
the raft is only an interval, and it is interrupted repeatedly by death
on the shore and even midstream, as anarchic primitivism is celebrated but also subverted by both Twain and Keillor. The life of
Huckleberry Finn, were he to grow old remaining as splendidly free
from "sivilization" as he is in his youth in St. Petersburg, would
closely resemble that of the Norwegian bachelor farmers.

Bachelor Farmers

The well-tended lawns and gardens of Lake Wobegon, not the open fields and what few uncultivated areas may surround it, symbolize the "middle state" pastoralism of *Lake Wobegon Days*. Young Gary's forced labor in the family garden precipitates his assault on his sister with a rotten tomato; he is goaded by sibling rivalry, but the deeper source of his irritation is the necessity of earning bread by the sweat of the brow.[38] Thus asparagus is Gary's favorite vegetable not just because it tasted good but because "it needed no planting, no weeding: it just jumped out of the ground by thousands" (*LWD*, 164). In his contempt for what he calls his "father's lawn compulsions" he resembles the bachelor farmers, who themselves take Thoreau's call to "simplify" farther than Thoreau ever took it himself. They are latter-day Virgilian shepherds, and while their rugged individualism is sometimes placed in a positive light to set off the effete manners of Cities people, they remain in the novel as they were originally used in early Powdermilk Biscuit spots: comic, rude peasants. Their version of escape from civilization's hypocrisies and deceits is explicitly branded as immature.[39] When Gary Keillor complains about having to do yard work on the primitivist grounds that "grass is *meant* to get long, it's part of nature, nature *is* growth," Clarence Bunsen tells him he has "a lot in common with the Norwegian bachelors," about whom he had once said, "In their hearts the bachelor farmers are all sixteen years old. Painfully shy, perpetually disgruntled, elderly teenagers leaning against a wall, watching the parade through the eyes of the last honest men in America: *ridiculous*" (*LWD*, 152).

95 Theses

Bachelor farmers scratch where they itch and spit when they wish, unconstrained by community opinion, but they are not so ridiculous as many of the exiles, including "the ones lured away by the pleasures of school and good money, who can afford to be nostalgic," who seem no happier than those who stayed put (*LWD*, 250). If the pastoralism of Lake Wobegon is best emblematized by well-tended lawns and gardens, that of the exiles is represented by the names of their streets and the pictures on the checks they send Harold Starr for their subscriptions to the hometown paper: "Violet checks, emerald checks, ... printed on a landscape, pictures of ocean or mountains.... The *streets*! Harold has readers on Melody Lane ... Arcadia Crescent ... Walden, Xanadu, Yukon, and Zanzibar, plus all the forestry variations, Meadowglade, Meadowdale, Meadowglen, -wood, -grove, -ridge" (*LWD*, 251-52): sentimental pastoralism run amok.

In the catalog of streets in the beginning of "News," Terpsichore Terrace is followed by an asterisk that calls attention to what Keillor said may be "the longest footnote in American fiction," the introduction to and text of "95 Theses 95." The note is a greatly expanded version of the complaint addressed to the town in general by "the Sneslund boy," who, when he turned 21 and was ready to leave town for good, nailed the note to the door of the Lutheran church in burlesque imitation of Martin Luther.[40] The author is older and anonymous in the novel, and his accusations address his parents, though they also apply to the town. Leaving the author anonymous invites identification of this character with the author of the novel himself – an association that is easy to make, even though the author's family is Lutheran and Gary's was not. Both he and Gary give evidence of having been raised according to the tenets of a narrow-minded, pharisaical version of Christianity, under a parental regime characterized by bad food, hollow conformity, emotional blackmail, and sexual repression.

In the author's numbered propositions we hear the angry, agonized voice of an aging Prodigal who, still brimming with unresolved anger, guilt, and self-loathing, has never negotiated a return and whose struggle to fashion a stable identity independent of his parents shows no signs of resolution:

12. You taught me to be competitive in matters of faith, to take pride in the great privilege of being born Lutheran, even at moments of contrition. Religious intolerance was part of our faith. (*LWD*, 256)

75. I wasted years in diametrical opposition, thinking you were completely mistaken, and wound up living a life *based more on yours* than if I'd stayed home. (*LWD*, 269)

90. I did listen to you, that's most of my problem. Everything you said went in
one ear and right down my spine. (*LWD*, 273)

In this counter-narrative we have an account, unreliable though it
may be, of the psychological struggle that must mark the undramatized middle of Gary's prodigality.[41] The conflict of Anonymous is the
sort that might take place in the gap between Gary's wayward flight
and his return as the Sojourner – a conflict from which he has
emerged less ravaged, having managed an accommodation with his
parents and his past. The other character has never been able to gain
the psychological strength he needs to be able to humble himself
and return to face his parents – necessary preliminaries before the
father can meet him on the road and fall on his neck and order a
celebration.

"I put that footnote in my book," Keillor commented during one
of his promotional readings, "because I thought I ought to include
some of the worst things that someone could say about my home
town." Presumably, his motive was his sense of an author's obligation to tell the truth – an ambition he inscribed in his epigraph:
"Dogs don't lie, and why should I? / . . . Now let me, by night or
day, / Be just as full of truth as they." The neurotic ranting of
Anonymous against Lake Wobegon must be held in balance with the
sentimental benedictions the Sojourner says over the place in other
passages; both narrators are imaginary constructs set to talking about
a fictional place, yet the clash between their antipodal attitudes creates an intensity that points toward a kind of dialectical truth, at least
the kind of truth available in fiction. Thus while many readers find
"95 Theses 95" the darkest passage in the book, many others find it
the funniest. In "truth" it is both, and Keillor's public readings from
this passage evoked some of the loudest laughs.

Keillor told an interviewer, "I was pleased with the footnotes in
the book and that one in particular. . . . I think footnotes have a
place in fiction. There is supporting material which can be read in
sequence or earlier or just glanced at or eliminated entirely, and that
can go into footnotes. It really allows a person freedom of digression
that you want in a book. And I like the idea of a book being packed
and rich and having layers" (Roback, 139). His extensive use of footnotes throughout the novel shows how he reveled in the dissemi-
nating propensities of text, unavailable to him as an oral storyteller.

The longest of these footnotes exploits these possibilities most fully; indeed, it provides an *aporia* in the novel, a gap wherein the novel begins to deconstruct, if not to interpret itself.

Splitting in half every page but the first in "News," the footnoted text of "95 Theses 95" visually reinforces the thematic dissonance between itself and what appears above. The text above rambles episodically along, including accounts of Harold Starr's editorial philosophy, which boils down to "I have to live here too," and parodic news stories that reveal tidbits that the severely discreet *Herald-Star* passes over. It also includes fictitious news about the Sojourner's own career as a writer and radio purveyor of "the news from Lake Wobegon," such as the fabrication that his real mother was the fat lady in the carnival. The footnoted text below, after a brief introduction, is all the first-person, continuous, monochromatic rant of this character, whose incredible tale of persecution paradoxically carries more plausibility as a disclosure of Keillor's psychological makeup than anything the Sojourner reveals about himself above the hairline.

After commenting that he added the "95 Theses 95" to include some of the worst things anyone could say about the town, Keillor said, "Also I put it in in hopes that people who write about this book, the people who write about this show, would no longer use the word 'nostalgic.' But it didn't help."[42] In other words, the book anticipates its own misreading by incorporating into the text a self-reflexive denunciation of nostalgic imaginings that is harsher and more derisive than any likely to be launched by Keillor's subsequent critics:

> 18. You instilled in me a paralyzing nostalgia for a time before I was born, a time when men were men and women were saintly, and children were obedient, industrious, asked no luxuries, entertained themselves, and knew right from wrong. I, on the other hand, was a symptom of everything going to hell in a handbasket. I was left to wonder why I bothered to be born. (*LWD*, 257-58)

Thesis 18 disarms (if it does not nullify) the charge that the book is nostalgic, since in a sense the author admits both to being nostalgic and to hating nostalgia. Thesis 18 steals the fire of the critics and, with the rest of the footnote, counters sentiment elsewhere.

The dialogic potential exploited in this and the many other footnotes is in keeping with the layered complexity in the handling of
narrative and the narrator's identity throughout the novel. The
anonymous author of "95 Theses 95" presents a picture of what the
Gary as Prodigal Son might have become had he failed in his own re-
creation as author, just as the Sojourner presents a more positive
outcome. Yet the correspondence of either persona with the author
is deliberately blurred. Whereas the absence of any name for the narrator of "95 Theses 95" encourages his association with the author,
the inclusion of the names of Gary's siblings discourages too close an
association of Gary and the Sojourner with the presumably maskless
Garrison Keillor who narrates the Preface. "I lived in a white house
with Mother, Dad, Rudy, Phyllis," the Sojourner tells us in "Home,"
speaking in free indirect discourse as young Gary. In doing so he distances himself from the living author, whose elder brother is Philip
and whose sisters are Linda and Judy (LWD, 12).

Another cryptic dissociation is playfully ironic; "the crisis" that
shattered Gary's childhood conviction that his identity and place in
the universe were precisely designed by God was when he learned
that his parents intended to move to Brooklyn Park before he was
born and that he was born in Lake Wobegon "only on account of a
pretty casual decision about real estate" (LWD, 13). Keillor, of
course, lived in Brooklyn Park from 1947 until he went to the University of Minnesota. Yet there are so many obvious similarities
between the narratives of Gary, the Sojourner, the author of "95
Theses 95," and the Garrison Keillor of the Preface that the
temptation to seek additional clues there about the missing middle in
the Sojourner's variation on the paradigm of the Prodigal Son is
irresistible.

What is missing from the paradigm as it appears in the Preface is
the beginning, the rebellion of the son expressed through the struggle to redesign and rechristen himself as an author against the wishes
of his parents. Such a beginning is of course available in the tales of
Gary and Johnny, which in turn find their truncated middles and part
of the end in this Preface. As the Preface informs us, since Garrison
first left home to realize his rebellious ambition, he had married and
fathered a son of his own before managing to secure what was in his
own eyes the status of author. The Preface is ostensibly an apology
supported by a tale of loss. Yet in it we hear of how he was paid

$6,000 for his profile of the "Grand Ole Opry" and how on his cele-
bratory train trip to the West Coast he worked on his stories, thinking of himself as "a successful American author who provided good
things for his family" (*LWD*, vii). In other words, although he places
his ineptness in the foreground and itemizes his failures – that of his
first marriage, his still-born novel, and his inability to write anything
as fine as the two stories he absentmindedly lost in the lavatory – the
anecdotes of loss provide setbacks necessary to dramatize a success
story. Thus the self-deprecatory tale is comic, since no serious harm
has come, and *Lake Wobegon Days* is itself yet another sign that the
Prodigal has come into his own.

Lake Wobegon as Prodigal's Rest

The author of the Preface did not fail and fall back on the mercy of
his father. He negotiated his return to Lake Wobegon by virtue of his
independent identity as Garrison, his name as author. In the persona
of the Sojourner, he may be judged harshly by Wobegonians like the
telephone operator, Elizabeth (*LWD*, 270), but he accepts them.
Indeed, he conceived them in his imagination; he is their father and
mother and he can be philosophical when they berate him. How he
has traversed all this psychological ground so as to be in a position
to forgive their pettiness, how he avoided being overwhelmed by
guilt and anger like the author of "95 Theses 95" – all this remains
undramatized in the novel. The clues smuggled in through the Preface, plus the Sojourner's references to his radio show, might propel
us toward the conclusion that he refashioned himself through his
writing: through the imaginative creation of Lake Wobegon and his
own relationship to it.

Lake Wobegon is the idealized American home, a vision he
ridiculed at first but in which, as he imagined it more deeply, he
rediscovered verities and values he had experienced as a child,
before these were obscured by his adolescent sense of home's limitations and constrictions. Yet while we can accept that he has long
since stopped pretending among strangers that he was from somewhere else and has stopped avoiding acquaintances from the hometown when he sees them in the Cities, without more complete
dramatization of his trials away from home, it is difficult to compre-

hend the sources of his strength. This incompleteness may have much to do with the novel's ambivalent tone, its unresolved tension between the elegiac and ironic modes.

The excellences of *Lake Wobegon Days* from the point of view of craft are like those of so many humorous books – to be found in short compass, not in the overall coherence of the grand design. The novel's cyclical plan emphasizes the drama and thematics of eternal recurrence, articulated by Clarence Bunsen in "Revival": "Anything that ever happened to me is happening to other people" (*LWD*, 334). The similarity and overlapping of the various narratives of Gary, Barbara, Johnny Tollefson, and other characters contribute to the pattern and its central theme. Yet the particularity of each life story, and especially the hints of uniqueness and complexity that cling to the composite narrative of Gary, generate some expectations that are not satisfied by subsuming the stories to the curve of cyclical return.

The novel ends with a fable about an unnamed man who, over the pleas of his family, drove into town in a blizzard because he was desperate for cigarettes (a detail that may link him to the author, who famously renounced the habit on 17 February 1985). On his way home he drives into the ditch; the cigarettes are back where he bought them. Like Per Hansa, the intrepid immigrant hero of *Giants in the Earth*, he had left the warmth of home and family to brave the storm on a mission of dubious practical value. Per's body is found in spring, his dead eyes staring to the West. But as the Sojourner said of these Wobegonian descendants of Per Hansa and Beret, "all the giants are gone" (*LWD*, 23); the quest for cigarettes is not propelled by tragic necessity. But though Keillor shows the man starting out confidently through the snow on "the short walk to the house where people love him and will be happy to see his face," his safe arrival seems less than certain to those who may notice how his buoyant attitude echoes the last thoughts attributed to Ole Edvart Rölvaag's character Per Hansa as he skis off to his death: "No danger – the wind held steady. . . . At home all was well . . . and now mother was saying her evening prayers with Permand."[43]

Whether the man makes it home or not, his proximity to death yields an epiphany, phrased in the uneven cadence of Keillor's colloquial sublime: "Some luck lies in not getting what you thought you wanted but getting what you have, which once you have it you may be smart enough to see is what you would have wanted had you known" (*LWD*, 337). Such a thought would not necessarily be cruelly ironic, even should he not survive his walk; nor was Rölvaag such a thoroughgoing naturalist that he would rule out an unironic interpretation of Per's last thoughts: Per was out in the storm because he loved his dying friend; his home in the New World *has* been established; the saga of his family continues in two subsequent volumes – at home all *is* well, and with him, too, since all must die. The "luck" of the man in the blizzard remains ambiguous and may be interpreted in secular terms as chance or in sacred terms as grace. Will the man still feel lucky if he does not find his way home and freezes close by home? Is Keillor inviting us to believe that we should accept the absurdity of such a foolish end? The answer is probably yes, or at least maybe. In any case, it is clear what Sveeggen Ingqvist concluded about "the great experience of his life" when he nearly perished a century before trying to find his way between barn and house; he was grateful for the rest of his life because grace was extended to him even though he did not deserve it: " '*Hvor er Gud Fader mild, vi alle var fordervet i synd.*' ('How kind is God the Father, we were all lost in sin')" (*LWD*, 207).

It is grace and not luck that curves the lives of Wobegonians into a pattern, and it is grace that allows people to touch "the ungraspable phantom of life" even there. The Sojourner has realized that while he has achieved some stature in life independent of that place, he is at last no better than anyone else; that the father loves the wayward son; that love is not the same thing as justice. To critics who discount the salience or deny the philosophical validity of such religiously grounded reassurances, Keillor's parables of acceptance are tantamount to an endorsement of social and political quietism (Larson and Oravec, 240). Yet in his public life Keillor is not himself quietistic but says he is a Christian and so presumably believes that acceptance of a mediocre or even a bad lot in life can sometimes have a transpolitical validity.

The complex pastoral ideal of Lake Wobegon is at bottom an evocation of home, the Prodigal's rest. But home, like Lake Wobegon, is an imaginary construct, an act of faith, a work of art, a sustaining fable or a myth. The novel demonstrates that Lake Wobegon, taken as a Utopia and model repository of heartland virtues, is unendurable and invites satire. But taken as a myth of home it offers comfort, it requires the elegiac mode.[44]

Storm Home

The evocative power of Lake Wobegon as home is compressed into the episode in "Winter" set in Gary's school days. All the children were assigned a "storm home" where they could seek shelter in case of a sudden blizzard. He was assigned to an old Catholic couple, the Kloeckls, but while his family was "suspicious of Catholics" and no blizzard sent him to their door, "they were often in my thoughts," he recalled, "and they grew large in my imagination. . . . . Blizzards aren't the only storms and not the worst by any means. . . . If the worst should come, I could go to the Kloeckls and knock on their door" (*LWD*, 248-49). As the Kloeckls' place is in a microcosm, so the town is in a macrocosm, the place "where, when you have to go there, / They have to take you in" (Robert Frost, "The Death of the Hired Man" [1914]). Of course the comfort afforded by an imaginary home is on the order of what Robert Frost claimed for a poem: that it could be "a momentary stay against confusion." The only perfect rest for the Prodigal is in the Prairie Home Cemetery, where Clarence buried his Uncle Virgil in an episode in "Fall," one of the most Frostian of Keillor's tales.

There was "bad blood" between Uncle Virgil and his father when he left Lake Wobegon in 1925; Clarence recalled seeing him only once when the family visited him in Nevada where he lived, and Virgil was not hospitable then. The argument that had created the rift was never settled, and he died unreconciled in a state his daughter said he always hated. Yet it was Clarence who found himself driving his body from the airport to Lake Wobegon, arranging the funeral, helping dig the grave, and even presiding at the graveside. Virgil's wife was already dead and his daughter had offered Clarence money to make all these arrangements, excusing herself on the grounds that funerals depressed her and she had plans to take a trip to Hawaii. So while she was in Hawaii – the kind of paradise to which Lake Wobegon is the polar opposite – Clarence was reluctantly, like the farmer in Frost's "The Death of the Hired Man," dealing with the corpse of a man whose closer, less rustic relatives could not be bothered. His impromptu homily at the committal – which was not a part of the version of this story as told on air 5 March 1983 – provides a fitting moral not only for the tale of this Prodigal Uncle but to the comic pastoral as a whole: "I'm glad to have him back and I hope that he is finally at rest. I hope that all of us will take a lesson from it, to settle our arguments as quick as we can. I say this especially to the younger ones. Life is short. . . . It isn't true that time heals all wounds, sometimes they get worse if you don't do something about them. . . . I know I've done things to make people mad and I ask you to forgive me for them and I forgive you for anything you ever did to me" (*LWD*, 198).

Chapter Six

Amid the Alien Sweet Corn: *Leaving Home*

The ferris wheel is the same year after year. It's like all one ride to me: we go up and I think of people I knew who are dead and I smell fall in the air, manure, corn dogs, and we drop down into blazing light and blaring music. ("State Fair," *LH*)

Leaving Home was published in October 1987, less than four months after the oral version of its concluding story was performed on the last "A Prairie Home Companion" live broadcast. The dispatch with which the book sped through the editing and publication process no doubt was calculated to capitalize on Keillor's name recognition, which peaked after his dramatic announcement during a performance on Valentine's Day 1987 that the show would end in June. Three stories appeared in the *Atlantic* as prepublication excerpts in September; it was a main selection of the Book-of-the-Month Club and the Quality Paperback Book Club, and it was on the best-seller list for 22 weeks; by 1990 more than 1.5 million copies were in print.[1]

All 36 stories are titled, and all begin with the first sentence of his oral framing formula, "It has been a quiet week in Lake Wobegon," although none of them conclude with the closing line, "That's the news from Lake Wobegon, where all the women are strong, all the men are good looking, and all the children are above average." More than half are based on monologues from 1986, and 90 percent of the monologues used first aired in 1985 or later; the earliest is "The Royal Family" (13 November 1982), and the latest is "Goodbye to the Lake" (13 June 1987).[2] Even though many characters appear in several stories and some tales carry over narrative or thematic elements from others, and while many follow a seasonal progression, there was no attempt to provide bridges between tales or to restructure them radically to create a more unified whole as in the case of *Lake Wobegon Days*.

That the stories were being offered as reasonably close transcriptions of the monologues was inferable from the copyright page, where Keillor noted, "All of these stories were performed, in slightly different form on 'A Prairie Home Companion.'" There would have been little time to refashion them extensively, at least not the latest among them, since the book's introductory "A Letter from Copenhagen" is dated 13 July 1987, one month to the day following the last performance. Moreover, in the "Letter," after reflecting on his decision to end the show and move to Denmark, Keillor called attention to the oral character of the book, saying that the stories "were written for performance on the radio . . . , as you may see from the tone of them. They were written for my voice, which is flat and slow. There are long pauses in them and sentences that trail off into the raspberry bushes" (*LH*, xvi). Mark Twain pointed out how written things had to be loosened and limbered up for speech; conversely, these stories show how things written for speech may need tightening up and bracing if they are to work equally well in print.

The teller takes great risks in adapting for print what was essentially the working draft of an orally realized text. The published story is no longer a narrative act that took place under the constraints of a given time and place but is radically reconstituted and presented in physical contiguity to the other tales, all originally told on different occasions. In their new order and state the stories exert novel and often unanticipated reciprocal forces on each other. Nevertheless, it is a distinctive mark of Keillor's artistry that the tales work on the page remarkably well, even when only lightly edited. Part of the reason has to be that Keillor's oral stories make extensive use of literate techniques and strategies, just as most of the stories he has written expressly for the page make use of the skills he deployed as a monologuist.[3] Most of Keillor's best work – and it is nowhere more evident than in the texture of *Leaving Home* – is a felicitous blend of the expansiveness, fluidity, and intimacy of oral storytelling with the complex narrative geometry of contemporary written fiction. Still, it is also true that while unheard melodies may be sweet, the heard melodiousness of Keillor's performance of these stories was sweeter, and it is common for those familiar with his work to greatly prefer Keillor's telling to their own reading of these tales.

The rising curve of the popularity of "PHC" probably attained its peak on a Saturday evening in the summer of 1985, even though Keillor's widest acclaim and greatest exposure to listeners and television viewers and to readers of *Lake Wobegon Days* was still to come. In June 1985 Keillor won the Edward R. Murrow Award (given for outstanding achievements in broadcast journalism), but through the blazing lights of his fall 1985 book tour and the televising of "PHC" (experimentally in April 1986 and for seventeen of the last performances), Keillor's annus mirabilis gave way to a period that must have been one of the most stressful in his career. This is not to imply that the stories during those last years are in any way inferior to those that came earlier; there is no falling off. Yet the assumption that Keillor anticipated the end of "PHC" as early as fall 1985 seems evident, in hindsight at least, from the actions of many of the characters in *Leaving Home* who hear a noise in the gearbox below them and sense the slight lurch as they glide backward and down toward the ground. The seasonal ordering and cyclical imagery and themes of these contributions to the Lake Wobegon saga link the book to *Lake Wobegon Days*, but here the wheel turns primarily through a descending arc. There are few mentions of forebears and almost nothing on origins, but nearly all concern a departure, literal or metaphorical, including the poignant, autobiographical "A Letter from Copenhagen," which at least one reviewer preferred to the stories it introduced.[4]

Taking the Bus to Minneapolis

The characters in *Leaving Home* are the familiar Wobegonian innocents, fools, and a few tricksters; and we find more stories about prodigals and parents and more reflections and asides on the nature of storytelling. Lovable rogues appear in a story about a snake-oil merchant ("The Speeding Ticket") and a con man specializing in phony genealogies ("The Royal Family"); the arch con man, Satan himself, appears as a moustachioed snake who, posing as a bus driver, beguiles Adam and Eve to take the trip to Minneapolis ("Where Did It Go Wrong?"). As for tall talk, in "A Glass of Wendy," we learn that the bricks for brewery towers went into making the meandering road because the workers, with part of their pay in beer rights, "felt more comfortable on their hands and knees" (30). In "Chicken" there is a woman whose face does not quite stop a runaway headless bird but slows it down so its pursuers can grab it (48). In "Life Is Good" Benny Barnes was struck by lightning so many times that he takes to standing on top of a hill holding a steel pole but dies years later of pneumonia contracted from standing in the rain (86). Here as in *Lake Wobegon Days* there are plenty of descriptions of midwestern comestibles and inside references to Keillor's chums (and to an enemy or two).

Here and there, however, are passages that seem to allude broadly to events, many of them painful, that attended the last two years of "PHC" and the life of its star – as when in two successive winters Pastor David and Judy Ingqvist long for a week's respite in the sun, away from the narrow scrutiny of the Lutherans of Lake Wobegon: "It's hard work," Judy would like to tell the Board, "to stand up and say what people don't really believe but want to think they do; and it's tough when a man of faith suffers from depression in a town where nice people are expected to be upbeat" (*LH*, 189). And throughout, the motif announced in the title recurs: Roger Hedlund is "tired of being a dad" (9); Darlene is heading for the Cities now to find her absent husband and "wind up her business with him" (171); Dale Uecker is joining the Navy (65); David Tollefson and Agnes Hedder left their respective spouses and children and ran away together (119); Father Emil is retiring and later is ill with cancer (181); Gary Keillor is finally going to places where Tom Flambeau cuts his wider swath, in Europe and New York (236); and on the last page the storyteller sits eating a cheese sandwich in the Chatterbox and watches his characters dissolve in the mist over the lake (244).

Byron Tollefson's moody grousing about the food at the Chatterbox in the final story complements some of Keillor's own complaints voiced in his introductory "Letter." Finding no mushrooms in his soup, Byron says, "It's getting to be like everything else. You got decaffeinated coffee, soda pop with no sugar, pretty soon we'll have chemical sweet corn. Taste fresh year-round, and it'll be flat and round like a cracker" (243). Keillor is funny about sweet corn in "Letter," too: "People have wanted sex to be as good as sweet corn and have worked hard to improve it, and afterward they lay together in the dark, and said, 'Det var deligt.' ('That was so wonderful.') 'Ja, det var.' 'Men det var ikke saa godt some frisk mais.' ('But it wasn't as good as fresh sweet corn')" (xiv-xv).

Part of Keillor's lament over recent "improvements" in his home-town sounds more alienated than funny, however:

> If I had eaten more sweet corn, maybe I'd still be in Minnesota . . . but I lost touch with people who raised corn and with their church and wasn't invited to Sunday dinner anymore and slowly lost my bearings and felt lost at home. . . . And all the little truck farms around the Twin Cities disappeared that sold fresh tomatoes, squash, and sweet corn at roadside stands or off the tailgate of a truck. Immense shopping malls sprang up in their place like fungus on the grass. (*LH*, xv)

But it was in St. Paul itself that "the worst occurred. The hometown newspaper decided that, being a published author, I was a credit to the community and should be paid close attention, so it announced my romance with my wife and published a photograph of our house, our address, and interviews with the neighbors. I felt watched. Felt mistaken for somebody else. It dawned on me that life might be bet-ter elsewhere" (xv).

A similar chord is struck in the story "Post Office." When the Sojourner goes to pick up his mail in Lake Wobegon one day, he notices that the postmaster keeps a kettle steaming on the stove, even though he does not drink coffee or tea: "I wrote about 187 love letters a year ago, and if I thought the old snoop had steamed the flaps open, reading my words to that lovely woman . . . should I have been thinking of him . . . reading my mind, stealing my life" (206). This story was told 15 November 1986, just short of a year after his marriage to Ulla Skærved (29 December 1985), which followed a courtship that was not only announced by the hometown papers but was a recurrent subject in the monologues from August 1985 into the next year.

The seeming suddenness and impulsiveness of his new romance (the first editions of *Lake Wobegon Days* carried a dedication "To Margaret, my love") in conjunction with the resounding success of the book and "PHC" made Keillor's personal life a hot subject in the press. The *Time* cover on Keillor was dated 4 November, and on 5 November columnist Nick Coleman (who was already persona non grata at MPR) announced the departure of Margaret Moos and the impending Keillor/Skærved marriage in the *Minneapolis Star and*

Tribune, and the *St. Paul Pioneer Press Dispatch* carried the news the following day. Keillor's feelings of distress, resentment, and frustration at the loss of privacy that accompanied his increased newsworthiness, evident in "Letter" and stories such as "Post Office," were also expressed in a number of contemporary interviews.[5]

Love Stories

By no means do all of the biographical echoes in these stories carry a moody or resentful tone; some are downright passionate and even ebullient. In "David and Agnes, a Romance" Val Tollefson works through his deceased father's love letters to Agnes Hedder, the woman with whom he ran away many years before, although both of them were already married with children at the time. His emotions are understandably mixed as he reads through the letters that reveal his father's adulterous love for the woman for whom he abandoned Val and his mother. He burns all of them; the only exception is a love poem that his wife slips into her purse – she "seemed to tremble when she looked at it" (*LH*, 123). The inference that the scandalous passion and love of David and Agnes allegorizes Keillor's courtship of Ulla Skærved appears irresistible, especially as it was told 17 August 1985, the week following a thinly fictionalized account of the twenty-fifth-anniversary reunion of Keillor's Anoka High School class. At the fictional reunion of the Lake Wobegon High School class of 1960, the Sojourner dances with and finally tells the former foreign-exchange student from Denmark, *"Jeg elsker du"* ("I love you"). Later that same month, Margaret Moos, producer of "PHC" from the beginning and the woman with whom Keillor had been living for years, left "PHC" and moved out of the house.

Even though Keillor was severely irked to have his personal relationships subjected to review in the press, he nevertheless continued to allude openly on the air to his romance with Skærved. In such a context, the image of "true love" evoked by Daryl and Marilyn Tollerud lying in each other's arms after burying their 68 pigs in "Hawaii" (*LH*, 218) invites a biographical association, particularly since its original telling (16 November 1985) was followed by a monologue that centered on what Keillor directly acknowledged as acute love sickness for the woman in Denmark. The same "lovesickness" tale strengthens the case for reading biographical resonances not only into the love stories of David and Agnes and Daryl and Marilyn but into those of Senator K. Thorvaldson and his silver-haired lady from Maine (in "Corinne," "Darlene Makes a Move," and "New Year's" [aired 12 April 1986, 6 December 1986, 3 and 10 January 1987, respectively]) and David and Judy Ingqvist.

David Ingqvist's vulnerability to criticism from parishioners and townspeople as pastor and preacher at Lake Wobegon Lutheran Church parallels Keillor's own as host and storyteller of "PHC." On a more intimate level, the church building committee's curious appraisal of Judy Ingqvist's underwear when they come to inspect the parsonage furnace (*LH*, 203-4) and the board's annual reluctance to budget money for Judy and David's participation in the pastoral retreats in tropical climates (in "Post Office" and "New Year's") parallel the press and the public's scrutiny of the private life of Ulla and Garrison. Keillor may even be empathizing with some of the real-life models for characters in his stories when he takes the point of view of Judy, who has to sit in a front pew, as David works her into his sermons: "It's always some dumb thing . . . but he quotes this with a big cheesy smile, and I have to smile up at him in a modest girlish way, when inside I'm thinking, 'You bastard, you didn't even quote me correctly'" (*LH*, 190). But he was not empathizing with Nick Coleman when he made up Rick the TV Dog.

The TV Dog

In Rick's single mention in the book (*LH*, 193) he is blamed for infesting the Ingqvist house with fleas, one among several plagues visited on the parsonage, including a balky furnace, children sick with the flu, and a persistent mouse ("New Year's"). Nick Coleman interprets Rick as a less-than-humorous reference to himself; he also assumes that the "Coleman Survey of 1866," responsible for Lake Wobegon's omission from the map of Minnesota, is another of several kindred allusions (*LWD*, 90-91; in the "Corner Lot" manuscripts of 1975 the survey was headed by a Mr. Berg).[6] Rick appeared in a monologue delivered one month after Coleman had reported that Margaret Moos was leaving "PHC" after ending her living relationship with Keillor and that Keillor planned to marry Ulla Skærved.

According to Coleman, Keillor told another reporter that "I was like a mangy dog that had crawled into bed with him after I wrote the story" (Fedo, 181).

In the monologue, Keillor tells how Val Tollefson tricked soft-hearted Pastor Ingqvist into sheltering the old Irish setter from the cold, but how the Pastor finally sneaks him back into Tollefson's house in the dead of night. The problem with Rick is not only that he loves to crawl onto your lap to watch television (Coleman had been a television critic) but that he loves garbage, not merely to sniff or study it "but to actually eat it. . . . A dog who now more recently has taken to climbing into bed with people" ("PHC," 7 December 1985). This tale went over extremely well with the audience, few of whom probably had any inkling at the time of its inside references. These are not necessary to its enjoyment but are relevant in a critical discussion largely because they illuminate the theme of departure that runs throughout *Leaving Home* and is linked in many ways with Keillor's discussion in "Letter" of his final years with "PHC."

The Valentine's Day Announcement

Keillor's ultimate decision to end "PHC" and to leave the Midwest probably had as much or more to do with stress and fatigue as with anger and annoyance at the downside aspects of celebrity. Indeed, in his formal announcement on Valentine's Day 1987, weariness seemed foremost among his stated motives:

> The show has had a good long run of 13 years in Minnesota, and we're very grateful to all of you who made it seem worthwhile. . . . It simply is time to go. I want to resume the life of a shy person and enjoy with my affectionate family a more peaceful life. . . . We want to live for a while in my wife's country of Denmark. I want to be a writer again. And it is time to stop.
>
> This business is so much fun, it's easy to hang around too long, which you know if you've ever stood up and made a speech. You're terrified at first, but then they seem to like you. . . . Their affection and approval inspire you to remember so many wonderful stories, and so you lavish yourself upon them, and then, in a moment of silence, you hear the unmistakable sound of car keys jingling in the dark. ("PHC," 14 February 1987)

Although Keillor refers to the fun of show business, the mention of the "long run of 13 years," the three uses of "time," and the image of "car keys jingling in the dark" accentuate his fatigue. Looking back in June 1988, he commented that it was sad to see the Department of Folksong end, "and then the old radio show itself came tumbling down, toppled by weariness and the natural stress that comes from playing one town for so long."[7] In "Darlene Makes a Move" Darlene's exasperation with her dead-end job in the Chatterbox, her unsatisfactory marriage to Arlen, and the staleness and constriction of her life in her parents' home in Lake Wobegon parallels Keillor's own feelings toward his work and life in the Twin Cities, down to the very number of years on the job: "This job is like being married to Arlen: you wait for something that isn't going to come. It's taken her too long to find this out. Fifteen years ago she got up the courage to go to Minneapolis and try to find something for herself, and what did she find? Arlen. Come back home with him, and now, thirteen years later, she's right where she started from" (*LH*, 168). This story was told 6 December 1986 – 15 years after Keillor moved from Freeport to the Twin Cities to work at KSJN and 13 years and five months after the first live broadcast of "PHC" (Lee, 151).

The pressure of writing, rehearsing, and performing "PHC" had increased after national broadcasting had begun in 1980 and as the size of the radio audience had continued to grow. As his notoriety increased, so did the demands on his time and energy. In the fall of 1985, for example, in the midst of his romance with Ulla Skærved, he was faced with opening a new season of the show without its long-time executive producer, just at a time when public interest was peaking and while he was also busy promoting *Lake Wobegon Days*. New producers Chris Cardozo and Steve Schlow lasted only about six weeks each, and personal relationships backstage suffered under the accumulated tensions. Musical performers Butch Thompson and Peter Oustroushko – both longtime regulars – left the show in spring 1986. Howard Mohr, who first read his poetry on a road show in Marshall, Minnesota, in November 1975 and had become a regular writer and performer in 1984, was gone by mid-October 1986, leaving even more work to be done.

The Other "PHC" Writers

Keillor had always written virtually all of the Lake Wobegon material (and almost everything else except the musical numbers) – all the spots, skits, and monologues – for more than 40 shows per season. Though he quit his four-day-per-week morning show in 1982 to allow more time to write, and although the season was somewhat shorter by that time, the much larger national audience expected a monologue – each one three or more times as long as those in the late 1970s – in every show. Mohr became a heavy contributor and frequent performer of his own work when Keillor was writing *Lake Wobegon Days* in 1984-85. *How to Tell a Tornado*, a collection of Mohr's humorous prose and poetry, was published by MPR in 1981 and marketed as "A Prairie Home Companion Book" through *Wireless* (the MPR-related direct-mail catalog). By 1983 he was writing material specifically for "PHC" (though almost none of it concerned Lake Wobegon). In all Mohr wrote more than 200 scripts, including "Raw Bits," "Worst Case Scenario," and "One Minute Romances." He would often drive up to St. Paul on Saturdays from his rural home near Cottonwood, Minnesota, to confer with Keillor during the day on scripts and later appear on the show. Mohr performed his own material as Howie Humde (owner of the Walleye Phone Company) and in other roles and was especially well-known for his "Minnesota Language Systems" spots, which formed the nucleus of his book, *How to Talk Minnesotan: A Visitor's Guide* (1987).[8]

Keillor told an interviewer in early 1985 that he got a lot of his monologue ideas from other people, saying that he needed "a few images" to get himself started since he spent so much time in an office (Hemingson, 22). Often ideas simply "passed on" informally from Mohr or another acquaintance to Keillor, who might find a use for them in the monologue. For example, a conversation with Mohr about his daughter's confirmation may have been part of the inspiration of "Aprille," with its long Bible text on the celebratory cake. On the copyright page in *Leaving Home* Keillor credits Joe O'Connell with the mouse episode in "New Year's" and Ulla Skærved with the bus story in "Aprille." Contributors were sometimes paid for significant ideas, even if no actual scripts had been submitted; for example, MPR paid Mohr for ideas used in monologues aired 13 October 1984 (published as "Homecoming" in *Leaving Home* and on *More News from Lake Wobegon* [MPR, 1989]), 25 May 1985, and 31 August 1985.[9]

After the publicity blitz of fall 1985, however, Keillor reportedly found some idea sources seriously diminished: "I used to get a lot of wonderful ideas for stories and characters from people I knew casually, for example, the people who empty your wastebasket or the men who come in and fix the lights in the office," he said (Thomas, F10). But he found that once people in supermarkets and cafes recognized him as a celebrity, they did not talk to him about ordinary things, such as fishing or gas mileage. He felt that he was treated in St. Paul the way Elizabeth Taylor is treated in Hollywood – as a phenomenon: "It's like you're a display of creamed corn," he said (Meier, 8A).

By the late fall of 1986, without Mohr as contributing writer and without a producer equal to his expectations, this writer who had written so voluminously for so long might have feared coming up dry. In any case, the *New Yorker* issue for 8 December 1986 carried an advertisement "seeking a creative, fresh and original writer" for "PHC." It seems likely that Steve Schlow placed the ad, since it asked that résumés and writing samples be addressed to him at MPR. Whether or not Keillor approved of this move, he did make use of some of the ideas that subsequently poured in. Freelance writer Gordon Mennenga was paid for an idea taken from one of his stories he sent in response and also for – what is so rare as to be perhaps unique – the use of an entire story, titled "February 3, 1959" (commonly referred to as "The Buddy Holly Story"), which Keillor adapted and told 21 February 1987. According to Mennenga, it was Margaret Moos and not Schlow who contacted him to say that his story might be used.[10]

MPR had announced in January 1987 that Moos would return to produce the remaining shows, which involved the added complication of working with a television production crew, which videotaped most of the last season from 14 February through the final show of 13 June. Ninety-minute versions of the shows were cablecast over the Disney Channel on a tape-delay the same evening as the live radio broadcast. The 21 February show was one of those videotaped; portions from it were televised nationally by the Public Broadcasting Service on or about 29 November 1991 as part of an hour-long special titled *Garrison Keillor's Home*.[11]

The Buddy Holly Story

Mennenga had originally submitted "February 3, 1959" to the *New Yorker*, but the editors rejected it on the grounds that it sounded too much like Garrison Keillor (Mennenga). Although it was not published in *Leaving Home*, Keillor's collaboration with Mennenga and the way he adapted his story shed light on his working methods and narrative strategies used in the stories collected there. The action in Mennenga's original manuscript unfolds quickly in a compact, chronological sequence. The point of view is that of a middle-aged adult reliving as he tells in the first person the events of a day long ago when he and fellow Pharaohs of Rhythm – his three-member rock band – heard of the plane crash near Mason City, Iowa, that took the lives of Buddy Holly, Ritchie Valens, and J. P. Richardson, "The Big Bopper." The three Pharaohs were preparing to go to high school, but decided instead to set off on an impulsive adolescent pilgrimage, driving to the scene of the wreck. The crash site is a winter blend of the ordinary charged by their sense of the momentous, and the narrator gains an ineffable recognition after he accidentally comes upon the neck of Holly's broken guitar poking out of a snowy cornfield. He leaves the iconic bit of wreckage undisclosed, and the three drive back to Lake Wobegon, hardly speaking, listening to Holly's music on the radio, each of them silently dealing with the realization that this was "the day the music died."

Mennenga says that his is a "straightforward, A-to-Z sort of story," and that when Keillor telephoned him two days before the show, he told Mennenga that he did not work that way, that he was going to "jump around" and make his own story wrap around Mennenga's. Keillor also questioned him about how he had felt about Buddy Holly and his songs when he was a teenager and what reasons he might have had for preferring Holly to Elvis Presley. According to Mennenga, Keillor had asked another friend about how an adolescent might have felt about The Big Bopper. Keillor used the ideas he gathered in such conversations as he wrote a frame tale for his own voice and persona as Sojourner that is about 2,050 words, as compared with Mennenga's inner story of 2,600 words.[12]

Mennenga's tale centers on the narrator's realization – inchoate at the time but discernible from his adult perspective – that an era had come to an end and that his own adolescent dream to make it big as a Pharaoh of Rhythm was lying in the snow with Buddy Holly's broken guitar. Keillor keeps the inner story essentially intact but supplements it with additional narrative incidents and oral effects (e.g., he sings Holly songs and imitates The Big Bopper). In a sense he takes Mennenga's story as a melodic theme, which he envelops within his own distinctive variations, adding harmony and deepening its resonance. Keillor's telling begins with his standard formula, followed by talk about the weather in Lake Wobegon, mentioning by-the-way that the Ingqvists are back from their winter vacation in Florida looking tanned and fit. In the course of such "news" he mentions the current standings of the Leonards basketball team, which prompts him to recall his youth when he and his friend Jim used to dream of state championships as they played on into the night on the Mennengas' gravel driveway. Thus he tips his hat to his collaborator as he introduces one of the other Pharaohs, and begins a tale about youthful hopes for glory on the basketball court – the first of several successive minor narratives on the theme of lost illusions, each of which adumbrates and so intensifies the core epiphany in Mennenga's story.

Keillor's reports on the current, real-time activities of the Ingqvists' (here he updates their doings from the monologue printed as "New Year's") – a practice with analogues back at least to the Bunsen letters – heighten the illusion of reality by seeming to give his fictional characters an extratextual existence. Traditional oral narrative is seldom either so complex or abstract in its handling of time. Keillor often pretends playfully to have a limited point of view, claiming to depend on the news he hears from informants or observes on visits. His true perspective on Lake Wobegon and its characters, however, is both panoramic and panchronic – he can see everything and in multiple planes in time (Kline, 139-40). Thus his introduction touches not only what the Ingqvists did in stories told and untold but what they are doing in their ongoing lives at the moment of narration. This means of blurring the line between fiction and reality bears a close relationship to his direct comments and asides to the listener/reader about his role as storyteller (as when he expresses his disappointment at not being able to describe Clarence Bunsen's heart attack because he is not really having one in "Collection" [*LH*, 79-80], or as in "Hansel" when the wife would get too angry with her husband if she went directly into her house, "so the writer is going to send her around the block" [*LH*, 224]).

Oral narrators often carry a double role by virtue of their physical presence before an audience, but Keillor's "narrative ubiquity" is often redoubled since he not only steps out of the frame to comment in the first person on the telling but also presents himself in the third person as a character or even as the protagonist within the same tale and then impersonates that fictionalized self in dialogue (Kline, 136).[13] The redoubled points of view foster the illusion that Keillor, too, exists both inside and outside the tale. Such narrative strategies have more in common with postmodernist literary technique than with oral narrative tradition or the practice of local colorists and literary comedians (Kline, 136; Lee, 161).

One of the embedded narratives that follows the story of basketball dreams is a family romance of sorts that is entertained by all three Pharaohs of Rhythm. The narrator and his friends Jim and Paulie imagined that some day they would write and record songs and become as rich and famous as Buddy Holly, and they would "all live together in a big house out in the country, outside Lake Wobegon, and we'd be rich but we'd still be very nice people and we'd still go to the Lutheran church and I would be married to Jim's sister, Jeannette" ("PHC," 21 February 1987). Thus Keillor wrapped not one but several narrative strands around the Mennenga tale, and the resulting whole seems more Keillor than Keillor. His careful yet casual-seeming nesting of stories within stories is one of his characteristic strategies as described by Michael Kline, who writes, "The impression that his sub-tales seem to wander away from each other is only apparent. Successive narrations, even embedded ones, are held together thematically as well as by replication of content. They usually evolve organically, each succeeding narrative arising from the preceding one. The main theme is typically rejoined at the end of the story" (Kline, 136).

Again, even though the paratactic style of Keillor's telling is classically oral, the strategy of multiple embeddings is another technique much more typical of literate practice. Kline illustrates his paradigmatic description of this strategy with references to the oral version of "Out in the Cold" (*LH*, 207-11), but Keillor's reworking of "February 3, 1959" would have served him just as well, even though the main narrative was supplied by another writer.

A Tale of Two Tanks

Keillor's adaptation in "Homecoming" of material Howard Mohr supplied about a faulty septic tank follows the same basic plan, though in this case he wrapped his successive narratives around an anecdote as opposed to a complete story. In Mohr's reworked and indepe:..lently published version (about 400 words), Harold Mire is climbing a ladder but notices that though he keeps stepping up, his head stays level with his kitchen window. The ladder is disappearing into the ground. After a friend with a backhoe digs into the sinkhole, they discover instead of a proper septic tank, a 1937 Chevy that had been buried to replace an even earlier wooden septic tank. They fill up the Chevy with rocks and bury the whole mess, and the man with the backhoe settles for 40 bucks, cash, no receipt.[14] Keillor's story opens with news about the Leonards football team, which played its homecoming game as an away game because their field had developed a huge sinkhole.

This adumbrative narrative is followed by a second, the story of Queen Carla Krebsbach and the homecoming parade. Carla, in the Lake Wobegon tradition, will ride in a National Guard tank, preceded by marching Guardsmen with rifles. This detail allows the narrator to offer confessional, self-deprecating, mock-autobiographical asides on his lingering tendency to associate beautiful young women with threatening weapons. He blurs the boundaries of fiction and reality even more by "confessing" that the Wobegonians know stories about him that are shameful to contemplate and that he was called by a nickname that "wild horses couldn't drag out of me now." Then he seals his intimate bond (with millions) by saying, "But I'll tell you: it was Foxfart" (LH, 148).

The next narrative concerns Carla's father, Carl Krebsbach, who while the parade is getting under way is out in his parents' yard probing another sinkhole with a backhoe and discovering a '37 Chevy, overflowing with "thirty years of family history" (LH, 150). As Carl loads the Chevy onto a wagon behind his tractor and heads across town for the dump, the head-on meeting of the two tanks with Queen Carla looking daggers at her Dad from the front hatch and the entire town assembled along the street is not really just another complementary narrative on a parallel theme; it is the consequence of careful plotting (not a typical feature of oral narrative), complete with inevitability, a reversal in expectations, and concluded with a comic recognition. In the closing vignette Carl, nursing a beer, decides that if this disaster had to happen, he is glad it happened "where everyone could see it," an attitude that prompts the story-teller to agree, asking rhetorically, "Who needs dignity when you can be in show business?" (*LH*, 151) – a bit of homespun wisdom that coyly acknowledges the artifice of the whole.

Hohman, Indiana

The small town parade is a familiar institution with enormous poten-tial for climactic comic action. Jean Shepherd (born in Chicago, 1929) used the Thanksgiving Day parade in the fictionalized town of Hohman (based on Hammond, Indiana, where he was raised) as the setting for a comic plot convergence similar to that in Keillor's "Homecoming" in his "Wilbur Duckworth and His Magic Baton," one of the stories collected into his episodic novel *In God We Trust: All Others Pay Cash* (1966).[15] Shepherd's career bears many resem-blances to Keillor's, since both come from working-class midwestern families, both are veteran radio deejays and raconteurs, and both write and publish but also tell and perform stories about their fic-tionalized youth in their own updated variations on the tradition of humorous local-color realism. The fall 1991 *Wireless* even advertised Keillor's *More News from Lake Wobegon* cassettes (which includes four stories printed in *Leaving Home*) on the page facing *Jean Shep-herd: Shepherd's Pie*, a set of four audiocassettes of the humorist reading from "his most popular stories," most from *In God We Trust* and his story collection *Wanda Hickey's Night of Golden Memories and Other Disasters* (1971).[16]

Just as Keillor's performances of his Lake Wobegon stories have been more widely known than their printed versions, Shepherd's radio storytelling and the televised dramatizations of his stories were better known in the 1970s and 1980s than their printed versions in *Playboy* and in his several collections. In the early 1960s Shepherd was so well-known in the East as an "underground" radio storyteller that media theorist Marshall McLuhan made no mention of his writing in his eagerness to characterize what he understood as Shepherd's postliterate orality:

Jean Shepherd of WOR in New York regards radio as a new medium for a new kind of novel that he writes nightly. The mike is his pen and paper. . . . It is his idea that, just as Montaigne was the first to use the page to record his reactions to the new world of printed books, he is the first to use awareness of a totally new world of universal human participation in all human events, private or collective.[17]

Asked some years later if he used his microphone as his pen, however, Shepherd demurred, saying that many of his stories took three or four months to finish and that he worked at *In God We Trust* for six years.[18] Since, like Keillor, he is a virtuoso reader of his own work, his stories benefit from his interpretive skill, and his printed stories, too, for all the labor he has put into them, go better as performed than read. Shepherd's stories often have more oral flourishes of the "Gluuummmp . . . Bluuuummmp" (Shepherd 1976, 72) variety than those that punctuate *Leaving Home* (which has more than enough for printed stories). Still, invidious comparison of the printed stories of both men to their oral performances would probably not be made so often if the latter were not so well-known. It is no doubt the continued accessibility of Keillor's oral storytelling, including recordings of several of the stories in *Leaving Home*, that keeps the comparison fresh.[19]

Both Keillor and Shepherd transplanted themselves from the Midwest to Manhattan, and leaving home is a central theme in the best known work of each. Both look over their shoulder a lot, but whereas Keillor's work has a powerful elegiac strain, Shepherd indulges much more heavily and consistently in hyperbolic irony. Cedar Lake (the name of an actual lake near Hammond) is the site of his youthful protagonist's initiation into manhood, but in "Hairy Gertz and the Forty-seven Crappies" (Shepherd 1972) the men are crude louts and the lake as Shepherd describes it is even more polluted than Lake Wobegon was said to be in an early Jack's spot in which it had a trash mound in the center ("PHC," 7 February 1976). Gary Keillor hears dirty jokes and pees outside with the men when he goes ice fishing ("PHC," 15 January 1983; "Guys on Ice," *News from Lake Wobegon*), but the men are sincere Christians, and the lake can seem like Walden Pond in later years, as when Keillor told of a fishing trip with a fellow named Arnie on a quiet, foggy morning ("PHC," 29 May 1982). And while Lake Wobegon has its seedy sides, Hohman, though only minutes away from fields of corn and tomatoes, is relentlessly antipastoral: "Nestled picturesquely between the looming steel mills and the verminously aromatic oil refineries and encircled by a colorful conglomerate of city dumps and fetid rivers, our northern Indiana town was and is the very essence of the Midwestern industrial heartland of the nation."[20]

Shepherd's stories about Indiana, like Keillor's Minnesota tales, are often called nostalgic. Yet although Shepherd typically employs a youthful perspective and the backward glance, he underplays the poignant and exaggerates the grotesque. Shepherd may be almost as nostalgic for his youth as latter-day Wordsworth, but his regret is more narrowly for the "clouds of glory" attendant on youth itself, not for pastoral haunts of his youth that have passed away. The wistful strains of Keillor's Sojourner often have the same causation, yet in tales like "Lyle's Roof" the context is only faintly ironic when the narrator describes a Lake Wobegon that in the very early morning "is so shining and perfect, so fresh, so still, if you took eleventh-grade English from Miss Heinemann you would think of Wordsworth"; he then recites the first stanza of Wordsworth's "Ode: Intimations of Immortality from Recollections of Early Childhood" (*LH*, 95, 96).

The Great Midwestern Joke

Despite the relatively caustic tone of Shepherd's material, he too has made "the Great Midwestern Joke" his central subject.[21] His midwesterners, like Keillor's, feel doomed to insignificance, to lives of provincial obscurity and sameness. They yearn to escape as soon as they are old enough to have interesting yearnings, yet the joke involves a backward tug, a longing for what they left behind in the great void of the heartland when they moved away to the fabulous coasts or the great cities where tragedy and passion are possible. Today the Midwest is "fly-over land," even to those who live there, but the joke is anything but new. Shepherd articulates its contours, at the same time demonstrating its venerability, in his Introduction to *The America of George Ade*, an anthology of fables and stories by his fellow Hoosier, the turn-of-the-century (1866-1944) humor columnist and crackerbarrel wit: "The thing about the Midwest is that hardly anybody really feels part of something. Everyone is always leaving. No one ever comes except on business or to see ailing rela-

tives. The city is too close to the farm, while beyond the last Burma
Shave sign the prairie rolls flat as a tabletop endlessly to the horizon."[22] Turning to the trope of the world as stage, Shepherd writes,
"The Midwesterner practically by definition is a born Audience
Member. When in the outside world he feels he is eternally a guest,
allowed only to participate in the proceedings because of the polite-
ness of those around him. Or because they aren't on to him yet. In
this respect Ade was a true Midwesterner. Although he was proud of
his birthright he was very conscious of it and wrote numerous articles in his later days defending and explaining Indiana" (Shepherd
1961, 17).

Shepherd follows in the Ade tradition with his own double-
edged pieces about Indiana, just as Keillor alternately ridicules and
celebrates Minnesota. Yet the distinctiveness of Keillor's *Leaving
Home* stories becomes evident in a close comparison of a story by
each that shares a common subject – the family trip to the fair as
described in "County Fair!" (Shepherd 1976, 49-90) and in Keillor's
"State Fair" (*LH*, 109-15). According to the autobiographical narrator
of Shepherd's story, it is the common lot of the Midwesterner to look
forward to the county fair as the shining moment of the year, only to
be jostled by the crowds, sickened by the food, tortured by the rides,
and insulted by the concessionaires.

Gary Keillor has similar experiences, but in "State Fair" his futile
yearning to break free from working-class privation and routine is
further complicated by his family's special estrangement from the
masses. The "good part" of the fair was the same as that anticipated
by young Shepherd – "a loud place with bad food and stink, music
and sex blaring – listen – it's gorgeous" (*LH*, 110); "the bad part,"
however, "was that I had to wear fundamentalist clothes to the Fair,
white rayon shirt, black pants, black shoes, narrow tie, because we
had to sing in the evening at the Harbor Light gospel tent near the
Midway gate. We sang 'Earnestly, tenderly, Jesus is calling, calling for
you and for me,' and fifty feet away a man said, 'Yes, she is absolutely
naked as the day she was born. . . .' I wanted to be cool and wear a
T-shirt" (*LH*, 111).

Shepherd represents his youthful protagonist and his family as
average Midwesterners in every way, from their steady diet of meat-
loaf and red cabbage to Dad's interest in cars, to kid brother's constant whining and runny nose. When these Hoosiers go to the fair,

Mom wants to see the quilts, but Dad goes for the stock car races and Midway rides, a passion he shares with the two boys. Gary Keillor's family is just as working-class in matters of housing, food, Mother's interest in the Home Activities Building, and so on, but while they are representative Minnesotans in most respects, their fundamentalism lends them a singularity, which paradoxically renders them all the more credible and realistic, as it simultaneously establishes a comic disparity between their piety and the worldliness of the setting. The young Shepherd files away his father's curses for future use as his Mom reprimands the Dad for swearing in front of the children, but Gary's father never takes the Lord's name in vain. The dad in "County Fair!" tests himself against the wildest rides, but Gary's family "gave a wide berth to the Midway" because they were Christians (*LH*, 110).

"County Fair!" makes use of a simple frame structure, beginning with a first-person Shepherd as a middle-aged New Yorker who, against his will, is launched in a reverie about the fairs of his Indiana youth because the late movie on television features an "archetypal Hollywood state fair." The unglamorous real fair recollected from the perspective of "kidhood" then unreels in an uncomplicated narrative sequence about traveling to, trudging about, and returning home from the fair. Cloture is provided by a return to the frame, as the adult narrator discovers that, though it is 4 A.M., he has to rush out into the Manhattan night to have a taffy apple.

Keillor's frame in "State Fair" begins with his formula, which instantly invokes his role as Sojourner. The original monologue was evidently broadcast from the grounds of the Minnesota State Fair, as the Sojourner says that it is a pleasure to be there and that he has gone to the fair "every year since I was five." Like Shepherd's narrator, he tells about his family's ritual preparations for the journey and uses Gary's youthful perspective as he describes the typical and the most memorable events from his years in attendance. Except for the frame in "County Fair!," the young Shepherd retains the point of view and is the protagonist throughout the tale. But inside Keillor's frame, after a few pages of autobiographical reminiscence, the Sojourner retains Gary's point of view but uses it to narrate an embedded tale about how one year his aunt Myrna was talked into entering the Minnesota State Fair Cake Baking Sweepstake.

Myrna's cake was undoubtedly the best, but the combination of Christian humility with her "supernatural" baking produced a cake that was too angelic to win on Earth, where people feed on corn dogs and pizza. Gary tells how when the judge (a drunken newspaper columnist) tasted her cake and moved to embrace her, she shrank back and protested, "It's gummy," and he took her at her word (*LH*, 113). Her tale is warm and funny, yet it serves to demonstrate how aunt Myrna is "in the world but not of it," and thus complements Gary's sense of estrangement as he itches in his fundamentalist clothes.

In the conclusion narrative the Sojourner talks of Gary's rides on the Ferris wheel, which he invokes as an emblem of constantly changing continuity:

> Every summer I'm a little bigger, but riding the ferris wheel, I feel the same as ever, I feel eternal. The combination of cotton candy, corn dogs, diesel smoke, and sawdust, in a hot dark summer night, it never changes, not an inch. The wheel carries us up high, high, high, and stops, and we sit swaying, creaking, in the dark, on the verge of death. . . . Then the wheel brings me down to the ground. We get off and other people get on. Thank you, dear God, for this good life and forgive us if we do not love it enough. (*LH*, 115)

Shepherd prefers the coruscating distance of irony and allows only the faintest hints of sentiment, like a breath of Walgreen's perfume, to linger over the last lines of his fictionalized reminiscences. There is nothing in his story that approaches the emotional intensity of such a passage, with its complex point of view, its subtle convergence of several narrative threads, and its deliberate and frank use of symbolism, sentiment, and even prayer.

Storytelling as Séance

The theme of recurrence voiced by Clarence Bunsen near the end of *Lake Wobegon Days* and paraphrased by the narrator – "our lives are being lived over and over by others" (*LWD*, 334) – not only finds symbolic expression in the stories proper, as in the image of the Ferris wheel, but is suggested by the dedication to the author's parents and stated explicitly in his prefatory "Letter from Copenhagen," in which he reflects on the implications of their lives and the lives of his more distant ancestors with his own. The sense of continuity is temperate, since children reincarnate their parents, but the generational rotation instructs with certainty that we owe a death. Once again Keillor memorializes his great uncle, Lew Powell, "the storyteller of my family," now deceased, and declares that while the stories in *Leaving Home* are not about his own family, "I hope they carry on our family tradition of storytelling and kitchen talk, the way we talk and what we talk about" (*LH*, xx).

"Letter" ends with a poem, a ballad of sorts, about his "Great-grandma Ruth, her husband John," who left Newburyport (Massachusetts?) aiming for Oregon but "pulled up in Wobegon, / Two thousand miles short" (*LH*, xx-xxi). They never reached their destination, and the poet offers the poem as a way of perpetuating their dream of arriving, since "we are the life that they longed for, / We bear their visions every day" (*LH*, xxiii). Such a motive for poetry and storytelling is very much in the tradition of singers and bards in oral cultures, who function as the living vessels of their people's memory. The individuality or creativity of the singer – qualities for which a fiction writer is celebrated – are irrelevant since "a singer effects, not the transfer of his own intentions, but a conventional realization of traditional thought for his listeners, including himself."[23]

The oral performance is always situational, an interaction with the audience, and as such it is often ritualistic – the word serving miraculously to bond the hearers into a community. In Trinitarian Christian theology Christ is the Word, spoken by the God the Father (Ong, 75). The quasi-religious role of the bard is equally evident in non-Christian oral tradition, in the sense that bard or singer is not understood as the creator of the word but as a medium or channel through which the divine afflatus passes to circulate through and animate the community. Thus Odysseus praises the bard Demodokos not for his creative imagination and verbal fluency but for the character of his inspiration: "Surely the Muse, Zeus' daughter or else Apollo has taught you."[24] Thus the power of the singer or storyteller is associated with the divine or its cognates in the realm of magic and the occult.

The similarity of "PHC" to Protestant worship has already been noted, but in "Letter" Keillor compares his storytelling not to sermonizing but to conjuration, as he remembers his 13 years with the show as a "sort of séance," a communion with the spirits via the magical intimacy afforded by storytelling and radio: "Standing at stage center with your toes to the footlights, you're as close to a thousand people as you can conceivably be. Out there on the prairie where even close friends tend to stand an arm's length apart, such intimacy on such a grand scale is shocking and thrilling and a story-teller reaches something like critical mass, passing directly from solid to radio waves without going through the liquid or gaseous phase" (*LH*, xvii). As James Traub wrote in 1982, "Keillor is a conjurer of spells, a weaver of white magic" (117).

Keillor cast his spells under the sign of comedy, however, and so the spirits that he called forth are unlike the pitchfork-toting "gigantic man with no eyes and chunks of his face falling off and big clods of brown dirt stuck to his bib overalls" whom he describes in "The Killer" (*LH*, 125). There is no ghastly killer because Keillor is "a storyteller who, for better or worse, is bound by the facts" (*LH*, 125). His metanarrative comment at this point about why he has no such characters in his stories recalls his earlier remarks about why in his stories the Lundbergs are tormented by beasts and demons only in their dreams and not in reality, since "life is a comedy" and God is its author. (The theme echoes in "*Du, Du Liegst Mir im Herzen*," a story about a married couple who have fought up to and during their golden anniversary celebration: "But this is a play, and they're actors" [*LH*, 230].)

Nevertheless, Keillor was, as he admits in "Letter," conscious of evoking in the audience something that might not be too far distant from what classical scholar Eric Havelock called the "paideutic spell," the enthrallment supposedly produced in the audiences of epic poetry or tragic drama. The Socrates of Plato's dialogues attacks sophistic rhetoricians such as Gorgias for their similar use of word magic (anticipating by more than 23 centuries the contemporary attacks on the witchery worked by television). In his objection to the then-new technology of rhetoric, Plato objected to what he under-stood as the passive sleep of reason produced by the uninterrupted, mellifluous speech of the practiced orators, which, by their own admission, worked on the audience like a witchcraft or a powerful drug.[25]

If Demodokos could sing today, he might strum an amplified lyre; similarly, Keillor has not been shy about enlisting the latest technology to heighten the spell. In the World Theater after it was reopened in 1986 he had the assistance of a state-of-the-art recording system, which permitted the use of "panned mono," a technique in which a mixing board is used "to take a monaural signal coming from Keillor's mike and play it in varying levels over the left and right stereo channels. . . . The effect is called 'directional depth.' . . . Script preparation and broadcast techniques are combined to create the effect of being present in a room where someone is telling stories directly to a group" (Larson and Oravec, 234).

Reduced to a bare paradigm and formulated in terms from archetypal criticism, the narrative pattern of the middle and late monologues of "PHC" corresponds to "the drama of the green world," seen in some of the romantic comedies of Shakespeare, in which the plot discloses "the ritual theme of the triumph of life and love over the waste land. . . . The action of the comedy begins in a world represented as a normal world, moves into the green world, goes into a metamorphosis there in which the comic resolution is achieved, and returns to the normal world" (Frye, 182). Each monologue begins with Keillor on stage in the normal world, invoking the ritual entry into the green world of Lake Wobegon by means of the formulaic opening line, inviting the audience to sojourn there together with him, until the séance is over. At the story's end the spell is undone with the ritual conclusion, absent in these printed tales. The line in a live performance was, like all ritual language, not as significant for what it said as for what it did. It is not needed in print because the printed story is not séance, not a communal experience or event but a text to be read. The blank space at the end of the story provides sufficient cloture to any reader who has not already sensed an ending.

Keillor's success at casting his spell, primarily through his live broadcast but also through the dissemination of printed versions of the Lake Wobegon stories, was attested to by Charles Larson and Christine Oravec, who called attention to his use of panned mono. Instead of seeing him as a harmless entertainer or as a closet evangelist, they see what they term his "fabrication of a community" as a moderately subversive kind of spellbinding that is potentially dangerous to the body politic. They expertly explain the rhetorical and technical means Keillor deployed in charging his listeners with the powerful sense that they were not just disparate individuals comprising an audience but members of a community. They contend, however, that by imagining themselves members of this "mediated community" the audience was succumbing to two potentially dangerous illusions: first, that the idyll of Lake Wobegon has affinity with the world of experience; second and far more sinister, that since all's well in Lake Wobegon, all is well in the world we live in. The baby boomers (the chief audience they identify for the Lake Wobegon works) are especially vulnerable to such delusions, since their days of activism and spirited involvement are far behind them; thus they are ready to be lulled by Keillor's artful assurance that "life is good."

Despite all the manifest deficiencies Keillor attributes to Lake Wobegon, the audience yet "may prefer to be sharing common but generalized feelings of exile, nostalgia, and acceptance with projected others whom they never need to meet, rather than sharing more particularized emotions with those with whom they interact." Still worse, since the boomers can see their "own experience of community as a trajectory from innocence, to rejection, to nostalgia [the attitudinal sequence the authors read in Keillor's dramatized stance toward Lake Wobegon], members may in turn apply an attitude of acceptance to their immediate communities. . . . By reproducing the fatalism of the Protestant ethic on a less literal plane, a strategy of acceptance forestalls both utopian idealism and critical activism as alternative approaches toward the building of community" (Larson and Oravec, 240).

The Epistle to the Baby Boomers

The case of Larson and Oravec resembles that made by Plato and other logocentrists against the sophists who used their honeyed words and practiced voices to sway listeners by supposedly illicit means. Pathos, ethos, and melos were seen as illicit appeals because they were alien to the emerging literate, analytic consciousness exemplified in dialectic. Socrates may well have believed in the old gods, but his new mode of inquiry certainly seemed to be at odds with oracular utterance and the spellbinding associated with not only worship of the old gods but the ancient drama and even (according to Havelock) early oratory.

Larson and Oravec seem analogously hostile to the elements of Christian doctrine and modes of discourse that are discernible in Keillor's storytelling. They assume that he has abandoned his fundamentalist theology (identifying his attitudes closely with those of the author of "95 Theses 95" in *Lake Wobegon Days*), but they insinuate that even though his stories do not overtly proselytize he fosters dangerous illusions. They do not, of course, claim that Keillor's theology or politics are those of the theocratic Right. But they do imply that, through his use of the biblical reassurances and the platform tactics of the spellbinders, Keillor helps to assuage the guilt baby boomers feel over the sucking vacuum that has formed in the place once filled with their spirit of commitment and social activism.

Keillor, as postulated by Larson and Oravec, is a man whose belief in a God who controls even the smallest events in history has given way to a godless fatalism, through which he manages to smile only because he has ceased to struggle, and out of which he recommends "a nearly religious quietism" (Larson and Oravec, 233). A possibility they do not appear to consider is that Keillor's biblical reassurances are offered out of genuine and revitalizing religious conviction – convictions, however, that remain both ambivalent and ambiguous since to become more specific would be to abandon humor and the motive to entertain in favor of outright sermonizing.

Keillor told Roy Blount, Jr., that "a certain feeling about preaching, and about the gospel, has been a liberating influence on the show" (16). Asked if there is "something about being funny that seems to you close to the religious impulse," he replied, "Well, I think so. I don't know what it is, and I think the moment you start talking about it, it's almost unbearable. It sounds like a term paper that you don't need to write anymore" (Blount, 16). Keillor's stories, in the way of traditional oral narrative, avoid abstract moralizing; he tends to embody his themes in concrete detail (Kline, 139). But his characteristic avoidance of abstraction does not mean that he has abandoned Christian faith; on the contrary, in a short piece titled "The Meaning of Life" Keillor says that "faith rules through ordinary things" (*WASM*, 217). His conjuring up the miraculous out of the ordinariness of Lake Wobegon can be seen as his ongoing form of testimony to what he recognized after the birth of his son, Jason, as "those small and frequent miracles by which we live" ("Jason's Birth").

It is true that Keillor's religiously charged catalogs of food, backyards, and hot afternoons in the garden tend at times to identify the faith with the contingent cultural forms with which it is embedded – a stance that prompted David Heim to call him "an elegiac poet of Culture Protestantism": "Keillor's remembrances of Lake Wobegon appeal to a certain complacency in our faith, a nostalgia for the days when religion and culture went hand in hand and did not need to be too closely distinguished." Yet Heim, in company with many other writers in the religious press, believes that Keillor's "humor has had an authentic religious resonance for Christians who are acutely aware of the tension between faith and culture. We know that the gospel relativizes all cultural forms; yet we also know that faith is always embodied in a particular culture. By embracing both points, Keillor's humor reconciles us, even encourages us, to live with that tension, confident that if grace can come through the 'Gospel Birds,' it can come through other mundane efforts as well. In any case, we have a faith serious enough to joke about."[26]

Chapter Seven

Exile and the Road Back

What's-their-names I knew back when,
Never liked them that much then,
But memory has been kind and they weren't bad,
I'd love to see those folks again.

("The Song of the Exiles [the Lake Wobegon Anthem]")

When Keillor left Minnesota in search of a job as a writer in either Boston or New York in 1966 his feelings about his native grounds were relatively uncomplicated. When he failed to land a job with either the *New Yorker* or the *Atlantic* he simply turned around and went back home. When in 1987 he left "PHC" "to resume the life of a shy person" and writer, however, he was acting like the anonymous author of "95 Theses 95" in *Lake Wobegon Days*, a 45-year-old Prodigal Son leaving Lake Wobegon and the United States for what proved to be the rather tiresome fleshpots of Denmark. After only four months he was settling into New York City, still resentful toward Minnesota and feeling like the Prodigal's elder brother with the people of Minnesota cast in the role of an unfair father.

Remembering how afraid he had sometimes been during the "PHC" years to sing and perform, Keillor wrote that he had relied on the charitable bosom of St. Paul, feeling that he was theirs, "that Minnesota people were people you could hurl yourself bodily from the stage at and they would catch you and not let you go, but the sad truth is that they only catch you if you fail; if you do well, then you're on your own. . . . The prodigal son's brother knew that: it's failure and disgrace that win the parent's love. You blow the song and people will be nice to you; you make it a big hit and the newspaper will walk up to pee on your roses" ("Who Do You Think You Are?," *WASM*, 129).

Less than eight months after getting on the plane to Denmark Keillor had discovered that he still wanted to perform and work in

radio but felt that he would never live in Minnesota again: "It was
not my choice to leave," he told an interviewer. "It was a choice that
other people made for me, and I'm not happy that they made that
choice . . . , even though I may be very happy about the move."[1] Five
years after his flight, however, he was feeling less sanguine about
living and working primarily in Manhattan, and during a broadcast
from Concordia College in Moorhead, Minnesota, on 28 March 1992
he announced that he would bring his radio show back to the World
Theater in the fall. He told the press that he had bought land within
commuting distance of St. Paul and would soon be living there in an
old log cabin (though he would hold onto his apartment on Central
Park West). In a sense, he would not be living in Minnesota, since his
land was on the Wisconsin side of the St. Croix River. But it was
close enough.

With his fiftieth birthday fast approaching, he said, "I think five
years of exile solves a person's problems very neatly," even though
he would be coming back to live within miles of

> all of the people you've ever disappointed. . . . All of the musicians you didn't
> book for your radio show. . . . All of the people whose writing was turned
> down. . . .
>
> After five years away . . . it's like moving back to a new place, except some
> of my best friends are here, people who've known me long enough and know
> me well enough to be able to tell me when I'm wrong, tell me to cut it out.
>
> A person *counts* such people. My best critics are here. That's reason
> enough to come back.[2]

Whether the people of Minnesota would kill their fatted calves to
celebrate his return and offer an auspicious beginning to a third,
postexilic phase of his career lies beyond the scope of this study.
This penultimate chapter examines the writing and performance of
what may turn out to be the exceptional middle period of Keillor's
career – the years away from the Midwest. First it takes up *We Are
Still Married* (1989), a transitional collection of that includes works
from both the first phase (the years leading up to and inclusive of
"PHC") and the middle phase (the years of "exile"); second, it
reviews the "American Radio Company" (ARC), the nationally broadcast radio variety show Keillor premiered in the fall of 1989. Detailed
discussion of *WLT: A Radio Romance* (1991), completed near the
end of his period of exile, is reserved for the final chapter. Taken

together, these works and performances show broad continuity with what had gone before. But they also demonstrate a more pronounced liberality in the choice of subjects and a renewed interest in forging ahead artistically, experimenting with new genres and modes of writing and expression.

The costume of the Sojourner now seems too tight, and Keillor opens the seams and makes alterations to accommodate a wider range of moods, an increased frankness and intensity. If for a while he played in public the role of late-blooming Prodigal Son and then an aggrieved Elder Brother, on his new radio show he was soon playing a retailored Sojourner as the Lonesome Lutheran, a Midwesterner in Manhattan. But the retailored pose of the rustic was more heavily laced with irony than his Crackerbarrel stance had typically been on "PHC." The Shy Person also appears as the Celebrity, rankled by nosy journalists. In some works Keillor even portrays himself as a Monster of Greed and Ambition, a self-caricature that allows him to ventilate his irritations while simultaneously reducing to absurdity some unflattering appraisals of his reasons for leaving Minnesota.[3] In the works of this period Garrison Keillor's complexity has grown to incorporate personas who can bless with the unction of the Sojourner or curse with the fluency of the Devil.

The work from his exile more openly and amply expresses his passions – lust, anger, frustration. Concomitantly, he became more outspoken and candid on politics, public affairs, and current events, not only in editorials or speeches but in sketches and radio monologues. He dramatized his readiness to be associated with partisan politics when he led the singing of the national anthem at the opening of the Democratic National Convention in 1988.[4] He wrote in praise of the power of passionate love and heaped scorn on President Reagan in the *New York Times* (sometimes in the same piece).[5] He sued National Public Radio over copyright violation; he lampooned *The Man from Lake Wobegon* (1987), the unauthorized biography by Michael Fedo; he testified in Congress in support of the beleaguered National Endowment for the Arts; he editorialized against the Bush administration's proposed flag-burning amendment to the Constitution; he satirized Vice President Dan Quayle.[6] He opposed the United States's role in what became known as Operation Desert Storm in the Middle East (his opinions about the brief war in a Fourth of July speech he gave in Denmark in 1991 so incensed the American ambassador that he denounced Keillor in the press).[7] When he resumed his Lake Wobegon stories on "ARC," the new mayor was a divorced mother of four teenagers who gives birth to a fifth with no husband or boyfriend in sight, and during the Gulf War as the Sons of Knute organized a Living Flag display in support for the troops, the Lonesome Lutheran talked of the need for dissent.[8]

We Are Still Married

The cover of the Penguin *Happy to Be Here* carried a photograph of Keillor sitting in the worn, prerenovation seats of the World Theater and touted him as "America's Tallest Radio Comedian." The jackets of the Viking *Lake Wobegon Days* and *Leaving Home* both carried paintings of the rustic village. But the dust jacket of *We Are Still Married: Stories and Letters* (1989) makes no allusions, visual or verbal, to Lake Wobegon or to Keillor's radio career, showing a beach scene that evokes a sea coast rather than one of Minnesota's 10,000 lakes. An old black typewriter with a sheet of paper under the roller rests on a sand dune in the foreground. The emphasis on Keillor as writer is redoubled by a blurb he apparently wrote expressly for the jacket. In place of a photo of the author, smiling above the tributes from reviewers, he offers instead "a few lines about the great and ancient invention you hold in your hand, the Book itself. . . . Ages before the loudspeaker and the camera, came this lovely thing, this portable garden, which survives television, computers, censorship, lousy schools, and rotten authors." And in the Introduction Keillor presents himself as a writer whose radio work was an interlude: "It was a long reach for a writer, to do a radio show all those years, like a dairy farmer sailing the Atlantic" (*WASM*, xv). Weary and sick after years at sea, longing for his fields and cows, the farmer returns to his farm. Just so, says Keillor, "I was glad to rejoin *The New Yorker* . . . and be back among *paper*" (*WASM*, xv).

Although he was now officially on the staff of the *New Yorker* and had a cubbyhole office there, he also maintained a personal headquarters called the "American Humor Institute" at Eighth Avenue and Fourteenth Street. While he was for a time writing many more unsigned pieces in "Notes and Comments" and "Talk of the

Town" (17 of these are reprinted in *We Are Still Married*, along with 14 additional "pieces" and "stories" that originally appeared in the *New Yorker*), he certainly had not given up performing or radio.

On tour with guitarist Chet Atkins on something called "The Sweet Corn Show" in the summer of 1990, he told a reporter in Hartford that after he left St. Paul, "I thought that I was going to lead a quiet and dignified life of a recluse, you know like Salinger, that over the years, I would become more and more revered by people. . . . I would be one of those writers at work for 20 years on his magnum opus."[9] But as early as March 1988 he had announced that he would be hosting a "Second Annual Farewell Performance" of "PHC" in Radio City Music Hall on 3 and 4 June. In February 1989 he performed in "A Pretty Good Night at Carnegie Hall," and that summer he toured with "The Third Annual Farewell Performance." Between the various farewells to "PHC" he performed in other shows as well, and before the "Fourth Annual Farewell" in 1990 he had launched his new Saturday evening show, "American Radio Company of the Air."

Despite his paean to the book on the dust jacket and his familiar protestation in the Introduction that he was first and last a writer, the author of *We Are Still Married* remained an artist committed to writing and performance. Unlike *Happy to Be Here*, which contained almost exclusively stories and burlesques written for print, this collection represents a broader sampling of Keillor's humor since something over a quarter of the pages are given over to material that might have been or actually was used on "PHC." As of January 1992 the Viking edition had sold 118,000 and the Penguin 80,000 copies.[10]

The section called "House Poems" includes 11 pieces of light verse, some of which had been set to music and sung on the old show. A ballad titled "The Finn Who Would Not Take a Sauna," for example, was one of the numbers included on *A Prairie Home Companion Anniversary Album* (MPR, 1980) and was also one of 13 poems published and distributed as a premium for MPR members in a very slim volume, *The Selected Verse of Margaret Haskins Durber* (MPR, 1979), supposedly brought out by Jack's Press in Lake Wobegon. The Sojourner of "PHC" could, however, hardly have been expected to recite on "PHC" "O What a Luxury," the first poem in the series printed here, since the luxury it celebrates is the joy of urination: " . . . what perfect bliss / so ordinary and yet chic / to pee to piss to take a leak" (*WASM*, 223).

"The Lake" section includes a selection of "Letters from Jack," leading with one occasioned by the beginning of national "PHC" broadcasts in 1980 and ending with one from January 1987. In "The Babe," a tall tale that was the monologue for 13 July 1985, Keillor recalls a Whippets player who used to preach in the dugout, "using the score of the ball game to quote Scripture; e.g., John 1:1: 'In the beginning was the Word,'" and rambles on to describe what happened when Babe Ruth played against the nine Schroeder brothers in Lake Wobegon in 1946. (The oral version was recorded on *Gospel Birds and Other Stories* and was published as "Lake Wobegon Games" in *Sports Illustrated* in 1986.) "Three Marriages" consists of letters written to spouses back home by three traveling Wobegonians; the third letter is by Clarence Bunsen, who writes to his wife from a fishing trip in Saskatchewan telling how he once ambushed an annoying squirrel and felt good about it until his daughter, Barbara Ann, said it was "her favorite squirrel." Though Keillor had used the epistolary format in the Barbara Ann Bunsen letters of the mid-1970s, these three letters may have been culled from an unfinished book about the town that he had begun as a sequel to *Lake Wobegon Days*. He told an interviewer in 1985, "I think the second book will be quite different [from *Lake Wobegon Days*], and it will be a book of letters written by exiles, back to Lake Wobegon, but the letters will all be about the outside world."[11]

"How I Came to Give the Memorial Day Address at the Lake Wobegon Cemetery This Year" is adapted from the "PHC" monologue of 30 May 1987 and 4 June 1988 (and probably various others as well). In it Keillor mixes pathos into the humor, giving a realistic description of the Battle of Gettysburg and concluding on a benedictory note by recalling his sadness over the deaths of all the combatants, noncombatants, and even his recently deceased friend Corinne (*We Are Still Married* is dedicated to Corinne Guntzel [1942-86], a cousin of Keillor's first wife). Though Keillor had touched on the Civil War in *Lake Wobegon Days* and in many monologues, his interest and the level of detail he commands in his description of the battle may have been reinforced by his association with filmmaker Ken Burns. Keillor read the part of Walt Whitman and various soldiers on the soundtrack of Burns's epic series, *The Civil*

War, "the most watched public-television documentary in history when it was broadcast in September 1990."[12] (Following in the footsteps of his "PHC" character, Father Emil, known for his vacation tours of Civil War battlefields, Keillor visited the Gettysburg battlefield during the Fourth of July weekend in 1988 and wrote about it in the *New Yorker,* a piece reprinted as "Gettysburg" in *We Are Still Married.*)

Lutheran Laughter

"The Young Lutheran's Guide to the Orchestra" is found under the rubric "Pieces" among 13 previously published works, most of which were written for the *New Yorker.* But while "Guide" was written after the end of "PHC," it is a script for a performance by speaker and orchestra that burlesques English composer Benjamin Britten's concert piece "The Young Person's Guide to the Orchestra (Variations and Fugue on a Theme of Purcell)" (1946). Keillor's "Guide" was commissioned by the Plymouth Music Series, Minneapolis (founded and directed by frequent "PHC" guest artist Philip Brunelle). The music was composed by Randall Davidson, and the piece premiered in Seattle in the fall of 1988; a performance in Orchestra Hall in Minneapolis can be heard on *Lake Wobegon Loyalty Days* (MPR, 1989) audio- and videocassettes.

This collaboration with Davidson soon led to another, which culminated in a comic oratorio, *A History of Evil,* which premiered 13 April 1991 in Minneapolis with narrator, soloists, chorus, and orchestra under the direction of Brunelle. The oratorio traces evil's history through adaptations of Bible stories, including that of the Fall, Noah's Ark, Sodom and Gomorrah, and the parable of the Prodigal Son, making some use of material Keillor had previously written for radio sketches on the same themes.[13] Even though some of the material had been previously written for other uses, in these two collaborations with composer Davidson Keillor was exploring new artistic horizons as a writer and performer.

After a preamble in which the narrator warns that Christ did not play an instrument and "the apostles did not attend concerts," the "Guide" takes up the various instruments serially in answer to the question, "Which instrument is the best one for a Lutheran to play?"

(*WASM*, 30-31). The clarinets are worldly, the oboes sensual, the first violins egotistical. Percussionists, however, must exhibit the Christian virtues as they wait patiently to play "a few beats," and harpists, too, are humble: having a harp "is like living with an elderly parent in poor health – it's hard to get them in and out of cars, impossible to satisfy them" (*WASM*, 34).

Keillor had been exploiting the humorous potential of the presumably dour and guilt-wracked Lutherans for almost two decades, throughout "PHC" and "ARC." The denomination is particularly strong in the Upper Midwest, owing to the large numbers of Scandinavian and German immigrants whose state churches in the old country had been Lutheran. In a sense, Keillor used "Lutheran" as shorthand for the bland and moralistic dimensions of midwestern culture in general. "I never knew a word like that that would get a response from an audience," he said in a 1982 interview; "just say 'Lutheran' and people break out laughing."[14] For years on "PHC" Wobegonians had been teaching their dogs to roll over and play dead when they heard the word *Lutheran*; they joined support groups for ex-Lutherans from small towns when they moved away. In the "95 Theses 95" Keillor published a whole series of his quips about Lutheran stolidity, intolerance, abstemiousness, and abhorrence for the body: "As Lutherans, we viewed pleasure with suspicion. Birth control was never an issue with us. Nor was renunciation of the pleasures of the flesh. We never enjoyed them in the first place" (*LWD*, 259).

In addition to "The Young Lutheran's Guide to the Orchestra," *We Are Still Married* has two other pieces that draw on the comic capital in Lutheranism: a "Talk of the Town" piece titled "Lutheran Pie" and, in "The Lake" section, "Who Do You Think You Are?" The latter piece stands almost at the center of the book; it is also in the center thematically, since the first-person narrator's hometown is Lake Wobegon, yet the piece also treats Keillor's departure from St. Paul for the East and his life as a former radio host and storyteller on "PHC" with convincing verisimilitude.

Janteloven

The title "Who Do You Think You Are?" correlates with what Keillor refers to in his Introduction as the "Law of the Provinces": *"Don't think you're somebody. If you were, you wouldn't be here, you'd be on the Coast"* (*WASM*, xviii). This of course is the "Great Midwestern Joke" of George Ade and Jean Shepherd and one of the standing jokes of "PHC"; it is the joke at the heart of James Thurber's self-portrayal of the artist as a Midwestern Little Man character in *My Life and Hard Times*: "Nobody from Columbus ever made a first class wanderer in the Conradean tradition."[15] Keillor once remarked that the pervasiveness of this repressive ethos in Minnesota might have to do with the state's Scandinavian ethnic heritage.[16]

Anthropologists may demur, but the letter and the spirit of the Minnesota law is strikingly similar to *"Janteloven* (the Law of Jante)." Jante is a Danish Lake Wobegon based on the hometown of Aksel Sandemose (1899-1965), a Danish-born Norwegian author famous in Scandinavia for his "ten commandments" of Jante, which he enumerated in his novel *A Fugitive Crosses His Tracks* (1936).[17] The first of the 10, for example, is "Thou shalt not believe thou *art* something"; the seventh is "Thou shalt not believe *thou* amountest to anything." The anonymous author of "95 Theses 95" (*LWD*, 251-74) had denounced just such unwritten laws before Keillor courted Ulla Skærved, but his calling these taboos the "Law of the Provinces" in the 1989 Introduction to *We Are Still Married* after having lived in Denmark may have been influenced by an awareness of what is no laughing matter to the Scandinavians, the "Law of Jante."

Nor does Keillor keep smiling all the way through "Who Do You Think You Are?" Yet while he treats his regrets about leaving St. Paul and settling in Manhattan very candidly, the piece resolves warmly enough in a self-deprecatory confession: "Ever since I left home and came to New York, I've known exactly who I am. *Ich bin ein Minnesotan*. In Minnesota, it's never really clear what that means, but living in Manhattan, I know *exactly* what Minnesotaness means – it means *moi* – and I plan to stay right here and enjoy it" (*WASM*, 134).

The piece is not only at the center of the collection in a physical and thematic sense; structurally considered, it is half-way between personal essay and a Lake Wobegon fiction. It opens with the words of the monologue's framing formula, *"It has been a quiet week in*

Lake Wobegon, my hometown," but instead of using that line as the "open sesame" to narrative, Keillor begins with a commentary about his use of the formula itself, saying how it "was such a sweet line all those years on the radio, the standard opening of each week's story, a pleasant, modest, *useful* sentence" (*WASM*, 119). This "meta-monologual" mode continues for more than two full paragraphs, as the piece develops into what seems a chatty critical analysis of the literary possibilities his framing sentence had afforded and precluded: "One problem with *It has been a quiet week in Lake Wobegon* is that you couldn't go straight from that into talking about dreams of boundless grandeur . . . , but, then, it was that way when I lived there, too" – and here, notice, he has segued back to narrative: "Dreams we did not discuss, they were embarrassing in normal conversation. . . . 'I'm going to college,' I stated. My sister laughed: Who d'ya think *you* are? She was right, I didn't know" (*WASM*, 120).

But who is this "I"? Gary, the boy and future Sojourner from Lake Wobegon? or the boy from Anoka and Brooklyn Park who grew up to tell stories about a fictional place called Lake Wobegon? It turns out that just as the piece is neither fiction nor nonfiction but a blend of the two, so the distance between the Sojourner of the former "PHC" and the maskless author has virtually disappeared. What remains is a complex blend, new in some ways but pure Keillor. It was this Keillor, in any case, whose on-stage persona, more frequently than in the past, was virtually interchangeable with the "I" who narrated his prefaces, speeches, and his more intimate "Talk of the Town" pieces in the *New Yorker*.

Following his metafictional opening gambit in "Who Do You Think You Are," this rather complicated narrative "I" supplements anecdotes that had been used previously on "PHC" with some that went beyond the limits of propriety that normally bounded "PHC" stories. One of the main topics, for example, is the narrator's sexual awakening. The Sojourner had not completely ignored sexuality, but here (and hereafter on "ARC") the subject is treated more candidly and in greater detail. And some of the details do not really fit within the frame of Lake Wobegon. The import and tone of the central theme, "You shouldn't think *you're* somebody" (*WASM*, 122), is complicated by statements that sound not merely rueful but brutally frank, even bitter: "Minnesota was a repressive place to grow up in and there's a lot I'd change, even as I think about sunny bygone days in Lake Wobegon" (*WASM*, 127).

"Lake Wobegon" in this context is not the fictional town that the reader is supposed to picture in imaginative collusion with the story-teller but a figure used to invoke the smiling aspects of Minnesota life ironically: "People there didn't have fun. Above all, we learned to repress the urge to achieve and be recognized, because the punishment for being different was so heavy. It might be postponed for a while, but when it fell on you, it fell hard, as when I wrote a book about Minnesota, called *Lake Wobegon Days*, and the local newspaper put me in my place but good" (*WASM*, 127). The "I" at this point has stepped entirely out of the fictional frame, since he refers to himself as the author, and the piece is neither completely story nor preface. The "I" is a character in the anecdotes he relates but is also the Author who wrote *Lake Wobegon Days*, hosted "PHC," and felt persecuted by the St. Paul newspaper. This "I" is Keillor, sure enough, but a Keillor who has as much in common with the anonymous author of "95 Theses 95" and the prefatory "Letter from Copenhagen" in *Leaving Home* as he does with the Sojourner.

"Who do you think you are?" considered as one of the Laws of Lake Wobegon instead of as a mere interrogative was identified also as a fundamental commandment of Lutheranism in a Keillor *New Yorker* story published a year after *We Are Still Married* (and two months after the *Christian Century* noted that Keillor had joined the Evangelical Lutheran Church in America). In a postmodern fable titled "Zeus the Lutheran," the wayward eye of the Lord of Olympus falls on Diane, a tourist he spots on a cruise ship in the harbor at Rhodes. Zeus feels "the old familiar itch in the groin," and, used to having his way with women and goddesses alike, he translates himself into the body of Diane's husband Wes, a Lutheran pastor from Pennsylvania. Hera, tired of Zeus's numberless infidelities and newly determined to share her husband's power equally, lays a curse on Zeus that confines him to the body of Pastor Wes. The incongruity of the pagan god doomed to live the life of a Lutheran minister is the essential joke of the piece, and his dilemma highlights the coincidence of "Lutheranism" with the "Law of Lake Wobegon."

Alone for the first time with the pastor's wife, Zeus must "steer his passion through the narrow twisting mind of Wes. All he wanted was to make love enthusiastically for hours, but dismal Lutheran thoughts sprang up: Go to sleep. Stop making a fool of yourself. You're a grown man. Settle down. Don't be ridiculous. Who do you think you are?"[18] The figure of Zeus imprisoned in the body of Pastor Wes may also be considered as a comic expression of Keillor's sense of being doomed by his success to being perpetually known for his role as the Sojourner, a character whose versatility and artistic range must be confined after the manner of those hapless Lutheran musicians, to percussion, the harp, and perhaps the piano or organ when there are all those other sensual instruments to be played.

"The Talk of the Town Squad"

From 1927 on E. B. White wrote more than 200 items for "Notes and Comments," the unsigned lead column of the "Talk of the Town" feature, which more than any other has epitomized the style and character of the magazine. "Talk of the Town" typically looked out on turbulent political affairs and social upheaval and then wrote about less disturbing miscellaneous events – matters worth reading about not because they were intrinsically newsworthy but because the writing was elegant and witty. "I read Talk," says Keillor of his own first encounters with the magazine, "as the voice of inexhaustible youth, charged with curiosity and skepticism, dashing around the big city at a slow crawl, and tried to imitate its casual worldly tone, which for a boy growing up in the potato fields of Brooklyn Park township, was a hard row to hoe, but I tried" (*WASM*, xiii).

The apolitical demeanor of "Talk" changed somewhat during the Vietnam era, when the anonymous authors of "Notes and Comments" began to write in opposition to the United States' continued involvement in the war. The column continued to editorialize on portentous issues, though the balance of "Talk" directed its attention away from front-page concerns, taking up issues such as sneezes, the robotic voice in an airport shuttle, a film crew shooting in a cemetery, the feel of the subway, or the way assorted pedestrians hop puddles on Manhattan sidewalks – all topics represented in "Talk" pieces reprinted in *We Are Still Married*.

In a piece reprinted as "The Talk of the Town Squad" Keillor revels in the famous marginality of the department itself and the anonymity of its writers. Noting how every obscure trade seems to have a convention or festive self-promotional event, he announces an imaginary, upcoming "Copy Carnival" for the "unsigned-writing trade," complete with a "big Prose Parade down Fifth Avenue." In the procession, along with the photocopiers, ad writers, authors of catalog copy and bumper stickers will be "the tiny Talk of the Town Squad, marching triple-spaced and chanting, 'Roses are red, so are balloons. We write the gray stuff around the cartoons'" (*WASM*, 192-93).

Just how many "Talk" pieces Keillor has written is difficult to determine, since the *New Yorker* has a policy against disclosing the authorship of its unsigned copy (though it is clear that his output increased significantly after the end of "PHC" and before the beginning of "ARC"). Yet in many of his "Talk" pieces, Keillor takes no pains to preserve his anonymity; indeed, many of his pieces were so intimately personal that many readers had no trouble at all identifying him as the author. In "Nineteen," for example, Keillor starts out anonymously enough, telling about a visit he paid to an office-machine shop to buy a new typewriter. In one of the machines he found a sheet of paper covered with the experimental keystrikes of various patrons. Starting from this screed of random letters, words, and nonsense, he exercises his ability to write eye-humor and springs off from this abstract text into a personal narrative, incorporating the misspelled words and random letters into his tale: "I traveled for a couple weeks in Denmark and went a litle ququ there, too. I don't eat hambarugers in foreign countries, because I'm proud to be an unugly American. . . . I am a good citizen, just as my mamama-mamamamamamama taught me to be." As the details accumulate about how he spent his summer, anyone reasonably familiar with the career of Garrison Keillor would have no trouble identifying him as the author as he discusses Copenhagen, where when "people walk up to me and say, '*Aldjksfjsadhfjsdjfkjsdkfwewewewewe*,' I answer (in Danish), 'I am sorry. I am an American. I do not understand you'" (*WASM*, 203).

In another piece about a trip he took to Greece, Keillor could be any anonymous "Talk" writer traveling abroad, missing the *Times* and news about the 1988 presidential elections. But as he describes his days on Patmos, he mentions the cave where the apostle John "dreamed about the end of the world and wrote the Book of Revelation and told about the Lake of Everlasting Fire that so absorbed my entire youth"; near the end he tells how, as he rides around on a motor scooter, his mother never let him do such dangerous things, and he hears her voice: "Be careful, Gary! Not so fast!" (*WASM*, 208). Though he does not disclose his first name, "Home Team" is even more personal. In it he not only discusses his feelings about the Minnesota Twins baseball team but talks about a fight he had with an old friend in the driveway of his former home in Marine on St. Croix and explains that his wife "is a city girl, born and bred in Copenhagen, and she never really took to Minnesota" (*WASM*, 166). As Anonymous sits in Manhattan in fall 1987 watching the Twins play in the World Series, his attention drifts to a church league softball trophy that he has brought with him from Minnesota, and he talks about how the league had long since broken up, since "by the early sixties so many players . . . had been lost to heterodoxy. . . . I left the church as soon as I could, sooner than most of the others" (*WASM*, 171).[19]

Not only were his "Talk" pieces frequently identifiable from their frank personal content and characteristic tone, but quite a few (especially those written in 1987 and after) concerned partisan politics. Indeed, an early version of a passage in the Introduction to *We Are Still Married* in which Keillor discusses how he has voted in every presidential election since 1964 appeared first in "Talk."[20] In "Reagan" he tells of his visit to a celebration in Grovers Mills, New Jersey, commemorating the fiftieth anniversary of Orson Welles's radio broadcast of "The War of the Worlds," a show that created havoc when thousands, confused by the news-documentary style, mistook the play for real news about a Martian invasion.

The Republicans in the presidential elections of 1988, Keillor then observes, ran a "mean-spirited campaign in which the distinction between real and unreal, news and entertainment, seems blurred beyond recognition, and in which politics seems dangerously out of touch with the world we inhabit." As a consummate entertainer Reagan knew how to create comforting illusions but sapped the nation's fundamental strength in doing so. George Bush followed Reagan's lead by running on a campaign based on "his personal showmanship about the Pledge [of Allegiance], the ACLU, murderers, and a few other matters that will not concern him as President." This is an interesting indictment, based as it is on a professional entertainer's conviction that, in a democracy, creating illusions is not the proper business of the head of state: "All Mr. Reagan's artistry cannot change the world, which remains real. . . . The world is not the sum total of our impressions of it, and it cannot be charmed by political entertainment." The 1988 campaign was known for the way it capitalized on slick imagery on the television screen, and in his concluding sentence Keillor as much as left his signature in his allusion to the medium Welles had used to such great effect in 1938 and in which he himself had made such a mark: "The voters who walk into the booth on Tuesday will find it unlit, as pitch-black as a radio show" (*WASM*, 209-13).

In many of these political pieces, while he departs from the affable and apolitical example of most of E. B. White's "Talk" pieces, Keillor is not so ardent a Democrat that he can be considered an ideologue sooner than an individualist. His political opinions seem to flow – like those expressed by White writing about fascism during World War II and Thoreau on the Mexican War in his day – from his ferociously independent spirit, his "middle-state pastoralism," and his disdain for materialism, ostentation, and the arrogance of the rich and powerful.

"Pieces" and "Stories"

Of the 23 short works collected under the headings "Pieces" and "Stories," 14 first appeared in the *New Yorker* and most of the rest were reprinted from the *Atlantic* or *Harper's* or were appearing in print for the first time. All but "After a Fall" (1982, in its third appearance in print) were published between 1983 and 1989 at a rate of about three per year (*We Are Still Married* was officially published in April). "Pieces" includes unusual items such as "The Young Lutheran's Guide to the Orchestra"; "The End of the Trail," a spoof on the antismoking frenzy; and "When You Kick a Liberal: A Post Election Parable." Collectively, these works are probably less deserving of the designation "Stories," the heading under which narratives such as "Lonely Boy," "The Art of Self-Defense," and "After a Fall" are gathered. These two sections at the beginning and end of the volume show that Keillor continued to write short humorous works with the same basic forms, subjects, and satirical targets represented in *Happy to Be Here*. For example, there are more burlesques of media hype and get-rich-quick rhetoric ("Maybe You Can, Too" and "Lifestyle"), of baseball writing ("Three Twins Join Club in Spring" and "What Did We Do Wrong?"), of self-righteous social movements ("The End of the Trail"), and of social scientese and social relativity – or what a social worker refers to as "the entire values-delivery infrastructure" ("The Current Crisis in Remorse," *WASM*, 25).

Yet Keillor's increased willingness to risk political partisanship is also evident. "Everything's Up-to-Date in South Roxy" (1984), the original version of "Lifestyle," was a fable for our times about the wasteful hedonism and laissez-faire entrepreneurialism at the middle of the Reagan presidency. It told the tale of Bob and Nancy Niles, a married couple who sold their teenage children because they were "just not the right children for us. . . . We're all the time being parents, we don't have time to grow" (*WASM*, 53). In the reprinted version Keillor focused the satire a little more tightly on Reaganism by changing Bob Niles's name so that the pair who put their own well-being ahead of their duties as parents were now Ron and Nancy. In 1988 Keillor wrote, "I took an eight-year vacation under Reagan and didn't have a political thought, except to admire the old masseur as he applied his craft" (*WASM*, xviii).[21]

The vacation from politics was over, however, when Keillor published "He Didn't Go to Canada" on the eve of the 1988 elections. This tall tale turns out to be a satirical indictment of its windy narrator, a fellow named Dan, whose military exploits lampoon the service career of Vice President Dan Quayle. A former member of the Indiana National Guard, this Dan was ordered during the Vietnam War to dress in loud clothing, "play good golf, drink cold beer, and make love to beautiful women" – sacrifices he underwent to help conceal what was in reality the "biggest secret army in the free world," ready to invade North Vietnam using equipment stored in bunkers beneath the placid golf courses of Indiana (*WASM*, 62, 64).

The Celebrity

In the title piece, "We Are Still Married," a bus driver named Earl tells how overnight he became an unwilling celebrity and the victim of voyeuristic media attention that almost ruined his marriage. There is no accounting for why the national press, the networks, and even the Pope should be interested in Earl's mundane transgressions against his wife. Nevertheless, she makes the rounds of the talk shows criticizing his grooming and television preferences and accuses him of being "stubborn and unreasonable" (*WASM*, 328). Earl is a neo–Little Man of the sort that populate the surreal fables of Donald Barthelme or Woody Allen; his absolute lack of newsworthiness is of the essence since the joke is at the expense of the gossipy sort of media attention that Keillor was already experiencing when he first published the piece in 1984. Indeed, the story seems almost uncannily prescient – so much so that one reviewer wrote that "surely the basis for the title story" was his loss of privacy at the hands of the local press between 1985 and 1987.[22]

Keillor's experiences in those years with the negative aspects of celebrityhood do seem the likely basis for at least three subsequent short pieces published within a year and a half of his leaving St. Paul in 1987. Only the last of these is overtly autobiographical, but the others offer numerous signs that they too have confessional (or mock-confessional) dimensions as well. "Your Book Saved My Life, Mister" is the account of Dusty Pages, a writer of westerns, who ruefully tells how he used to haunt the public library in hopes of meeting readers who would tell him how much his work has meant to them. After many disappointments, he meets a man who claims that one of Dusty's books literally saved his life – by stopping a bullet. The man was so moved that he read the book and found that it was his life story "down to the last detail." He sues Dusty and wins big.

"Meeting Famous People" is a burlesque of a "how-to" feature that offers illustrative anecdotes and recommendations to "sensitive fans" so that they can prevent "personal rejection by an idol [from becoming] ... a permanent scar," including such tips as, "Never grab or paw the famous. ... Personal dirt ... can wait for later" (*WASM*, 256). It opens with a cautionary tale about what happened when a fan named Tim ran into his idol, country singer Brian Johnson, in an airport. Brian fled, Tim pursued; Tim cornered Brian and told him, "You saved my life." Brian pushed him away, replying, "vampires like you ... make me regret ever becoming a performer," and slapped him. Tim sued. En route to the trial, Brian was arrested for possession of narcotics, and after a series of painful and humili-

ating mishaps he dies among strangers and is buried under a tomb-
stone that spells his first name "Brina" and gives his year of birth as
1492. A newspaper columnist tapes an epitaph of sorts to his stone
reading, "His name is Brian," and recommends some of his records,
though he also warns that one of them is "too pretty, too nostalgic,
too *self-conscious*" (*WASM*, 254-56). 1492 scrambles Keillor's birth-
date of 1942, and the columnist's critical judgment was just the sort
that prompted him to write the "95 Theses 95" as a preemptive
strike to prevent reviewers from calling *Lake Wobegon Days*
"nostalgic." "PHC" featured a lot of country music, of course, and
Keillor's burlesque of a cowboy ballad, "Whoopi Ti-Yi-Yo" (recorded
on *Lake Wobegon Loyalty Days* in 1989), was built on the pun of
"writer/rider," the author as cowboy.

No such clues were needed to link the author's personal experiences with those suffered by the bedeviled celebrity of "My Life in
Prison" (first published in the November 1988 *Atlantic*), since it is
narrated by Keillor himself. Like Earl in "We Are Still Married," Keillor explains how he was lured to lunches with reporters whose stories magnified minor blemishes into moral leprosy and foresees how,
like Brian in "Meeting Famous People," he is headed for jail. He
grovels in guilt like K in Kafka's *The Trial*, confessing that not only
was he selfish when he lived in St. Paul but his actual sins remain
unilluminated by the moral spotlights of the media. Overcome with
mock-remorse, he proceeds to admit the truth he has concealed ever
since the day in his childhood when his cousin foretold, "You're
going to go to prison for the rest of your life." He said this right after
Keillor had hit him in the head with a pair of stilts. "I offered him the
stilts and he accepted them, but that didn't change anything," Keillor
explains. "It would be prison for me: no trial, no judge, or jury"
(*WASM*, 321).

"My Life in Prison" parodies gossip rags and muckraking biographies in general but aims smart bombs directly at Michael Fedo and
Nick Coleman. Fedo's *The Man from Lake Wobegon*, which advertised itself as "An Unauthorized Biography of Garrison Keillor," is
retitled *Geek: An Unauthorized Biography of You Know Who (the
Big Jerk)*. Nick Coleman had been quoted in the press some months
earlier saying that Keillor had not been forced to leave St. Paul but
went because he wanted to live in New York among "the literary
lions and the glitterati" (Colford). Keillor's parody of a story by a

"newspaper columnist back in St. Paul" includes a passage about how Keillor "sleeps all day and spends his nights cavorting with the glitterati in the niteries of Sodom" (*WASM*, 318).

"My Life in Prison" demonstrates that Keillor had gained sufficient distance from his sense that he had been hounded out of St. Paul to translate his outrage into humor. Still, his self-caricature as the guilt-ridden, penitent Celebrity/Victim depended in part on the fact that Keillor was now a rich celebrity whose actions, feelings, and opinions were matters of public interest. The "I" of this piece was not the simple Shy Person or the Sojourner but a complex Garrison Keillor, the famous Author and Radio Personality, now vulnerable to portrayals in the press as a Monster of Greed and Ambition. It was a new complexity that Keillor would use again in his oblique self-caricature as Francis With, the boy from Mindren, North Dakota, who in *WLT: A Radio Romance* becomes the Showman, a television celebrity stalked on the streets of New York by a venal biographer with a poison pen.

Postmodern Shadings

Though *We Are Still Married* includes orally based tales such as "The Babe" and other essentially realistic, traditional narratives, many of the more recent burlesques and stories reveal a cartoonlike vigor and harder-edge comedy reminiscent of experimental writers of the 1970s and 1980s. The blurring of the line between fiction and nonfiction in "Who Do You Think You Are?" is only one instance among several where generic boundaries are purposely indistinct.

Another case in point is "A Liberal Reaches for Her Whip." The piece originally appeared in the January 1989 *Harper's* under the heading "Miscellany" and the title "When You Kick a Liberal: A Post Election Fable." The piece develops a thesis of sorts, in the manner of an opinion piece, and concerns the terrible drubbing liberals and liberalism took in the presidential election campaign of 1988. But while it begins with a discussion that equates liberalism with "niceness," presumably in Keillor's own voice, it develops through a series of bizarre scenarios as it illustrates the theme that the liberals were metaphorically kicked down the basement stairs. Considered as a fable the piece seems to suggest that in the future they should

avoid becoming actors in "The Old Story: jerks rewarded, nice people abused."

The "Old Story" is illustrated with three scenarios. The first
depicts how America would forgive Adolf Hitler if he acted suffi-
ciently contrite and nice on the talk shows, since, as the narrator
puts it, "people can forgive anybody for just about anything but they
don't respect *nobody*, and so a miserable sinner with one redeeming
virtue is equal to a righteous person with a secret fault." His primary
illustration of this point is another retelling of the Prodigal Son, with
emphasis on the ill-treatment of the nice, liberal Elder Brother (a figure who had, as we have seen, great personal resonance for Keillor).
In the concluding scenario, the mother of Ronald and George Reagan and the final personification of the nice, Christian, liberal, is
kicked down the cellar stairs by her sons. The piece inverts the
import of the biblical parable – that abnegation and forgiveness are
the better course – to propose that liberals fight back. At least this
seems the moral of the bizarre conclusion: Grandma Reagan does
not just lie down and suffer on the cellar floor. "Liberal," she says.
"I'm going to liberate you boys from ignorance or die in the
attempt," she growls as, "clad in a black spandex bodysuit," she
springs up the stairs to avenge herself in fury (*WASM*, 43-48).

This intermingling of political commentary, surreal fantasy, biblical parable, and action comic book parallels the work of black
humorists and experimental writers such as Donald Barthelme,
Robert Coover, John Barth, and Kurt Vonnegut. Away from "PHC"
and living in New York, Keillor's antic exuberance expanded as he
no longer needed to take the role of the *eiron* Yarnspinner on a
weekly basis. Uncollected *New Yorker* stories such as "A Christmas
Story," "How the Savings and Loans Were Saved," "Zeus the
Lutheran," and "Lonesome Shorty" published after *We Are Still
Married* seem as a group to have more in common with the post-
modernists than with the burlesques and sketches the literary comedians or the classic *New Yorker* humorists Keillor most frequently
mentions as his idols. Among the stories in this collection, this
antimimetic comic mode is most evident in one of the "Stories" titled
"Yon."

Originally published in the *New York Times Magazine* as "My
Name is Yon Yonson," the title and central character derive from the
self-replicating doggerel rhyme, "My name is Yon Yonson, / I come

from Wisconsin," the same rhyme invoked by Kurt Vonnegut in *Slaughterhouse-Five* as an expression of his failure to extract meaning or find form in his experience of the World War II destruction of Dresden.[23] Keillor begins "Yon" by repeating the verse on itself several times, then he breaks out of the loop into a cartoonlike fantasy in which lumberjack Yon leaves Wisconsin "to visit my sister Yvonne and her husband Don Swanson" in New York. The flat characters with silly and sometimes rhyming names (Gary Chalet, Vanelle Montage, Raoul Cassette, Bob Bobson) and the use of doggerel rhythm in the opening and closing function to eliminate expectations of consequentiality, narrative cohesion, or even authorial self-disclosure.

Since the story first appeared just six months after Keillor left Wisconsin's neighboring state, the stupefied awe of Yonson is readable as a verbal cartoon based on Keillor's own Midwestern self in collision with Baghdad-on-the-Hudson. Yonson emerges from the obscurity of the pine woods to learn street-smart hustle, and by grace of extravagantly impossible entrepreneurial opportunities he becomes wealthy and retires to Connecticut with the newfound love of his life. While some of these elements might begin to shape an arabesque on Keillor's move from St. Paul (via Copenhagen) to New York, made possible by the fabulous success of "A Prairie Home Companion" and the sales of *Lake Wobegon Days*, such autobiographical traces are just flecks in the flat, neon-colored episodes of a tale that is mostly surface, which, like the Möbius-strip "Frame-Tale" that heads John Barth's *Lost in the Funhouse*, leads only into itself endlessly.[24] "Yon" concludes almost as it began, with rhyme, as Yonson tells us that he keeps in touch with his sister Yvonne mostly through answering machines. His machine says, "This is Yon Yonson, I've gone to Wisconsin to visit my aunts in Racine. I'll come back – when I do, I'll get back to you. Tell me what is your name" (*WASM*, 290).

"A Christmas Story," published eight months after *We Are Still Married*, is a first-person story in which the "I" narrator is presumably the famous host of a radio show. For all his allusions to "PHC," however, this "I" is no Sojourner. The story calls attention to its artificiality by introducing a patently unrealistic action and then repeatedly interrupting it with authorial intrusions. The narrative portion is a reworked version of one of Keillor's serial dramas, "Buster the Show Dog" (from the last years of "PHC"), which concerns the adventures of Buster and his friend, Timmy, "the sad, rich teenage boy" (here the dog is Tony and the boy is Jim). The plot is stretched even farther than the already far-fetched radio version. Whatever temptation the reader may feel to enter into the world of the characters is arrested when the author repeatedly breaks in with self-promotional messages: "As I mentioned," he says in the second of these interruptions,

> DioNate is picking up most of the tab for *publication* of "A Christmas Story," but, of course, corporate underwriting can't hope to cover all of the *writer's* costs. None of the $21,600,000 went to me, and I've had to spend a lot of time writing and rewriting and rewriting to make sure the story is phenomenally good, and that's why I'm coming directly to you, my readers.[25]

In their wild improbability, both the "story" and the comically crass intrusions by the author prevent the reader from sinking beneath the surface of words into the spell of a narrative. In one of his messages the author advertises a Caribbean cruise exclusively for "readers. Not John Jakes' readers or Danielle Steele's or Stephen King's. *My* readers. Such as you, for example." Not only is the narrative progression about the lost boy and dog broken every 150 words or so by the author's self-mocking mock-commercials but in the impossibly contrived and hurried denouement, the author confesses that he has become personally involved in the life of one of the minor characters: "Jim is headed for college, and Sharon split up with Vince, who was an illiterate brute, and – how can I say this? – she is marrying me on Wednesday morning" ("Christmas," 42). This last facetious blurring of the line between the story's and the author's worlds can hardly be taken as a metafictional gesture that seriously calls into question the boundary between reality and fiction – no narrative illusions had been allowed to rise high enough to merit challenging.

We read "A Christmas Story" in a magazine that advertises itself as "perhaps the best magazine there ever was," yet what we have paid our money to read exposes itself as a travesty and its author reveals himself as a hack, devoted not to his art but to making money. Such reflexivity or self-apparency is not pretentiously calculated to make the reader think twice about the nature of narrative and its role as commodity in the publishing industry. Rather, Keillor seems to place in the foreground the commercial context of his art and authorship in order to create amusement. But this is a complexly structured amusement, and the self-awareness and opacity of such a fiction mark it clearly as a postmodernist work.

"American Radio Company"

In spring of 1989 Keillor announced publicly that in September of that year he would be starting another radio show that would "pick up where 'A Prairie Home Companion' left off plus a couple years." As his main reason for returning he cited the public radio audience of "decent, generous, and intensely loyal" people. Not everyone in this audience reads books or the *New Yorker*, he continued, "so that's why you go back on the radio – because you've got more to say." Keillor said the show would resemble "PHC" and be meant for the same audience but would be called "The American Radio Company of the Air." "I like the redundancy in it," he said of the name; "it has an element of pretension." After the first season the name was shortened to "American Radio Company" ("ARC"). The show would include sketches along the lines of "Buster the Show Dog" from the last years of "PHC," and it would have "classic American music," including not only music for orchestras but film music, show music, country music, the music of Cole Porter, Leonard Bernstein, and Lefty Frizzell – music "that every American should hear at least twice." It would also have a monologue with "something about Lake Wobegon," perhaps viewed in retrospect or with characters from the town transported to New York.[26]

"ARC" premiered its 20-week first season on Saturday, 25 November 1989, broadcasting live to a national audience over the APR network from the Brooklyn Academy of Music from 6 to 8 P.M. (EST) – the same slot formerly filled by "PHC." The opening had been pushed back two months owing to difficulties finding a suitable theater in the New York area. This difficulty was the first of many that MPR and Keillor had to confront in trying to do the show in New York instead of St. Paul in a theater they already controlled. Everything cost more in New York, and ticket sales to the live performances lagged. Across the East River from Manhattan, the theater was hard to reach for many people and located in a neighborhood that discouraged tourism. The opening had been delayed, and then there were only four live shows before "ARC" after 16 December went on furlough until February. Moreover, the live "ARC" shows were interspersed with rebroadcasts of old "PHC" shows – a pattern that confused would-be ticket buyers and listeners alike. Asked why it was produced in New York, considering the costs and the necessity of flying out sound-effects man Tom Keith and other technical personnel for each show, MPR president Bill Kling said, "Because that's where Garrison lives."[27]

Though at no point during the first three years did the audience grow as large as that for "PHC" had been at its peak, during the fall "ARC" had an estimated 1.3 million listeners, a number that increased to 1.5 million during March 1990 (about half as many listeners as "PHC"); 225 stations across the country carried "ARC" during 1992.[28] In its second season "ARC" moved its home base from Brooklyn to the 350-seat Lamb's Theater just off Broadway but was on the road a lot. Out of 26 live broadcasts, 14 originated from all around the country – San Francisco, Chicago, St. Paul, Seattle, Memphis (and around the world, as the 9 March 1991 show aired live from London).

In the third season the show moved uptown to Symphony Space but was on the road for 23 of its 29 live broadcasts. Budgetary considerations played a significant role, of course, since while ticket sales in New York did little or nothing to keep the budget in the black, "ARC" could sell out large halls at its live performances on the road. Regional stations that carried "ARC" typically hosted the show and helped out with local arrangements and underwriting, since the stir and publicity boosted their local support and because they received a percentage of the ticket revenues.[29]

At the "ARC" premiere Keillor joked about putting on his show in a city where so many cars have signs on the windows that say, "No radio in car." The location was infinitely seedier than the Macalester College setting of the first live broadcast of "PHC" in 1974, but whereas "PHC" had sounded amateurish partly out of necessity in its early days, "ARC" was from the start wholly professional. Keillor's established reputation ensured solid financial backing, and New York afforded a ready pool of musicians, actors, writers, and music librarians and other support staff whose experience and expertise supplemented his own. As a reviewer said in a comparison of the old to the new, "This one is more structured: more scripts, less ad-libbing. And instead of country and folk music, there is rock, jazz and . . . powerful American mainstream music, with 'a crack orchestra' led by Rob Fisher and a focus on piano rather than guitar."[30]

Keillor auditioned and hired experienced actor/singers Ivy Austin and Richard Muenz as regulars in his Broadway Local Theatre Company; soon Bob Elliott of the former radio comedy team Bob and Ray became a regular. Keillor continued to write most of the show but relied on several other writers including Ken LaZebnik, Russell Ringsak, and writer/performer Dan Rowles. Notable guests included such nationally and internationally known performers as Eileen Farrell, Maureen McGovern, Peter Schickele, Victor Borge, and Pete Seeger.

"ARC" was better rehearsed, jazzier, and of consistently higher quality than the early "PHC"; however, as Keillor's radio station manager in *WLT: A Radio Romance* said to Slim Graves when he switched from singing weepy ballads with Little Buddy to cheating songs with The Blue Moon Boys: "Lots of performers improve their act and lose the public's favor . . . and that is exactly why the successful performers try so hard not to improve" (157).

The Lonesome Lutheran

In place of the country-western "Hello Love" on "PHC," the uptown riffs of the "Tishomingo Blues" opened each show and helped to define Keillor's retailored radio persona:

> Way out in New York City
> The buildings touch the sky.
> I don't know anybody low or high –
> I'm just a lonesome Lutheran
> Whose luck is runnin' thin.[31]

The monologue on the first "ARC" show did not use the familiar framing formula from "PHC," but, unlike quite a few other monologues on Keillor's show that first season, it did include news from Lake Wobegon. In the introduction Keillor told how he had recently defended New York for the first time, saying that, to his amazement, he had already become a New Yorker. He thought it would take longer, but he had also discovered that "it's still possible to love two places at one time and to belong in two places . . . just as one has two parents." He had recently visited the town, of course, and his news centered on Pastor Ingqvist's sermon at the Lutheran church. The pastor had stunned the congregation by quoting Martin Luther's injunction to "sin boldly," elucidating it in the context of I John 4:18: "There is no fear in love; but perfect love casteth out fear." Thus Keillor gave a theological rationale to account for his boldness in starting up another radio show armed only with "pretense" and "a tremendous talent for lying": "We don't draw nearer to God by being careful" ("ARC," 25 November 1989).

As the Lonesome Lutheran he was still touting his credentials as Amateur and Shy Person, and his signature song placed him in one of the hoariest stock situations in the history of American humor, "Adam Slick from Pumpkin Crick" in the big city (as he quipped on "ARC," 27 November 1990). The slow-talking, naive midwesterner's perspective on the culture of New York – the high prices, the brusqueness, the famous streets and sites, the squalor – provided the substance for many of his monologues. On some occasions during the first season Keillor not only dispensed with the familiar framing formula but entirely omitted allusions to Lake Wobegon. The narrator of these talks about New York was not really the same old Sojourner from Lake Wobegon, since that character was never completely interchangeable with Garrison Keillor, Author, Celebrity, and Public Figure.

"Thoreau on the Subway"

In the monologue for 17 February 1990 Keillor talked about how the pulse of New York life was affecting his daily life, how he feels the pace pick up every day as he heads down the stairs to catch the subway. He tells how frustrated he becomes if he just barely misses a train and how he inwardly berates himself for not dawdling: if only, for example, he had not stopped to look up that quotation from Thoreau: "Simplicity, simplicity, simplicity! Our life is frittered away by detail. A man must live by dead reckoning on this chopping sea of civilized life if he would not founder and go to the bottom."[32] After declaring that Thoreau was a preacher and comparing him with Pastor Ingqvist, he goes on to tell about an encounter he had with an

evangelical preacher he made the mistake of smiling at on the subway, after which the man just "pounded" him, shouting, "Man is
degenerate with no good in him!" "Yes," Keillor replied, "I know
that. I live here now" – a one-liner that maximized the potential of
his Yon Yonson-in-New York pose. But the momentary pose hardly
defined the complicated persona, since this simple rube joke was in
the mouth of the Author and Radio Celebrity who lived on the upper
West Side, who enjoyed soaking up the culture of the subway on his
way about town, bound for the *New Yorker* on Forty-third Street or
for his American Humor Institute at Fourteenth – a man who quoted
Thoreau. He was a Minnesotan all right, but also a New Yorker, using
the words of the New England icon in his chat with a national radio
audience.

That the on-stage persona by this point had become more fully
interchangeable with Garrison Keillor as he presented himself in
speeches, prefaces, interviews, editorials and so on was especially
evident at the "Fourth Annual Farewell Performance" the week after
the first "ARC" season ended. This special show was broadcast live
on Saturday, 16 June 1990, from Iowa City, Iowa, but there had been
another nonbroadcast performance the previous day. Though the
shows were the same in most respects, the monologue Keillor told
on Friday was not the same story by "the man from Lake Wobegon"
that he told the next night; it was instead a story by Garrison Keillor,
the writer and performer living in New York. It was about his anxiety
as a father over the welfare of his son, who, he reported, had
recently broken his arm in a bicycle accident. The Friday night
monologue also illustrates the intimacy of many of Keillor's unsigned
pieces for the "front of the *New Yorker*," since the same material
used in this oral performance appeared in print as "Notes and Comments" a few weeks later.[33]

In the first year of "ARC" it seemed almost as if Keillor was
building a show on the lines of "PHC" but with New York substituted for Minnesota as home base and primary source for the local
color in Keillor's spots and tales. Before the end of the first season,
however, it was clear that regional humor about New York would
never displace Lake Wobegon, and the extensive tour schedule made
it equally apparent that "ARC" was trying to appeal directly to as
many geographical and cultural regions with the country as possible.
To the extent that New York could be used as a common cultural

reference – the capital of everywhere – it served well as the base for a program that named itself after the familiar reference to the whole nation and that featured "classic American music" of all sorts and a variety of guests. But even during the latter half of the first season, "The News from Lake Wobegon," complete with framing formula, was making a comeback as a regular feature. Looking back at the end of the second season, Keillor said, "I started out the first season assuming that listeners wanted to hear me talk about New York. Maybe some of them did, but an awful lot of them wrote in to say, 'Thank you, but that's enough.' They wanted Lake Wobegon, so I changed and went back to that. I've done that all this season."[34]

Yet Keillor did not invariably talk about Lake Wobegon even in the second and third season. One notable departure was his special broadcast of 1 December 1990 when "ARC" originated from Mark Twain's house in Hartford, Connectictut – a show that featured anecdotes about and readings from Twain's work. In his talks about Twain and his house and in the monologue, it was not the Sojourner speaking but Garrison Keillor the nationally known humorist: "I'm so happy to be one of Mark Twain's children in my own way," he said. "He is the father of us all who write humorous and semi-humorous stuff." Aware that critics might find his bringing the show to Hartford House a sign of hubris, he posed as an *eiron* to affirm his association with the legend but subvert possible carping:

> Many people have compared me to Mark Twain, and I was pleased of course and then I met some of those people who had and then I saw that it wasn't such an honor; they tended to be people with very short socks and a lot of lint on their pants. . . . But it's a pleasure to think of yourself as being in the same line of work as Mark Twain was. ("ARC," 1 December 1990)

This show was considered important enough to be made available in its entirety in a set of two audiocassettes; prior to the production of this set two other cassettes from "ARC" had been produced, but both gathered selections from various shows.[35] Doing the show in Twain's house was another way of appealing to a national, as opposed to a midwestern, audience. At the same time it clearly worked to affirm the artistic kinship of Keillor with Twain. The following season Keillor did another live show along the lines of his tribute to Twain from the Red Cloud, Nebraska, home of Willa Cather ("ARC," 7 December 1991). Two months later, as if to head off the impression that he was trying too hard to associate himself with icons of high culture (Thoreau, Twain, Cather), Keillor did a live show from the Surf Ballroom in Clear Lake, Iowa – the site of rock singer Buddy Holly's last gig in 1959 ("ARC," 15 February 1992).

Even though he returned to reporting "The News from Lake Wobegon" regularly, Keillor allowed himself greater freedom to talk about things the Sojourner had seldom so much as mentioned on "PHC," such as what went on beyond the bedroom walls or how national political events looked from the perspective of Lake Wobegon. Nearing the end of the first season he said that "ARC" was "freed somewhat from this sentimentality about the Midwest" that had characterized "PHC." Explaining how the new show was "jazzier and it's got some color," he added, "Or maybe it's that I really feel loose and free and feel as if I have nothing to lose and nothing to protect" (Catlin, E2).

During the heyday of "PHC" Keillor often said that the show was not a forum for political topics, but talking about his "ARC" mono- logues in 1992 he said, "I don't mind using the show as a plat- form. . . . It's not right, but I still do it."[36] In three monologues dur- ing the first quarter of 1991, for example, Keillor talked extensively about United States involvement in the brief war in the Persian Gulf. On 26 January, a little more than a week after the United States began air strikes on Iraqi positions, he satirized the "plague of televi- sion" that had swept over the nation, raising the stress levels so high that Lyle Krebsbach drove down from Lake Wobegon to the Dales in search of gas masks, spooked by the news that the Iraqis might use poison gas. On 9 February he talked about how "You Can't Say That" is a sacred principle in Lake Wobegon, but that the U.S. policy in the Gulf necessitated dissent. And on 2 March, working the tour location into his act (his usual custom), he told how David Tollerud discovered on a high school class trip to Chicago that "Lake Wobe- gon is not his home." This epiphany came in the wake of the boy's refusal to be coerced into a wearing a yellow ribbon in support of the war effort.

Keillor was looser and feeling freer, but he had tried at the out- set of "ARC" to write his way straight past the invisible boundary of Lake Wobegon into new territory altogether, and he had not suc- ceeded in taking his audience along with him. He could not have expected to keep playing the Lonesome Lutheran encountering the

city for very long, but he had invested more heavily in "The Story of
Gloria, a Young Woman of Manhattan," a serial musical featuring the
acting and singing talents of Queens-born Ivy Austin.

Thirteen years before Keillor had explored the artistic possibilities of exile from Mist County by taking the perspective of Barbara
Ann Bunsen, a young woman of Lake Wobegon. Again at an artistic
crossroads, interested in writing about something other than Minnesota life in a new genre, he chose once more to take a woman's
perspective. "The idea was to do a serial musical," Keillor said midway through the experiment. "That's the part that appeals to me; I
don't believe that anybody did that before. Of course, 'Gloria' is
complicated by the fact that I am trying to write something I don't
know anything about, trying to write about a single woman in her
early 30s."[37] Like Garrison, Gloria came from the heartland to live
the life of a performer in New York; unlike him, she was still struggling in obscurity, hoping for a break. Unlike the Sojourner, she did
not care a bit for the Midwest. "It's full of extremely polite, extremely
calm people – like trees with hair," she said. Gloria sang and spoke
in the dialect of New York, a place that, for all its dirt and "all this
sadness right out where you can see it," she preferred to "Out
There – where the cows are" ("ARC," 25 November 1989). Keillor
said, "It's the most difficult piece of writing I've done," but when it
failed to generate sufficient enthusiasm after the first season, he
reluctantly gave it up.[38]

In May of 1990 Keillor said that while it had usually been easy
for him to write about Lake Wobegon prior to his exile from the
Midwest, he felt "lost" writing "ARC" monologues in New York and
that he was "groping my way toward something and I'm not sure
what it is. . . . It just didn't feel right to stand up in front of Brooklyn,
in front of this audience, and talk about the wonders of small town
life. It seemed cruel."[39] Less than two years later, weary of all the
road shows and suspicious that he was acquiring a New York accent,
he talked about his reasons for bringing the show back to St. Paul,
saying that "I can't talk about Lake Wobegon and not live here. . . . If
you talk for a living, you develop an ear. You soak up what you hear
around you, and you imitate people unconsciously." Moreover, he
would not have to rely on the *New York Times* for news about the
weather in Mist County. In New York in 1989 he had imagined himself on the subway preaching "out of Thoreau to anybody who could

use it"; by spring of 1992 he had made plans to spend more time emulating the life of the author of *Walden*, whom he had called a "suburban man" who "commuted to work out in the country" ("ARC," 25 November 1989). Keillor had picked out a cabin and his own country acreage where he would site it along the St. Croix, and, like Thoreau in his house by the pond, he was planning to use the place to write.

Chapter Eight

WLT: A Radio Romance

We used to listen every night,
The radio our only light.
We were poor, but we could always close our eyes and see
Cowboys and sweet guitars,
Funny men and opera stars.

("The Family Radio")

Overheard in October 1992 as two senior citizens in the World Theater in St. Paul awaited the start of the season opener of "American Radio Company": "I hope he doesn't do any dirty jokes," says one. The other replies, "He *never* tells dirty stories or anything like that." On sale in the lobby below were copies of *WLT: A Radio Romance* on tape, already available in advance of the official publication date of 6 November 1991 for the hardcover of what one reviewer called Keillor's "saltiest book." Had the two seniors listened to the *WLT* tape for more than a few minutes they might have echoed the *Vanity Fair* reviewer who asked, "Who does he think he is . . . Garrison 'Dice' Keillor?"[1] Yet while the novel does plow up earthier comic ground than any Keillor had previously worked, as Jim Lehrer wrote, "There is sex, violence of a sort and cussing, but Keillor is no Danielle Steel of the prairie, no Elmore Leonard of Minneapolis."[2]

Not only does the book venture into "dumb jokes and toilet humor,"[3] but there are some scenes where the humor is as black as Nathanael West's *Miss Lonelyhearts* (1931). Widowed when her husband is scalded to death in a train wreck, Francis With's mother drifts in and out of mental institutions, pleading with her son to remember her; "her only friends were on the radio" (*WLT*, 106). Such scenes, along with other less mordant vignettes of listeners who believe that Dad Benson's Elmville on "Friendly Neighbor" is a real place, certainly suggest that Keillor was indeed knocking some breathing holes in the crackerbarrel where so many fans who believed in the reality of Lake Wobegon had mentally confined him. Yet for all the discontinuities of *WLT*'s new raunchiness, the dark shadows in some of the corners, and its pervasively satiric attitude toward small-town culture and stodgy midwesterners, most of the book is tonally and often thematically consistent with many of Keillor's earliest *New Yorker* sketches and with mock-commercials from the days of his morning show from Collegeville, however discordant it is with the elegiac strains of the "PHC" monologues.

The antic mode of the book is so old in Keillor's repertoire that it should surprise only those unfamiliar with his non–Lake Wobegon fiction. Moreover, while Keillor claims that to entertain is his supreme aim in *WLT* and that, finally, "a good time is tasteless" (Holston, 1F, 7F), the book, for all its scatological humor and cartoonlike energy, in some ways resembles a moral fable. While rewarding virtue and assailing vice is hardly the central business of the narrative, some of the most egregiously covetous, prideful, and lecherous sinners suffer deplorable ends. On his promotional tour Keillor said the book is "a cheesy story about rascally people who knew they were sinners and pretty much enjoyed it to the end."[4] Even more succinctly, during its latter stages of composition, he called it "an erotic Christian novel about radio."[5] None of his characters – and radio could be included as a character of sorts – escape unscathed from satiric barbs. But in the ancient Christian tradition that includes Dante, the incontinent sinners (the lecherous, adulterous Ray Soderbjerg and Wendell Shepherd) seem less twisted and evil than the malicious sinners (the increasingly sullen Art Finn, the avaricious Richard Shell). The retribution wreaked on the archlecher, Ray, is devastating: rushed to the hospital emergency room after his dentist has discovered a malignancy in his jaw, the man next to Ray starts paraphrasing Revelation: "And God will come upon us with fire and a sword. And God will open the book. And our torment will be great" (332). While this chiliastic warning and concept of sin may be comically undercut, issuing as it does from the lips of a drunken derelict, the scene nevertheless balances against those that display the sexual exploits of characters like Ray.

The novel takes swipes not only at sensual excess but also at those who have demonstrated a rigid, sometimes religiously motivated abhorrence of the flesh (such as that shown by the woman who imprisons Francis With and his childhood playmate in her cellar when she discovers them lying together naked [*WLT*, 120-21]). The Golden Age of Radio is, in sum, presented as at best a Gilded Age. As the narrator of *WLT* says, "To speak through the air on radio! It was so wonderful – and so awful" (*WLT*, 24). Radio merely amplified and multiplied its creators' capacities for good and ill and was itself qualitatively and morally ambivalent – no better or worse than any number of other media in its capacity for simultaneously delighting and exploiting its devoted listeners.

Critical Reception

Promoting the book in Minneapolis, Keillor was asked to reply to the reviewer's question: Who did he think he was to write such a racy book? He answered that he thought of himself as

> a novelist who has freed his characters to be whomever [*sic*] they are. . . . Keillor acknowledged that the novel's raunchy side is a departure for him, but said he considered it "to be such a cheerful and old-fashioned sort of ribaldry that I don't have any reluctance about springing it on the readers." (Holston, 10F)

Asked in the same interview if he had been "practicing self-censorship" back in the days when he first published the WLT short stories, he said, "I suppose maybe I was," after explaining how the book in an early draft had been "a sentimental novel about the early days of radio, and that just killed it. . . . Nostalgia is not a strong enough impulse to keep a novel afloat – certainly not nostalgia for an era you don't have first-hand knowledge of. So the second time through I put some overripe characters in it and wrote it from the standpoint of those characters, not the powerful and sentimental and moralistic narrator I had the first time" (Holston, 10F). He added that he had "always accepted the decorum of speech on radio. . . . And I've also never had a problem with the decorum of the *New Yorker*. But in writing the novel the first time through, perhaps I was inhibited by a decorum that did not apply to me as the writer of a book" (Holston, 10F).

WLT had a first printing of 250,000 copies and net sales of 166,000 as of 24 June 1992 (a paperback edition was scheduled for November 1992); prepublication excerpts appeared in the *New*

Yorker and the *Gettysburg Review*. It was a Book-of-the-Month Club featured alternate in November 1991, a Quality Paperback Book, and appeared among the top 15 on the *New York Times* best-seller list for seven weeks.[6] Most reviewers read the book as fundamentally in keeping with characteristic Keillor themes and humorous techniques (18 of 22 reviews sampled were favorable to strongly favorable). Several, however, not only saw this book as a departure from his previous radio and written work but as an angry reversal: "Keillor uses 'WLT' to clear his throat with a vengeance, depositing a large gob of phlegm directly on the heads of his too-adoring fans. This is assault literature," said the reviewer in the Minneapolis newspaper.[7] Such an assessment is surely over the mark, yet those who found evidence in *WLT* of Keillor's post-"PHC" desire to move ahead in a new direction could find considerable corroboration in the text.

Castles in the Air

The novel begins and ends with possible allusions to the author's sense that this book marks the emergence of a new Garrison Keillor, freed from old constraints and mightily invigorated. The epigraph from *Walden* – with its emphasis on advancing "confidently in the direction of his dreams" and passing "an invisible boundary" – may have been chosen to suggest Keillor's feeling that the novel denotes a fresh direction in his work and life, under "new, universal, and more liberal laws." The whole passage, especially the Thoreau saying "If you have built castles in the air, your work need not be lost; that is where they should be," seems to allude more directly to the life and radio career of Keillor than to station WLT, "The Air Castle of the North."[8]

The last chapter, "Epilogue," can also be read as Keillor's declaration of independence from his previously established public image. Even though a few reviewers found this section an unnecessary and excessively bitter authorial intrusion, its essential mode is comic invective and humorous self-deprecation. Still in the third person, the section is a flash forward from the 1950s to 1991. Frank White (whose name is Francis With until he changes it after graduating from high school), now retired from a long career as television announcer, is a rich celebrity who is being stalked by his dirt-seeking

biographer, Richard Shell, a junior college teacher with the soul of a
tabloid press reporter. Just as Keillor after the summer of 1987 had
enjoyed the freedom of being anonymous in New York after being
treated like Elizabeth Taylor in St. Paul, so White had gone to live in
Paris, "for the freedom" (*WLT*, 393).

On the assumption that the violent death of his subject would
boost sales of his nearly finished book, Shell stakes out his hotel and
plots White's murder; lost in imagining how he would write about
White's sudden demise, however, he is knocked into the vegetable
kingdom by a truck. With its not-so-disguised complaint on the part
of the author against the ills of celebrityhood, "Epilogue" has a good
deal in common with two other bolts of comic invective written
during Keillor's exile from St. Paul – "My Life in Prison" and "That
Ol' 'Picayune-Moon.'" The former seems principally inspired by *The
Man from Lake Wobegon*, Michael Fedo's 1987 "unauthorized biography" (like Shell, Fedo teaches communication at a junior college);
the latter may aim particularly at the *St. Paul Pioneer Press
Dispatch*.[9]

WLT as History

While Keillor discounted any claims to historical accuracy or
verisimilitude and said he did no research on old time radio, the farcical chronicle WLT nevertheless presents a surprisingly credible
evocation of radio's early days (granted generous allowances for
comic license and exaggeration). That a major regional radio station
should originate as a promotional gimmick in a sandwich restaurant
seems pure Keilloresque whimsy. But this and many other details
and nuances of plot or character may have been based, however
loosely, on Keillor's knowledge of the historical development of
radio. In *Empire of the Air: The Men Who Made Radio* (1991), a history of radio centered on the lives of three inventors and
entrepreneurs, Tom Lewis provides a list of early stations sponsored
by organizations just as unlikely as the Soderbjerg Court restaurant.
Stations were run by "newspapers, banks, public utilities, department stores, . . . pharmacies, creameries, and hospitals. . . . In New
Lebanon, Ohio, the Nushawg Poultry Farm started one; . . . in
Clarksburg, West Virginia, Roberts Hardware opened WHAK."[10]

While WLT's general conformity with the historical record may be serendipitous (the restaurant origins of WLT were part of his 1976 story "WLT [The Edgar Era]"), details, incidents, and characters may have been influenced by the account of radio history as presented in Lewis's book and in the Ken Burns documentary film based on the book in which Keillor appeared talking about old-time radio.[11] Aspects of the character and career of Roy Soderbjerg, the dreamy inventor, for example, may in part be inspired by Lee De Forest (1873-1961), one of Lewis's three main characters and the self-proclaimed "Father of Radio," whose more than 200 patents for electronic devices failed to enshrine his name indelibly in public memory. De Forest's exalted expectations for radio resemble those of Keillor's character Vesta Soderbjerg; during the 1930s he bemoaned the commercialism of and poor quality of radio programming, quipping that radio broadcasting was in the hands of "uncouth sandwich-men" (Lewis, 242).

More details and anecdotes about early radio may have been gleaned from incidental published sources that came to Keillor's attention. Two such possible influences are the *WLS Family Album: 1933*, a promotional booklet published by the Chicago radio station, and Jane Woodfin's *Of Mikes and Men* (1951). A copy of the former is filed in the "PHC" archives, and a copy of the latter was on the bookshelves in Keillor's New York office in 1991.[12]

The "WLT Family Album" that Art Finn sends his nephew Francis With when he is still living in Mindren, with its pictures of "Bud & Bessie and Leo and Dad Benson and Little Becky visiting an orphanage and giving a wheelchair to a crippled boy" (*WLT*, 114), must have looked a lot like the *WLS Family Album: 1933*. With false sincerity to match that of Roy Soderbjerg, Jr., the WLS booklet proclaimed its purpose to introduce its listeners to the "Prairie Farmer-WLS family circle," and it featured photographs of an inspirational preacher, a sound-effects man, a cowboy band for "The National Barn Dance," a male quartet like the Shepherd Boys, and their own "little cowboy" – 13-year-old George Goebel – who doubtless sang better than Little Buddy did on WLT.

Of Mikes and Men is a fictionalized memoir of the author's career in early radio on Portland, Oregon, station KUKU from just after the crash in 1929 into the late 1930s. The writer's narrative persona, Woodie, is a counterpart to WLT's Patsy Konopka: both write

ceaselessly to feed the radio goat. Woodfin's chronicle of KUKU parallels Keillor's tale of WLT in its depiction of predictable radio-station
types – unsociable technicians, illiterate announcers, egotistical
actors, decadent musicians – and a listening audience of invincible
gullibility. Just as the Shepherd Boys drink Everclear, "the rocket
ship of the barroom" (WLT, 298), and bedevil the announcers in
Studio B, the band leader at KUKU drinks sweet spirits of niter and is
an irrepressible practical joker. Whereas WLT is said to be haunted
by the ghost of Price Waterman, the announcer who lost his voice in
Studio B (WLT, 4), KUKU has a "ghost" of its own – an apparently
homeless woman who haunts the reception room.

KUKU has a Rev. Albert H. Kramer, greedy-eyed, tight-lipped
cleric of dubious religious standing. Unlike WLT's Reverend Irving
James Knox, the man who seduced Little Becky (WLT, 279), Reverend Kramer does not engage in sex with other employees; nevertheless, he too is fired – in his case for selling "splinters from the
original manger" (Woodfin, 178).[13] KUKU has a child actor just as
irritating to the adult members of the troupe as WLT's Little Buddy
and Little Becky. Both books include humorous descriptions of
improbable sound-effects paraphernalia, and the tightfisted tactics of
a KUKU manager – who attempted to use train rails and snaked wires
through sewers to avoid paying the phone company for connections
to remote locations – also finds a parallel in Buck Steller, who, since
"WLT couldn't afford the long-distance line charges . . . did his play-
by-play from the studio, reconstructing a big colorful game from the
skinny little facts that came in over the tickertape" (WLT, 259).
KUKU's sports announcer not only drinks as much on the job as
WLT's Buck Steller but demonstrates similar visionary talents by giving a spirited blow-by-blow account of an eastern prize fight by
elaborating extemporaneously from the Western Union wire service
account (Woodfin, 210).

Keillor turns up the volume and the pace in his account of the
events at WLT that seem to parallel those at KUKU; he greatly elabo-
rates the earthier dimensions of life that are barely suggested in
Woodfin's openly nostalgic memoir. The markedly different handling
of material that is in many cases quite similar reveals the pains Keillor
took to purge nostalgia from the novel. Said Keillor in a postpublica-
tion interview, "The old radio shows that people collect on tapes

and traded at conventions – it's like people collecting plastic purses. It's perverse" (Warren, 2C).

Roots in the Early Short Stories

The call letters of station WLT and their significance ("With Lettuce and Tomatoes"), along with many of the main characters and basic situations, comic premises, and even the book's satirical tone, were used in several stories Keillor published before "PHC" went on the air. Even so, like Keillor's "PHC" monologues, *WLT* takes a long, backward look at the lives and culture of ordinary Minnesotans. It derives in part from two burlesques of listeners' tributes to old-time radio – "The Slim Graves Show" (1973) and "Friendly Neighbor" (1973) – and from two more directly satirical stories about the radio station's citified illusionmakers – "WLT (The Edgar Era)" (1976) and "The Tip-Top Club" (1981). (All but the last, which was first published in the *Atlantic*, were first published in the *New Yorker*, and all four appear together in all editions but the first of *Happy to Be Here*.) *Lake Wobegon Days*, deriving from the "comedy in slow motion" of Keillor's monologues, was loose-jointed and episodic and had to be counterweighted against excessive sentimentality. *WLT*, even though based on several short stories, is more coherent and internally consistent – possibly because for Keillor writing *WLT* was a matter of expanding and extrapolating from just a few tales, whereas writing *Lake Wobegon Days* had been complicated by the availability of hundreds of pages of manuscript. The relative paucity of preexisting material allowed Keillor more room to maneuver and greater freedom to experiment with various narrative strategies and plans for structuring the work.

An interviewer mentioned that Keillor's agent had proposed that he expand his WLT stories into a book as early as 1976 (Letofsky, 1976), and during his tour in 1991 he said that he had an advance from Harper & Row to write such a book in 1981: "I was living out in Marine on St. Croix then, and I just sat down and started. . . . I never bothered to write an outline or think about form or characters. And I quickly got myself into a series of blind alleys" (Holston, 10F). While more formally coherent as a novel than *Lake Wobegon Days*, the finished product still threatens at times to break into pieces. But the humorist's tendency to work best in short compass fails in this case to compromise its cohesion seriously. Chronicling the life of a radio station provides an organic fictional premise: various subplots can be grafted onto the trunk of an infinitely expandable series of developments as they appear to be necessitated by changing times, new programs, or changing personnel.

Provided with the novel's enlarged scope for complication and character development, and uninhibited by the constraints of what he could treat on air or in the pages of the *New Yorker*, Keillor not only increased the number of characters but introduced previously unmentionable dimensions to the lives of those he had already created. None of the original stories is preserved fully intact, and the use of a third-person, omniscient narrator allows Keillor to switch from one subplot or scene to another more easily than might have been the case had he retained "the powerful and sentimental and moralistic narrator" he had used in his draft circa 1981. The dramatic potential of each revised story is greater in the context of the novel, since the events and characters combine and multiply in hybrid forms across the wider narrative plane, thereby enabling increased ironic counterpoint and comic juxtaposition. The paragons now sprout warts, the titillating lines are now indecent, and the overall effect is more deeply and resoundingly entertaining.

Two of the four ("The Slim Graves Show" and "Friendly Neighbor") are in the first person, ostensibly written by amateur authors who, in the tradition of Huckleberry Finn, are self-revealing characters in their own right – less sophisticated than their creator and unintentionally funny. While they are fools, they are amiable fools (in the tradition of the literary comedians) whose failings owe more to ignorance than to malice. The principal targets of these indirect satires is the banality of old-time radio – thus the narrators' praise for their favorite WLT shows registers inversely with the reader. The third-person narrative voices of the two later tales – "WLT (The Edgar Era)" (1976) and "The Tip-Top Club" (1981) – anticipate the more satirical mode of *WLT: A Radio Romance*.

"WLT (The Edgar Era)" more completely than any of the three stories contains in microcosm those portions of the novel that have to do with the origins of station WLT as a promotional gimmick thought up by two brothers in the restaurant business (named Roy and Edgar instead of Roy and Ray). Edgar shares precisely with Ray the abiding ambivalence toward the invention that puts him on easy street (of course in the story his career as a philanderer is never mentioned). The narrative crux of the story is Edgar's fear that someday someone will ruin them by stepping up to the microphone and uttering filth. Exactly as in the novel, this fear goads Edgar/Ray to write "The Principles of Radiation," a "code covering all aspects of broadcasting," ending with a quotation from Scripture. Despite the code, however, "the dread event" that he had foreseen comes to pass all the same. In both story and novel it is one Vince Upton on "The Story Hour" who reads a script that has been tampered with. In the novel the listeners hear about the erotic adventures of Cowboy Chuck from St. Paul who takes up "with a dark Paraguayan beauty named Pabletta, whose breasts were pale and small and shivered at the thrill of his touch" (*WLT*, 6; cf. *HBH*, 54), whereas in the earlier version "the story was the 'confession' of a young man named Frank who gains wealth in Chicago" (*HBH*, 54).

From his name and the few other details provided about his life, this incidental character from a story-within-the-story in "WLT (The Edgar Era)" would appear to be a progenitor of *WLT*'s Francis With/Frank White, the protagonist in a strand of narrative analogous to that provided by the tale of Gary Keillor in *Lake Wobegon Days*.[14] "I was born twenty-seven years ago in a place called Northfield, Minnesota, the dullest little burg in the dullest state in the Union," Frank says in the short story, "and as soon as I was old enough to earn the train fare, I set out to see what life was all about" (*HBH*, 54). In the novel Keillor moves the hometown of Francis With much farther away from Minneapolis than Northfield, all the way out to desolate Mindren, North Dakota – a Lake Wobegon in a minor key. This small change illustrates the pattern in Keillor's revisions, which tend toward greater comic exaggeration.

Amiable Idiots

While there are no other mentions of any character named Frank in the four stories, one of his narrative functions in the novel (if not his identity) is also anticipated by the first-person narrators of "The Slim Graves Show" and "Friendly Neighbor." The narrators of both stories are radio fans who adore their idols without a trace of irony.

They are essentially rustic innocents, whose wide, trusting eyes reflect actions that the reader sees as comic even when the reflector does not.

The diarist who keeps track of events on "The Slim Graves Show" enters wholeheartedly into the illusion that Slim's wife, his country music singing partner Billie Ann Twyman, is actually making plays on the air for the guitarist, Courteous Carl Harper. He chronicles the history of their affections, responds generously to Billie Ann's request to help her "decide which man is right for her" by buying "a box of SunRise Waffle Mix with the picture of the man we favor on the flap" (*HBH*, 49). In the first week, he buys four boxes for Carl, but as the contest for Billie Ann's affections continues on the show, he sides with Slim and buys nine boxes for him. Slim wins the contest, and he and Billie Ann retire from the air, leaving the diarist none the wiser and ready apparently to become involved in Courteous Carl's new troubles of deciding which of the Pierce Sisters, "identical sixteen-year-old beauties," he loves the best (*HBH*, 61). In the novel it is young Francis With who listens faithfully to Slim's morning show, though at this point in the novel Francis is not so utterly naive, having been inside the station often enough to know that Slim is a heavy drinker who has willfully injured his son, Little Buddy. Nevertheless, Francis serves to register a listener's reaction to Slim's on-air romance with his female lead singer as he concludes that Slim's love misery and other troubles actually improve his singing (*WLT*, 164-65).

"Friendly Neighbor" is written in the form of a newsletter or an amateur's account for a newspaper of the annual Friendship Dinner, hosted in alternate years by Chaffee, North Dakota, and Freeport, Minnesota, in honor of the memory of "Walter 'Dad' Benson, long beloved in the Midwest for his 'Friendly Neighbor' show from radio station WLT in Minneapolis" (*HBH*, 62). Dad's show as it is worshipfully remembered in the story is identical with a show of the same name in the novel, though in the novel it changes character after Dad runs out of ideas and the writing is turned over to Patsy Konopka. Francis, like the narrator of the short story, provides the perspective of the listener, of all "the friends and neighbors in radioland [who] thought of the Bensons as real people" (*WLT*, 76). Indeed, the first appearance of Francis With is when he writes an ingenuous fan letter to Little Becky, the character played by Marjery Moore on "Friendly

Neighbor" (*WLT*, 81). But unlike the deadpan narrators in the short
stories, Francis eventually learns not only to distinguish radioland
from reality but to enter into its illusionary world himself. Even following a visit to the station at age 11 when he learns that Little Becky
is a cigarette-smoking, eye-rolling teenager, Francis and his family
remain devoted listeners of the show (*WLT*, 82). His more decisive
disillusionment is delayed until he is in high school when, on
another visit to the studios, Little Becky gooses him and he retaliates
with a knee in her face (*WLT*, 142).

Francis's mother introduces a darkly comic dimension to the
representation of all those listeners who cannot distinguish radio
fantasy from real life. After her husband, Benny With, is killed in a
spectacularly horrible train accident that recalls the crash of the
Prairie Queen as described in "My North Dakota Railroad Days"
(1975), she loses whatever power she formerly had to discriminate
between radioland and reality. She follows all the shows, and as she
lapses into profound depression she writes letters to Dad Benson
and is even paid $3 for a poem read over the air on "The Tip-Top
Club" (an unremittingly upbeat show adapted directly from Keillor's
1981 story of the same name).

The Prodigal Son from Mindren

First introduced one-fifth of the way through the novel, Francis With
not only serves as a naive perspective on the shenanigans at WLT but
turns out to be the protagonist of an extensive bildungsroman subplot. Structurally considered, his story provides a narrative bridge
between the gullible listening public and the duplicitous realm of
show business as revealed in the farcical saga of WLT.

After his father's death, Francis's only diversion from grimness in
Mindren is the radio; his escape to Minneapolis and a job with WLT
is tainted by his realization that the Wizards of his richly imagined Oz
were only humbugs and worse. His story of Francis is another
retelling of Keillor's favorite parable, the Prodigal Son. "It was a
shameful thing to turn your back on your own name," Francis thinks
just after graduating from high school, on a last visit to Mindren,
preparing to leave for good:

> Especially with your father lying in the ground without a stone over his head. But he had no family left, not to speak of. And then he saw that by adding an *e* to *With* he could get *White*.
>   Frank White.
>   The names made a nice click like closing the bolt on a .22. (*WLT*, 175)

His reasons for changing his name recall those attributed to 13-year-old Gary Keillor when he chose Garrison as his nom de plume because "it sounded mighty, formidable, like someone not to be trifled with" (Letofsky). And, like the Gary character in *Lake Wobegon Days* who "ran a constant low fever waiting for my ride to come and take me away to something finer" (*LWD*, 15), so Francis has yearned for Minneapolis and an exciting life like that which he imagined while listening to the radio.

As he drives away from Mindren, having just rechristened himself Frank White, he hears Patsy Konopka's revised version of the parable in an installment of "Friendly Neighbor":

> Jo was feeling sorry for Mr. Lassen, whose boy Leon was living a sad profligate life in Chicago and driving his poor father to distraction. The boy was sullen and careless, ran up bills he didn't pay, wasted the gifts his father generously sent him, and took up with bad companions who meant him no good. (*WLT*, 176)

Frank's career does not align perfectly with biblical parable anymore than that of Gary/Garrison did in *Lake Wobegon Days*. In a sense, he had previously rebelled outrageously against his father when, pinned down by his Mindren schoolmates, he is ordered to sing the "Daddy song." He shocks and thrills them utterly by singing it loud, "grinning, arms out, and sang all their verses," even though the song is gruesome, scatological, and blasphemous and defiles his father by name (*WLT*, 116). Punished by the teachers for using "bad language," he becomes a "true hero" to the other boys, who nickname him "Showman" (*WLT*, 116). The Showman, who eventually lives up to his nickname by becoming Frank White, radio announcer and ultimately a television celebrity, confirms his initiation to what is in essence a duplicitous vocation by regaling the other boys with pornographic tall tales about his sister.

Thus his story includes a kind of Prodigal rebellion and flight, though it lacks the paradigmatic narrative of profligate ruination and the abject return. Since his father is dead, his mother insane, Grampa in a home, and his sister has gone off to live with relatives, there is no parental home for Frank to return to in Mindren. Even so, he does negotiate a symbolic return by periodically visiting his mother and writing letters to his dead father. The first of these letters he puts inside a bottle and buries it at the gravesite: "Daddy, I am going to Minneapolis and get a job from Uncle Art. I want you to be proud of me. I wish we were all here together" (*WLT*, 175). After hearing Dad Benson quip that "a thrifty father makes for a prodigal son" in response to Patsy's radio version of the parable, Francis thinks, " 'Was Daddy thrifty?' He didn't think so. Anyway, Daddy was dead and in his grave. Maybe a dead father makes for a lively son" (*WLT*, 176).

Frank is altogether too clean-living and earnest to make a perfect Prodigal. But his success as a showman is so deeply ambivalent that his achievements in radio and television constitute a paradoxical profligacy in which success is tantamount to moral failure. Radio, as Ray's counterpart Edgar in the "WLT (The Edgar Era)" always believed, turns out to be a "Pandora's box" (*HBH*, 49). Frank pays a price in disillusionment for every rung up on his career ladder, and when he finally decides to abandon the foundering vessel of radio, he steals $800 of the station's money and uses it to buy train fare to Chicago and live there until he fortuitously lands his first job in television. In transforming himself into Frank White, Francis With was, like Dr. Frankenstein, unwittingly creating a monster.

Even Frank's earlier thrill of achievement when he first became a radio announcer had been quickly dampened by his discovery that success in radio was largely a matter of "grabbing up handfuls of the ordinary" (*WLT*, 281) and by his dispiriting premonition that radio was doomed. When Roy Soderbjerg, sounding like Keillor himself on numerous public occasions, predicts the inevitable failure of television in 1950, Frank silently demurs:

> It is less than photography and less than radio and it combines the two to make something that is nothing but a minus. It is novelty, and it has its day, but when radio returns . . . television will go the way of Smell-o-Rama. . . .
> *He is dead wrong*, thought Frank. (*WLT*, 241)

Frank was certainly right in the sense that radio – that is, radio with real shows and live music – was "on the way out," as WLT announcer "Old Ironpants" had predicted in 1937 (*WLT*, 4). But Frank disagreed with Keillor if he meant to deny that television was a corruptive influence, as Keillor had been saying in person for many years.

Though in the novel Ray Soderbjerg is convinced that even radio destroys families (*WLT*, 26-27), Keillor, in words that echoed many similar statements over the years, contradicted his character by saying, "Radio, to me, was almost part of our family circle. I did not feel that it broke up our family to listen to radio – we listened together. . . . Television you watch solo." As for the likelihood of television fading away, giving new life to radio as Roy predicted, Keillor said, "Pictures destroy words. In a head-on battle between pictures and words, people will always go for the pictures."[15]

While Frank's story resembles Keillor's own in many ways, as a confession it is hardly apologetic or contrite. Moreover, Frank White, while he carries more than a passing resemblance to his creator, is in no wise unique in that respect within this text. Keillor is nothing if not circumspect about self-representation; what he said about his Lake Wobegon stories applies to *WLT* as well: "I'm more comfortable put into the third person. There's no one character that's more Garrison Keillor than another; there are a lot of characters to whom I ascribe what happened to me."[16]

"Hiding Out in Public"

Though Frank White – the Exile who becomes a Celebrity – may look more obviously like the author than any other character in *WLT*, Keillor has diffused his own attributes liberally through the book. Dad Benson, for example, ironically incarnates Keillor's pose as Crackerbarrel Philosopher/Preacher. Even the story of Marjery Moore, doomed by the adoration of her fans to keep on playing the saccharine Little Becky on "Friendly Neighbor," bears a resemblance to Keillor's own, "stuck out in St. Paul . . . , a victim of his own success," playing the Sojourner on "PHC."[17]

With Patsy Konopka Keillor satirized his addiction to writing and even burlesqued his penchant for slipping slightly disguised friends and enemies into his scripts: snubbed in the halls of WLT one day by Ray Soderbjerg's wife, Vesta, Patsy writes her into the next day's installment of "Friendly Neighbor," where she appears as a yammering opera enthusiast named Lester Plumbottom, wife of William Jennings Plumbottom (Ray's hero was William Jennings Bryan). The incident calls to mind the appearance of Rick the TV dog in "PHC" monologues during 1985-86 after Keillor was riled by newspaper television columnist Nick Coleman (see Chapter 6). Keillor's venture into vulgar humor in *WLT* may well be motivated by the same frustrations that Patsy claims drove her to write salty material for "Friendly Neighbor": it is so hard writing about "*taciturn* Midwesterners" since sometimes they "just plain *won't talk* . . . and sometimes it gets *so hard*, . . . and to keep yourself awake, you write a few pages of risqué stuff" (*WLT*, 232).

Keillor's long-standing ambivalence toward radio is probably the psychological source that inspired the polar antipathies of Soderbjerg brothers, Roy and Ray. Using the pair allows Keillor to personify his own internal contradictions, projecting them onto this duo of squabbling siblings. Whereas Ray is a city lover and ladies' man whose idea of a good time is a trip to New York on a Pullman with his latest mistress, Roy prefers living on a farm, dreamily puttering away at inventions that never quite work. Roy loves to tinker with radio, theoretically and in his shop, while Ray never trusts the medium in concept or as a mechanism, even after it has made him rich.[18]

Nostalgic for the era of Bryan, Ray prefers that bygone age of print and oratory to the radio age of his adulthood. He is sickened by radio's "trashiness," its commercialism, its disruption of family life, and by "the sheer bulk of it! After a year they had broadcast more words than Shakespeare ever wrote, most of it small talk, chatter, rat droppings. . . . *I hope to high heaven people don't listen to all this!*" (*WLT*, 29). Ray's complaint rehearses reasons Keillor gave in 1977 for resuming his writing for print after years of radio work: "the intangibility of radio is what makes some of us miserable and depressed sometimes. We think we are wasting our lives feeding words and music into a goat. Radio eats everything, it eats constantly, and when you are done with your shift at the zoo, what do you have to show for it? *Nothing, dear God*" (*DJ*, 1).

Ray's nostalgia for the heyday of oratory seems an ironized treatment of Keillor's own sentiment that contemporary politics and politicians have been diminished by electronic technology. Ray's recollection of the day in Fargo in 1896 when he heard William Jennings Bryan, "the Great Orator," hold thousands in the palm of his hand sounds surprisingly similar to a passage in a 1974 editorial in which Keillor contrasted the speechmaking of Ignatius Donnelly to the lackluster abilities of Walter Mondale and other lesser contemporary politicians: today "few are capable of making five or 10 minutes of pleasant remarks, and the others are sleepwalkers." Conversely, in Redwing, Minnesota, in 1868 Ignatius Donnelly gave a two-hour campaign speech to a jam-packed hall, and when it was over people "wept and cheered" and carried him through the streets in a torchlight procession. Now, Keillor claimed, "to be seen by crowds of people, politicians have to leech. They ride in parades and stand around at fairs, to be looked at by people who've really come to see queens and breeder cattle."[19] Ray laments that "nobody today would walk across the street to hear Bryan speak" (*WLT*, 153-54).

Between the two brothers Keillor has mouthpieces for humorous elaboration of some favorite themes. Ray's resistance to Vesta's belief that radio should be a tool for cultural progress, a "Classroom of the Air," allows him to indulge his long-standing animus against the pretentiousness of public radio. Their dispute over whether commercials should be allowed on radio may also be based on the historical corporate warfare between David Sarnoff of RCA and Walter Sherman Gifford of AT&T. In 1921-22 Gifford tried to take over the radio business by refusing RCA the use of AT&T lines for broadcasting and announced that his stations would sell commercials – he called this "toll broadcasting." Reluctantly, Sarnoff did the same, though, like Vesta Soderbjerg (and Lee De Forest), he had long believed that radio should be a public service, presenting programs " 'of substance and quality.' Radio had the power to be a public benefactor, like a library, 'only projected into the home where all classes of people may remain and listen.' "[20] Even Ray worried that the people would not stand for commercials intruding into the airwaves, but the money proved to be so good that he stayed in radio for that reason alone, even though he believed "radio had destroyed the world of his youth" (*WLT*, 51).

"Plato's Pharmacy"

While Roy is much more given to explicit theorizing about the nature of radio and its cultural effects, he and Ray apparently share the belief (not very different from that espoused in the pages of Walter Ong or Marshall McLuhan) that profound cultural changes often follow the displacement of one dominant medium by another. Thus Plato saw the invention of writing not as "medicine" (in Greek *pharmakon*) for the memory, a cultural benefactor and an enabler of progress, but as a "poison" (also *pharmakon* in Greek) that causes forgetfulness. The art of oratory – praised by early rhetoricians such as Gorgias for having miraculous powers that he compared to those of powerful drugs – was denigrated for the same qualities by Plato, who reasoned that any powerful drug is also a kind of poison.[21] Ray and Roy continue this ancient theoretical discussion, and both of them share Keillor's ambivalence about television.

"You could put Bryan on the radio," says Ray, "and there he'd be, the same as a comedian or the fellow who sells soap. Back then, that man could stand on a train platform and hold ten thousand people in the palm of his hand" (*WLT*, 154). Radio is the *pharmakon* of oratory. Roy predicts that television will not manage to poison radio, though Frank White believes he is "dead wrong"; the prediction of Old Ironpants in 1937 was more prescient. Though the venerable announcer did not know just what medium would kill off radio, he compared its action to that of a drug: "It'll have the same effect as bourbon but it won't give you headaches or upset the stomach, so it'll be used even by the kiddos" (*WLT*, 4-5). Prescient or not, however, Roy should win for Keillor the prize for Best Parody of Contemporary Media Theory (as written by Walter Ong, Eric Havelock, Julian Jaynes, Marshall McLuhan, and others). Under the spell of Norwegian philosopher Søren Blak, Roy contends that

> radio . . . was a raw primitive gorgeous device that unfortunately had been discovered too late. In the proper order of things, it should have come somewhere between the wheel and the printing press. It belonged to the age of bards and storytellers who squatted by the fire, when all news and knowledge was transmitted by telling. Coming at the wrong time, radio was inhibited by prior developments, such as literature. (*WLT*, 145-46)

Busting Out of the Crackerbarrel

There can be little doubt with all these self-deprecatory surro-
gates – Dad Benson, Marjery Moore, Patsy Konopka, the Soderbjerg
brothers, Frank White – and with his burlesques of old-time, wholesome family-oriented radio shows like "Friendly Neighbor" that
Keillor had dispensed with the kitsch and the heartland homiletics
that he sometimes stirred into his Lake Wobegon tales. Though its
early roots in pre-"PHC" short stories demonstrate that the book is
fundamentally consistent with Keillor's antic side – the irreverent
early-morning deejay and author of sharp satires and farcical burlesques – the book as a whole does show a writer who had passed
"an invisible boundary" and was now operating under the "more
liberal laws" within himself. During his exile Keillor had put a foundation under his "Air Castle of the North," WLT. Or, to draw on
Keillor's biography of Slim Graves instead of his epigraph from
Thoreau, Keillor's progress in finishing *WLT* was like that of his aging
guitar picker who, having had all he could take of singing "maudlin
ballads about dying children" on "Friendly Neighbor" and then his
own "Cottage Home Show," finally got rid of Little Buddy and
started doing cheating songs early in the morning with Billie Ann
Herschel. Though the public preferred the old songs, Frank White
knew better: "Now that Slim was in decline, drinking hard . . . a
moocher and a four-flusher and a louse to his wife and kids, he
became a better and better singer . . . the only really astonishing
singer at WLT, the only one who sang so true and naked that you
shivered to hear him. Sex and misery" (*WLT*, 166).

Conclusion

What new directions Keillor's work will take as he settles into his latest little house near the prairie is only a matter for tentative specula-
tion. That he will continue to write regionally based humor can be
safely assumed, since if there is any single recognition echoing
through his writing during his exile in Denmark and New York it is
that no matter where he may be living he knows that "*Ich bin ein
Minnesotan*" (*WASM*, 134). Before his 1992 announcement that he
would be moving back to the Midwest, however, distance was fun-

damental: the central running joke of "ARC," after all, was Keillor's pose as the Lonesome Lutheran, lost and down on his luck in Manhattan. This was a character who said of New York (in a *New York Times Magazine* piece that parallels the themes of his oral monologues of the same period), "For now I'm happy to be here." But while he could say with only a little irony that "New York is the greatest city in the world," he was also joking that as he moved about its streets he wore a dog tag that reads "I am an American Lutheran. Take me to the Swedish Hospital in south Minneapolis. I can pay."[22]

It seems equally clear that in the third major phase of his career Keillor will continue to perform and work in radio. As he said about why he came back to radio to start "ARC," "It's what I do. It's what I feel confident of, and what other people seem to respond to."[23] Certainly he might once again hear "car keys jingling in the dark" and decide, as more than once in the past, that it is time to "resume the life of a shy person" devoted more exclusively to writing. And while there is no reason he should be expected from this point forward to abjure sentiment and nostalgia altogether, it seems a safe bet that following his fiftieth birthday he may appear to have more in common with the likes of Slim Graves, trying to sing those cheating songs, and with Frank White, a wealthy celebrity from the Midwest who keeps a place ready in Manhattan. And he will have a lot less in common with Dad Benson, that proverb-spouting Poor Richard Saunders of the airwaves, who was memorialized by a Freeport minister as a radio "pastor of the flock" who sermonized through stories and "brought home spiritual truths far better than preaching ever could" on "Friendly Neighbor" (*HBH*, 64).

Keillor predicted in 1989 that "I will never have a book again that sells a third as many copies as *Lake Wobegon*," an assumption that gave him a certain satisfaction: "To have your success behind you is the most calming, most peaceful feeling. Why should one ever want to repeat something so tumultuous – this catastrophe of good fortune?"[24] Yet even if the bubble fame never bounces him so high again, he has already earned a permanent niche in the Hall of American letters – not in the central Canon Corridor where Mark Twain is ensconced, but certainly in a dignified place equal to that given in the adjacent wing devoted to humorists, among the likes of his *New Yorker* predecessors Thurber, Perelman, and his hero, E. B. White.

Many of Keillor's short works will continue to be anthologized and sometimes assigned in the schools, and his two novels, especially *Lake Wobegon Days*, will remain in print a long good while and can be expected to attract additional interest in the academy. The fate and popular longevity of Keillor's thousands of oral stories, songs, and sketches preserved on audio and video recordings is even harder to predict. But it is possible that these nonprint materials, many of which have been made commercially available to the public, constitute an archive that is his most extraordinary contribution to the tradition of American humor and letters. Twain's talent and achievements as a yarnspinner and performing literary comedian may have surpassed Keillor's, but since Twain's performances could not be preserved to enable a meaningful comparison, Keillor's compound mastery of the "carpentry of prose" and vernacular storytelling should set him ahead of most, if not all, the rest of those who in the history of American humor have undertaken such an ambitious dual career.

Appendix: Dates of Monologues Used in Leaving Home

"A Trip to Grand Rapids," 17 May 1986, with bits from 18 May 1985, and 14 June 1986. Published on *More News from Lake Wobegon.*

"A Ten-Dollar Bill," 8 March 1986.

"Easter," 28 April 1984.

"Corinne," 12 April 1986.

"A Glass of Wendy," 8 Feb. 1986.

"The Speeding Ticket," 21 March 1987.

"Seeds," 30 March 1985, with 13 April 1985.

"Chicken," 13 September 1986.

"How the Crab Apple Grew," 10 May 1986.

"Truckstop," 23 February 1985. Published on *More News from Lake Wobegon.*

"Dale," 7 June 1986 and 21 June 1986.

"High Rise," 31 May 1986, with a bit from 13 April 1985.

"Collection," 16 March 1985.

"Life Is Good," 28 June 1986.

"Lyle's Roof," 2 March 1985, published as "Smokes" on *More News from Lake Wobegon*; 6 September 1986, and 23 August 1986.

"Pontoon Boat," 19 July 1986. Published on *More News from Lake Wobegon.*

"State Fair," 30 August 1986.

"David and Agnes, a Romance," 17 August 1985.

"The Killer," 20 September 1986.

"Eloise," 4 October 1986.

"The Royal Family," 13 November 1982. Published on *News from Lake Wobegon.*

"Homecoming," 13 October 1984. Published on *More News from Lake Wobegon.*

"Brethren," 1 November 1986.

"Thanksgiving," 29 November 1986.

"Darlene Makes a Move," 6 December 1986.

"Christmas Dinner," 24 November 1984.

"Exiles," 27 December 1986.

"New Year's," 3 January 1987 and 10 January 1987.

"Where Did It Go Wrong?" 28 February 1987.

"Post Office," 15 November 1986.

"Out in the Cold," 1 February 1986.

"Hawaii," 16 November 1985.

"Hansel," 22 November 1986.

"Du, Du Liegst Mir im Herzen," 22 March 1986.

"Aprille," 26 April 1986. The opening of the remodeled World Theater commemoration, broadcast for PBS television and Disney Cable channels.

"Goodbye to the Lake," 13 June 1987. Published on *A Prairie Home Companion: The Final Performance* and *A Prairie Home Companion: The Last Show* (videotape).

Notes and References

Preface

1. William M. Dietel, audiotape of his introduction of Keillor at the Public Radio Conference, San Francisco, 18 May 1989, Archives of "A Prairie Home Companion" (APHC).

Chapter One

1. Keillor quoted in Bill Nelson, "Why Did Time Forget This Man's Town?" *Milwaukee Journal Insight*, 1 August 1982; hereafter cited in text.

2. Roy Blount, Jr., "A Conversation with Garrison Keillor," in *Farewell to "A Prairie Home Companion,"* Collector's Edition (published simultaneously as a supplement to *Minnesota Monthly* 21 [June 1987]) (St. Paul: Minnesota Public Radio, 1987), 17; hereafter cited in text. In some interviews Keillor has said he wanted to be a writer from age nine or ten.

3. In one of several speeches when he returned to give the commencement address at his alma mater, Anoka High School (Donna Halvorsen, "Keillor Tips His Hat to Anoka, a Place He Says He Never Really Left," *Minneapolis Star and Tribune*, 5 June 1990, 1B; hereafter cited in text).

4. Keillor purchased the house after it had passed out of the hands of the family (Cheryl Walsh, "Her 'Cheesy' Gift . . .," *Minneapolis Star Tribune*, 9 February 1992, 3B).

5. "What Do You Do? How Much Do You Earn?," in *G.K. the DJ* (St. Paul: Minnesota Public Radio, 1977), 31; hereafter cited in text as "What Do You Do?"

6. Irv Letofsky, "For Garrison Keillor, Fantasy Is a Lot More Fun than Reality," *Minneapolis Tribune*, 29 July 1976, 8C; hereafter cited in text.

7. Michael Fedo, *The Man from Lake Wobegon* (New York: St. Martin's Press, 1987), 1; hereafter cited in text.

8. Beverly Beyette, "Fishing for Meaning in Lake Wobegon Waters," *Los Angeles Times*, 18 September 1985, V2; hereafter cited in text.

9. Liner notes to *A Prairie Home Companion Anniversary Album* ("PHC" 404) (St. Paul: Minnesota Public Radio, 1980).

10. "There was once a Zenith console radio," "Broadside of the Tower," *Ivory Tower* 65 (9 March 1964): 7.

11. "The Boy Who Couldn't Have TV," *TV Guide*, 15 May 1982, 42; hereafter cited in text as "TV."

12. *We Are Still Married* (New York: Viking Press, 1991), 158; hereafter cited in text identified as *WASM*.

13. Alan McConagha, "The Making of Garrison Keillor," *Washington Times*, 10 October 1985, 1B; hereafter cited in text.

14. Sam Newlund, "Ingenuity Helps Keillor Take Crassness Out of Christmas," *Minneapolis Star and Tribune*, 15 December 1982.

15. "Stories you tell ought to be as common as dirt and yet try to raise people up a little bit" (Keillor to Peter Hemingson, "The Plowboy Interview," *Mother Earth News*, May-June 1985, 20; hereafter cited in text).

16. Audiotape, "A Minnesota Thanksgiving," Minnesota Public Radio, 24 November 1977, APHC.

17. "A Prairie Home Companion," Minnesota Public Radio, 8 November 1975; material from Keillor's Saturday-evening radio show are hereafter cited in text as "PHC," followed by the date of the original broadcast. Citations of unpublished radio broadcasts are, unless otherwise indicated, based on my own transcriptions of unpublished reel-to-reel and audiocassette tapes in APHC at Minnesota Public Radio (MPR) in St. Paul. First citations of published recordings will be in notes.

18. "To the Reader," in *G.K. the DJ*, 1.

19. Introduction to *Happy to Be Here* (New York: Penguin Books, 1983 [revised and enlarged paperback edition]), x-xi; hereafter cited in text as *HBH*. Recent reprints of *Happy to Be Here* have dropped the Introduction.

20. Diane Roback, "PW Interviews: Garrison Keillor," *Publishers Weekly*, 13 September 1985, 139; hereafter cited in text.

21. "Laying on Our Backs Looking up at the Stars," *Newsweek*, 4 July 1988, 30.

22. "Bush's Cynical Use of the Flag," *Des Moines Register*, 4 July 1989, 8A.

23. "I Once Was Lost, But Now I'm Churched," *Christian Century*, 8-15 August 1990, 727.

24. James M. Wall, "Door Interview: Garrison Keillor," *Wittenburg Door*, December-January 1984-85, 13. This interview provides the most comprehensive discussion of Keillor's religious background and belief.

25. Interview with the author, 10 August 1990; hereafter cited in text.

26. Alan Thurber, "Lackluster Career Spins Off into Prairie Stories," n.d., unattributed newsclipping, AMPR.

27. The quotation is from Letofsky, 1976; on Keillor's grades at the university see also Judith Y. Lee, *Garrison Keillor: A Voice of America* (Jackson: University Press of Mississippi, 1991), 6; hereafter cited in text.

28. During a live radio spot for Powdermilk Biscuits, Keillor said, "I'm just a biscuit. God coulda made me a croissant, but he made me a biscuit instead" ("PHC," 5 November 1982).

29. Keillor identified 30 unsigned *Ivory Tower* articles for Lee, whose bibliography is nearly comprehensive, though the actual number he wrote is probably higher. My bibliography lists only five undergraduate pieces, including one additional unsigned piece that he did not identify and four signed pieces omitted from Lee's bibliography.

30. Unsigned piece, "The Green Goose Awards for Impenetrable Prose," *Ivory Tower* 66 (11 January 1965): 13.

31. Letter to *Minnesota Daily*, 29 September 1964, 4.

32. "Means Magazine, Sneam Naieamgz," *Ivory Tower* 66 (5 October 1964): 20.

33. "Off to the Smut War," *Ivory Tower* 66 (7 December 1964): 8-10.

34. "God by Magic," *Ivory Tower* 65 (5 October 1964): 6.

35. The monologue aired on "PHC" 27 October 1984 and was published as "Gospel Birds," *Gospel Birds and Other Stories of Lake Wobegon*, Cassette no. 1 ("PHC" 1213), MPR, 1985.

36. *Lake Wobegon Days* (New York: Viking Press, 1985), 97; hereafter cited in text as *LWD*.

37. See "The Vulgarians" and "A. J. Liebling on Campus," *Ivory Tower* 66 (8 March 1965): 8-9. His later piece is (with Mark Singer) the Foreword to *The Honest Rainmaker: The Life and Times of Colonel John R. Stingo*, by A. J. Liebling (San Francisco: North Point Press, 1989), ix-xi.

38. For examples of "dark" Thurber stories, see "One Is a Wanderer" or "A Box to Hide In," in *The Middle-Aged Man on the Flying Trapeze* (New York: Harper, 1935), and "The Whip-Poor-Will" or "A Friend to Alexander," in *My World – and Welcome to It* (New York: Harcourt Brace, 1942).

39. "The Courtship of Eve," *Ivory Tower* 66 (13 January 1964): 18-22.

40. "Frankie," *Ivory Tower* 67 (2 May 1966): 30-37.

41. "Poet Garrison Keillor will read from his work at 11 a.m. tomorrow at the Sauran-Russoff Book Loft, 302 S.E. 4th St.," "Callboard," *Minneapolis Star*, 1 March 1974.

42. *Atlantic Monthly*, July 1968, 54.

43. Keillor celebrates some of his poetic mentors in the poem "On the Freshness of Poetry: For (of and by) Reed Whittemore," *Ivory Tower* 64 (3 June 1963): 14. John Berryman's "In Memoriam: Morgan Blum" appeared in *Ivory Tower* 66 (7 December 1964).

44. "On Waking to Old Debts" and "Nicodemus," *Ivory Tower* 66 (5 April 1965): 21; "At the Premiere" and "This Is a Poem, Good Afternoon," *Ivory Tower* 67 (7 February 1966): 20.

45. *Ivory Tower* 68 (6 February 1967): 26-28.

46. "Jason's Birth," "A Minnesota Thanksgiving," MPR, 24 November 1977; hereafter cited in text as "Jason's Birth." Keillor published another account of his son's birth near Jason's twenty-first birthday; see "Notes and Comments," *New Yorker*, 25 June 1990, 23-24. Keillor has reiterated at least five times – in print, interviews, and in stories told on radio – the idea that "we live by miracles."

47. Keillor, audiotape of his speech to the Public Radio Conference, San Francisco, 18 May 1989, AMPR. His short-lived attempt to support himself and his family through freelance writing out in the solitude of the farm is fictionalized in "Happy to Be Here," which before it was reprinted in his first volume of collected stories had appeared in the *New Yorker* (1971) and in *G.K. the DJ* with the ironic title "Found Paradise (A Midwestern Writer Nobody Knows and How He Found Peace of Mind)."

Chapter Two

1. Keillor as cited by James Traub, "The Short and Tall Tales of Garrison Keillor," *Esquire*, May 1982, 112; hereafter cited in text.

2. KSJR (St. John's Radio) first went on the air in 1967 from the campus of St. John's University, a liberal arts institution run by the Benedictine order. KSJR relinquished control of the station in favor of Minnesota Educational Radio in 1971; MER became Minnesota Public Radio (MPR) in 1974. See Patricia Weaver Francisco, "The Life and Times of MPR," *Minnesota Monthly* 21 (January 1987): 50-57.

3. "Garrison Keillor: A Decade of 'Prairie Home Companion,'" *Minneapolis Tribune Picture*, 1 July 1984.

4. Michael Schumacher, "Sharing the Laughter with Garrison Keillor," *Writer's Digest*, January 1986, 35.

5. Foreword to Marcia and Jon Pankake, *A Prairie Home Companion Song Book* (New York: Viking, 1988), xi.

6. Audiotape of Keillor's speech to the Public Radio Conference, San Francisco, 18 May 1989, AMPR. In this speech he also told a story about how he first got into radio (to impress a young woman in his American literature class); he used the same material in "The Announcer," *Lake Wobegon Loyalty Days* (MPR 15065), MPR, 1989.

7. Judith Yates Borger, "Garrison Keillor: Your Companion on the Prairie," *Lutheran Brotherhood Bond*, Winter 1975, 7.

8. Foreword to Pankake, *Song Book*, xii. Keillor's association with his musical mentors endured, and as early as 1968 he recorded their group and played the tape on *Radio Free Saturday*. They performed live on his morning show in 1972 and did "The Pankake Breakfast Hour" for him in 1976. In 1986 John Pankake appeared as "The Masked Folksinger" for "The Department of Folk Song" ("PHC," 1983-87). *Song Book* publishes the songs listeners submitted to The Department.

9. Attributed to Tom Kigin by Patricia Weaver Francisco, "The Life and Times of MPR," *Minnesota Monthly* 21 (January 1987): 52.

10. *Preview*, January 1969.

11. Will Jones, "After Last Night," *Minneapolis Tribune*, 3 October 1971, 6D; hereafter cited in text.

12. Audiotape, AMPR.

13. The increasing similarity of his voice to his father's was mentioned by Keillor in "A Letter from Copenhagen,"in *Leaving Home: A Collection of Lake Wobegon Stories* (New York: Viking Press, 1987), xvi; hereafter cited in text as *LH*. See also Roback (139).

14. A sampler of published descriptions of Keillor's voice is provided in "Notes and Comment on Keillor and His *Prairie Home*," in *Farewell to "A Prairie Home Companion*," 96-97.

15. *WLT: A Radio Romance* (New York: Viking, 1991), 44; hereafter cited in text as *WLT*.

16. "A Prairie Home Companion," *Preview*, July 1973, 20.

17. "Notes and Letters," *Preview*, October 1971. The story alluded to is the uncollected "Sex Tips," *New Yorker*, 14 August 1971, 31.

18. Untitled manuscript (1971?), Garrison Keillor Papers, American Humor Institute, New York (Summer 1991); hereafter identified as GKP.

19. Matt Damsker, "Heartland Humor Flows from Depths of Wobegon," *San Diego Union*, 6 March 1983, E12.

20. Cliff Radel, "Home on the Prairie," *Cincinnati Enquirer*, 4 March 1982, B9; hereafter cited in text.

21. Untitled manuscript (1971-73?), GKP.

22. Mike Steele, "KSJN: Giant Step for Public Broadcasting?" *Minneapolis Tribune*, 15 November 1970, E1, E4.

23. "Keillor's most frequent pose was that of the Amateur, a broadcaster unworthy to further the noble history of live radio" (Lee, 50).

24. In later interviews and in monologues (such as 4 December 1982) Keillor mentioned the influence of other family storytellers who inspired him, including his aunt Ruth (Blumer) Keillor and his paternal great-uncle, Lew Powell. The *News from Lake Wobegon* cassette set (1983) was dedicated to the memory of Powell and unnamed others to whom God gave "the gift of gab."

25. See "Keillor to Quit Daily Show; Others Leave KSJN," *Minneapolis Tribune*, 24 August 1973, 14B.

26. "Thanks for the Memories," *Farewell to "A Prairie Home Companion*," 36.

27. "Friendly Neighbor" was first published in the *New Yorker*, 31 December 1973, 23-25. Though this was not a radio show, some details about the January 1974 performance are taken from undated rundowns of

partial tapes of these shows in AMPR. The title of the show that played on 5 and 6 January 1974 was given in a review by Roy M. Close, "Humorist, Poet Create Show That at Best Is Wildly Funny," *Minneapolis Star*, 5 January 1974, 10A.

28. "Onward and Upward with the Arts: At the Opry," *New Yorker*, 6 May 1974, 46-70.

29. Liner notes to *A Prairie Home Companion Anniversary Album*, "PHC" 404, MPR, 1980.

Chapter Three

1. The nine monologues recorded between 1983 and 1985 on *The Gospel Birds* cassettes, for example, average around 19 minutes, and such published versions are usually edited down. *Gospel Birds and Other Stories of Lake Wobegon*, two audiocassettes, no. 1 ("PHC" 1213), MPR, 1985.

2. Bob Blackman, "A Prairie Home Companion," *Lansing Star*, 7-20 October 1982.

3. Ron Wolf, "Public Radio Enters Era of Competition," *Philadelphia Inquirer*, 13 February 1983, 11-I.

4. Eric Scigliano, "Prairie Fire: Garrison Keillor and the Radio Robber Barons," (Seattle) *Weekly*, 8 September 1983.

5. Patricia Weaver Francisco, "A Place to Go That's Just like Home," *Minnesota Monthly*, July 1984, 15.

6. Mark Twain, "How to Tell a Story" (1895), in *Selected Shorter Writings of Mark Twain*, ed. Walter Blair (Boston: Houghton Mifflin, 1962), 239.

7. This discussion of traditional American humor relies primarily on *Native American Humor*, ed. Walter Blair (New York: Harper & Row, 1960); hereafter cited in text.

8. "Ten Questions Most Often Asked about 'A Prairie Home Companion' and Ten Answers Not Given Previously," unpublished press release, MPR (14 February 1987), 1, AMPR.

9. *Garrison Keillor's Home*, MPR with A La Carte Communications, 1991 (videocassette).

10. Paul Fatout, Introduction to *Mark Twain Speaking* (Iowa City: University of Iowa Press, 1976), xvii; hereafter cited in text.

11. "Platform Readings," from the Autobiographical Dictation of 10 October 1907, in "Mark Twain," ed. Henry Nash Smith, in *Major Writers of America* vol. 2, ed. Perry Miller (New York: Harcourt, Brace & World, 1962), 107.

12. During 1974 "PHC" played in the 400-seat concert hall in the Janet Wallace Fine Arts Center at Macalester College in St. Paul from the first live performance through 5 October; other locations included the 82-seat Vari-

ety Hall Theater in Park Square Court (St. Paul), in the same building with KSJN; the 220-seat St. Paul – Ramsey County Arts and Science Center auditorium. It also toured, taping shows for rebroadcast from various locations, including Concordia College, Moorhead, Minnesota; St. John's University, Collegeville, Minnesota; Moorhead Community Theater; Augustana College, Sioux Falls, South Dakota; Worthington Community College, Worthington, Minnesota; and Southwest State University, Marshall, Minnesota. In March 1978 it moved into the World Theater in St. Paul, which then seated 650; it was purchased by MPR in 1981, and reopened in April 1986 after its deterioration forced the show to move into temporary quarters at the nearby 1,650-seat Orpheum Theater in January 1984. The World seated 925 after its major remodeling (1984-86). See "A Prairie Home Almanac," in *Ten Years: The Official Souvenir Anniversary Program* for "A Prairie Home Companion" (St. Paul: Minnesota Public Radio, 1984), 5-20. For a list of more than 20 venues in the Twin Cities where "PHC" played through 1984, see "*A Prairie Home Companion* Trivia Quiz Answers," *Minnesota Monthly*, July 1984, 38.

13. Betty Jean Robinson and Aileen Mnich, "Hello Love" (Nashville: Acuff-Rose Songs, 1970).

14. *A Prairie Home Companion Anniversary Album*, "PHC" 404, MPR, 1980.

15. Compare Keillor's account of visits to WCCO studios in "Drowning, 1954" (*HBH*, 208).

16. *A Prairie Home Companion Anniversary Album*, MPR, 1980.

17. Jack Thomas, "The 'Prairie' Tour Stops Here," *Boston Globe Calendar*, 19 March 1983, 10.

18. See John C. Gerber, "Mark Twain's Use of the Comic Pose," *PMLA* 77 (June 1962): 297-304. Compare Lee's use of Gerber's analysis in her extensive treatment (esp. 49-90) of Keillor's comic poses.

19. For samples see "The Perils of Success: Selected Letters from Jack," in *Farewell to "A Prairie Home Companion,"* 100-104, and "Letters from Jack," *WASM*, 69-79.

20. Compare this discussion of Keillor's poses to the analysis of Mark Twain's movement from the "Twain-Brown character axis" in his early travel burlesques, including *The Innocents Abroad* (1869), toward the more memorable "developing character," such as the narrator of *Roughing It* (1872), who incorporates elements of both the sentimental Twain and the unsentimental Brown characters into one, complex narrative identity (in Franklin R. Rogers, *Mark Twain's Burlesque Patterns* [Dallas: Southern Methodist University Press, 1960]).

21. Poses named and discussed by Lee include Announcer (or Professional), Amateur, Companion, Shy Person, Exile, Witness, Crackerbarrel Philosopher/Preacher (see Lee, esp. chap. 3). I find her designations worth

perpetuating. The Sojourner from Lake Wobegon is a name I have chosen for the persona that incorporates all of these poses with the exception of the Announcer; I have added to Lee's list the pose of Fatherly Host and Storyteller.

22. Henri Bergson, *Laughter* (1900), in *Comedy*, ed. Wylie Sypher (Garden City, N.Y.: Doubleday, 1956), 84.

23. I first encountered "Corner Lot" while listening to old broadcast tapes in January 1990 in AMPR. From my summary of the monologue, Rosalie Miller matched the tape with its undated manuscript versions. Lee never heard the tape or read the "Corner Lot" manuscripts (Lee, letter to the author, 13 December 1991). She cites a telephone conversation with Miller (8 May 1990) as her source for the date and titles (Lee, 191n20).

24. "Corner Lot Outside Town," undated manuscript (13 December 1975?), AMPR; hereafter cited in text as "Lot."

25. Another version was narrated three months later, when the news was that "the citizens have been down in St. Paul lobbying for a bill to correct . . . the old surveying error . . . when four surveying teams went out and made different maps which turned out to overlap somewhat and Lake Wobegon wound up right in the middle and consequently does not exist" ("PHC," 10 April 1976). One version of this anecdote, retold many times, was printed in the "*Sumus Quod Sumus*" section of *Lake Wobegon Days* (90-91).

26. Carolyn S. Brown, *The Tall Tale in American Folklore and Literature* (Knoxville: University of Tennessee Press, 1987), 11.

27. According to " 'Companion' Finds Friends," (Escanaba, Minnesota) *Press*, 11 June 1984, an anonymous Associated Press story in AMPR.

28. This spot was published as "Powdermilk Biscuits," *Prairie Home Companion Tourists* (audiocassette; "PHC" 808C) (St. Paul: Minnesota Public Radio, 1983). In the monologue aired on the same show, Keillor claims to have become so accomplished as a liar that he is troubled by the inaccuracies in his lies. The monologue was published as "Fiction," *Spring* cassette ("PHC 909), *The News From Lake Wobegon*, MPR, 1983.

29. Lee credits Rosalie Miller for locating versions on this pattern in the "Corner Lot" manuscripts and in monologues for 15 May 1982, 12 March 1983, and 17 November 1984. In the last two listed Keillor himself is the vain smoker (Lee, 81-83, 196n24). Lee did not list 8 May 1976.

30. These brief quotations are from an undated fragment of manuscript no. 306 in *Pre-1984 Monologues*, GKP, which is most likely the basis of the oral version of 8 May 1976.

31. Undated holograph manuscript, no. 404, in *Pre-1984 Monologues* binder, GKP (summer 1976?).

32. Undated holograph manuscript (summer 1976?), AMPR.

33. Undated manuscript, GKP (March 1977?).

34. Undated manuscript (November 1979?), GKP.

35. Manuscript (9 September 1980), GKP.

36. Undated manuscript (March 1981?), GKP.

37. Undated manuscript (March 1981?), GKP.

38. Interview with Bob Potter, "Midday," MPR, 13 November 1982.

39. First aired 13 March 1982, the story was published as "Letter from Lake Wobegon," *Los Angeles Herald-Examiner*, 16 March 1982, A1-A15, and as "Letter from Jim," on the *Spring* cassette, "PHC" 909, *News from Lake Wobegon*, MPR, 1983.

40. Manuscript no. 127 in *Pre-1984 Monologues* binder, 11 November 1982, AMPR.

Chapter Four

1. Peter H. Schreffler, "Where All the Children Are above Average: Garrison Keillor as a Model for Personal Narrative Assignments," *College Composition and Communication* 40 (February 1989): 82-85.

2. "Who's on the Right Track?" *Minneapolis Tribune*, 14 January 1974, 8A.

3. "Me and Myrtle and Harry"; originally published as "The Delights That Will Beckon Myrtle and Harry to the City."

4. The former was originally published as "Meeting the President in a Dream" and the latter as "Saving a Vanishing Species."

5. The former was originally published as "New Experiences ($) Artists Must Seek" and the latter was published in *Preview* as "A City Letter: What Do You Do? How Much Do You Earn?"

6. The latter was originally published as "Wearing Well in a Cornerstone."

7. The piece was originally published as "Getting Mileage out of the Metric System."

8. In "One of the Most Outstanding Columns I Have Ever Written about Education in My Own Life," originally published as "Why Not 'Goodness' in Education?"

9. George Orwell, "Politics and the English Language," in *In Front of Your Nose: 1945-1950*, vol. 4 of *The Collected Essays, Journalism and Letters of George Orwell* (New York: Harcourt, Brace & World, 1968), 139.

10. Curtis Hansen, "New York Stories," *Minnesota Monthly*, September 1989, 29.

11. In October 1992 Keillor "broke his long-standing contract giving the *New Yorker* an exclusive first look at any article or short piece of fiction he wrote" (Sallie Dinkel, "Keillor Cancels Contract with the *New Yorker*," *Magazine Week*, 16 November 1992, 3). Keillor's defection followed hard

on the appointment of Tina Brown as editor of the *New Yorker*. Brown had edited *Vanity Fair*, a magazine Keillor called a "trash pit."

12. The first edition was *Happy to Be Here: Stories and Comic Pieces* (New York: Atheneum, 1982); the paperback edition (*Happy to Be Here: Even More Stories and Comic Pieces* [New York: Penguin, 1983]) revised the order slightly and added five pieces: two previously printed in the *New Yorker*, two from the *Atlantic*, and one from *Twin Cities*. Recent editions have omitted Keillor's Introduction. As of January 1992 Viking Penguin estimated that there were approximately 600,000 copies in print (Leslie Hulse, telephone conversation with the author, 6 January 1992). The Penguin edition is cited in text as *HBH*.

13. Amanda Smith, "The Sage of Lake Wobegone [*sic*]," *Boston Phoenix*, 23 March 1982, sec. 3, pp. 1, 14; hereafter cited in text.

14. A 1988 piece reprinted as "Lifestyle" in *We Are Still Married* explores the same basic theme as a married couple agree their "lifestyle" would improve if they sold their two teenage children.

15. *New Yorker*, 10 October 1970, 45.

16. Jerome Klinkowitz, *The Self-Apparent Word: Fiction as Language/ Language as Fiction* (Carbondale: Southern Illinois University Press, 1984), ix; hereafter cited in text.

17. Larry McCaffery, *The Metafictional Muse: The Works of Robert Coover, Donald Barthelme, and William H. Gass* (Pittsburgh: University of Pittsburgh Press, 1982), 99-100; hereafter cited in text.

18. Lois Gordon, *Donald Barthelme* (Boston: Twayne Publishers, 1981), 132.

19. *Come Back, Dr. Caligari* (Boston: Little, Brown and Company, 1964), 109.

20. For a sample of one of these verses, see "Two-Nine-One-Nine-One-Nine-Oh," in *Farewell to "A Prairie Home Companion,"* 70.

21. Keillor transformed the story into a radio drama and it was performed (with Jason Keillor taking a role) as "Don the No-good Punk" on "American Radio Company," 2 March 1991.

22. In the original context of his remarks Keillor said he valued the two autobiographical stories more highly than stories such as "A Christmas Story," an uncollected *New Yorker* piece published in 1989 (interview with the author, 10 August 1990). Keillor chose the two stories to be among the 14 short works (most originally published in the *New Yorker*) to read aloud on *Stories* (HighBridge, 1992).

23. "If Robert Frost Had an Apple," *New York Times Magazine*, 20 November 1983, 80, 84.

24. "A Prairie Home Almanac," in *Ten Years: The Official Souvenir Anniversary Program for "A Prairie Home Companion"* (St. Paul: Minnesota Public Radio, 1984), 13.

25. This apothegm may derive from a more secular saying attributed to Oscar Wilde: "The world is a stage but the play is badly cast." Keillor's use of the trope "God is an author and has scripted our lives as comedy" is also invoked directly in a 13 February 1982 monologue about a marital fight between Naomi and Harley Barley and reworked for the "Summer" chapter of *LWD*. It is invoked obliquely in "The Killers" (*LH*, 125) and *"Du, Du Liegst Mir im Herzen"* (*LH*, 225-30).

26. *The Second Tree from the Corner* (New York: Harper & Row, 1989), 17; hereafter cited in text.

27. "Story of the Bad Little Boy" (1865), in *Selected Shorter Writings of Mark Twain*, ed. Walter Blair (Boston: Houghton Mifflin, 1962), 19-22. Keillor's poem "Obedience" seems more clearly related to Twain's fable, telling about the consequences of the deeds of a bad boy named Jim (*WASM*, 236-37).

28. *One Man's Meat* (New York: Harper & Row, 1982), 203.

Chapter Five

1. John Skow, "Lonesome Whistle Blowing," *Time*, 4 November 1985, 68; hereafter cited in text.

2. Kathryn Court, Keillor's editor at Viking Press, confirmed this estimate (of copies in the United States exclusively) (telephone conversation with the author, 6 January 1992.

3. Keillor's use of the pastoral is the focus of critical articles by Mark E. Vander Schaaf, "A Spark From Heaven: Garrison Keillor's *A Prairie Home Companion*," *Another Season* 2, no. 1 (Winter 1983): 6-18, and Stephen Wilbers, "Lake Wobegon: Mythical Place and the American Imagination," *American Studies* 30, no. 1 (Spring 1989): 21-34.

4. *Anatomy of Criticism: Four Essays* (1953; Princeton: Princeton University Press, 1973), 43; hereafter cited in text.

5. Because the Harper & Row editors rejected his *WLT* manuscript (around 1981) and were not interested in any book based on his "PHC" monologues, Keillor later went to Viking Press with *Lake Wobegon Days* (Noel Holston, "Keillor Says He's Freed His Characters," *Minneapolis Star Tribune*, 17 November 1991, 1F, 10F; hereafter cited in text).

6. Keillor said this in his monologue for the season opener of *American Radio Company* in St. Paul, 12 October 1991.

7. "Modern American Humor," *Studies in American Humor* 3, no. 1 (April 1976): 9.

8. James M. Tarbox, "Lake Wobegon Celebrating Its 10th Anniversary," *St. Paul Pioneer Press*, 1 July 1984, 3H.

9. Eric Ries, "Live, from Atlanta: It's Garrison Keillor," *Savannah News-Press*, 25 May 1990, D1.

10. Edward B. Fiske, "Small-Town America," *New York Times*, 30 October 1982.

11. Michael Schumacher, "Sharing the Laughter with Garrison Keillor," *Writer's Digest*, January 1986, 32.

12. Robert Barr, "Fear and Pride in Lake Wobegon: An Author with a Mission," (New Brunswick, New Jersey) *Home News*, 13 October 1985.

13. Charles Larson and Christine Oravec, " 'A Prairie Home Companion' and the Fabrication of Community," *Critical Studies in Mass Communication* 4, no. 3 (September 1987): 221-44; hereafter cited in text.

14. Richard Eder, review of *Lake Wobegon Days*, *Los Angeles Times Book Review*, 8 September 1985, 3.

15. For a detailed discussion of the blend of oral and literate stylistic features in Keillor's "PHC" monologues, see Michael Kline, "Narrative Strategies in Garrison Keillor's 'Lake Wobegon' Stories," *Studies in American Humor* 6, n.s. (1988): 129-41; hereafter cited in text.

16. Concerning the "agonistic" and "empathetic" properties of orality, see Walter J. Ong, *Orality and Literacy: The Technologizing of the Word* (New York: Methuen, 1983), 31-77; hereafter cited in text.

17. I have elaborated on an insight of Randall H. Balmer, "Religion Helps Explain 'Lake Wobegon' Appeal," *Des Moines Register*, 9 June 1987, 7A.

18. Liner notes to *A Prairie Home Companion Anniversary Album*, "PHC" 404, MPR, 1980.

19. Alison Lurie, "Plain Tales from a Garrison Town," *Observer Magazine*, 24 January 1988, 25.

20. " 'Companion' Finds Friends," (Escanaba, Minnesota) *Press*, 11 June 1984.

21. This is the only plausible translation according to Erwin Panofsky, "*Et In Arcadia Ego*: Poussin and the Elegiac Tradition," in *Meaning in the Visual Arts* (Garden City: Anchor Books, 1955), 295-320.

22. In the discussion of primitivism, he is citing Ortega y Gasset, *The Revolt of the Masses* (1930). See Leo Marx, *The Machine in the Garden: Technology and the Pastoral Ideal in America* (New York: Oxford University Press, 1964), 5-11.

23. "A Prairie Home Companion," *Preview*, July 1972, 7.

24. The influence of the magazine title was reported by John Bream, "Garrison Keillor: A Decade of 'Prairie Home Companion,'" *Minneapolis Tribune Picture*, 1 July 1984. The influence of the cemetery's name was reported by Roger Catlin, "Keillor Brings Bit of 'Prairie' to Oakdale," *Hartford Courant*, 6 July 1990, E1-E2.

25. Keillor had played the role of Harley Peters and used that name in "Sex Tips," and a real person named Harley (Refsal) "performed" as a

Norwegian-American woodcarver on "PHC" at least twice, but the name Harley Barley was apparently too rich for print.

26. Compare his use of this trope as discussed in Chapter 4 in the context of "After a Fall" and in Chapter 6 in the context of "The Killer" and "*Du, Du Liegst Mir im Herzen.*"

27. Kevin Klose, "The Keillor Instinct for the Truer-Than-True," *Washington Post*, 15 September 1985, K4.

28. Bruce Michelson, "Keillor and Rölvaag and the Art of Telling the Truth," *American Studies* 30, no. 1 (Spring 1989): 32; hereafter cited in text.

29. "ARC," 20 October 1990. Talking about Minnesota's soldiers in the Battle of Gettysburg, Keillor wondered, "would they have *liked* us? or would our America horrify them?" (in "How I Came to Give the Memorial Day Address," *WASM*, 117). The Gettysburg reflections draw on a "PHC" monologue of 30 May 1987. The Memorial Day episode in the novel mentions the soldiers but does not include the rhetorical questions (*LWD*, 120-22).

30. "Prodigal Son," *Antaeus* 66 (Spring 1991): 246-47. He also uses the parable in "Who Do You Think You Are?" (*WASM*, 129) and in "When You Kick a Liberal: A Post Election Parable," *Harper's*, January 1989, 72-74 (reprinted in *WASM* as "A Liberal Reaches for Her Whip").

31. Johnny's campus visit first aired 12 June 1982 and was published as "The Tollefson Boy Goes to College" ("PHC" 910), *News from Lake Wobegon*, MPR, 1983.

32. Keillor's father's name is John. The monologue mentioning the Keillorinis first aired 21 May 1983 and was published as "Uncle Al's Gift" on the *Love* cassette ("PHC" 14988), *More News from Lake Wobegon*, MPR, 1989.

33. Sigmund Freud, "Moses and Monotheism," *The Standard Edition of the Complete Psychological Works of Sigmund Freud*, trans. by James Strachey, vol. 13, *1906-1908* (London: Hogarth Press, 1964), 12-13.

34. Mark Twain, *The Adventures of Tom Sawyer and The Adventures of Huckleberry Finn* (New York: New American Library, 1980), 18 (chap. 2).

35. Versions of the "gumball" argument with a Providence-affirming conclusion aired on "A Minnesota Thanksgiving," MPR, 24 November 1977 and "PHC," 15 January 1983; the monologue was published in truncated form as "Guys on Ice," on the *Winter* cassette ("PHC" 912), *News from Lake Wobegon*, MPR, 1983.

36. Mark Twain, *Adventures of Huckleberry Finn*, ed. Walter Blair and Victor Fisher (Berkeley: University of California Press, 1986), 158.

37. The quotation from *Huckleberry Finn* is from chapter 12, a river idyll that parallels that in chapter 19 where Huck and Jim argue about the

origin of the stars. See Keillor, "Laying on Our Backs Looking up at the Stars," *Newsweek*, 4 July 1988, 30-31. Reprinted in *We Are Still Married*.

38. The tomato assault was first aired 31 July 1982 and published as "Tomato Butt," on the *Spring* cassette ("PHC" 909), *News from Lake Wobegon*, MPR, 1983.

39. "The typical Norwegian Bachelor Farmer is in many ways like the cyclops of Greek mythology, unwilling to offer hospitality and an ungrateful recipient of the same, lacking community and therefore subhuman" (Vander Schaaf, "A Spark From Heaven," 9).

40. The monologue first aired 14 January 1984 and was published as "Freedom of the Press" on the *Humor* cassette ("PHC" 14988), *More News from Lake Wobegon*, MPR, 1989.

41. My discussion of "family romance" and of the Prodigal Son as paradigm and theme relies on the theories of David Wyatt, *Prodigal Sons: A Study in Authorship and Authority* (Baltimore: Johns Hopkins University Press, 1980).

42. During a reading from *Lake Wobegon Days* aired 26 May 1986, MPR.

43. *Giants in the Earth: A Saga of the Prairie* (1927; New York: Perennial Library, n.d.), 452. Michelson observes that "those who have wintered in the northern tier of American states know how possible it is for a grown man to freeze a quarter of a mile from his own front door. The News from Lake Wobegon is ambiguous about his fate, just as the whole book seems reluctant to say anything for sure about inherited mythologies and their shifting relationship to the present" (33).

44. My views on Lake Wobegon as a mythic projection of home have been influenced by Wilbers and Michelson.

Chapter Six

1. Kathryn Court of Viking Press thought Lee's figure of 2.2 million copies in print sounded high and estimated the number at 1.5 million (telephone conversation with the author, 6 January 1992).

2. Of the 43 monologues adapted to make the collection, five first aired in 1987, 26 in 1986, eight in 1985, three in 1984, and one in 1982. Air dates for the monologues were supplied by Rosalie Miller from AMPR in June 1990, and a list is printed in the Appendix. Five of the monologues have been published by MPR on audiocassettes and disks (see Appendix).

3. "One of Keillor's greatest skills as a narrator is to use both oral and literate discourse features in complement, a practice which supports the view that there is no absolute dichotomy between written and spoken forms of language" (Kline, 129).

4. See Spalding Gray, "Plenty Wholesome and a Little Perverse," *New York Times Book Review*, 4 October 1987, 9.

5. The *St. Paul Pioneer Press Dispatch* published a story about and a picture of his newly purchased house off Summit Avenue on 27 December 1985. Keillor's feelings about his unwanted celebrity status and his treatment by the local press are quoted in Jack Thomas, "Weekend in Wobegon," *Boston Globe*, 9 March 1985, F8, F10; Peg Meier, "Keillor Has Had Enough of Celebrity," *Minneapolis Star and Tribune*, 22 March 1987, A1, A8; and Mary T. Schmich, "Goodbye to St. Paul: Tired of Stardom, Garrison Keillor Makes a Fresh Start," *St. Paul Pioneer Press Dispatch*, 22 March 1987, 1G, 4G, 11G. All are hereafter cited in text.

6. There were also references to a Nick Portland (February 1986) and to the Flying Coleman Twins (April 1986) in letters from Jack; see *Farewell to "A Prairie Home Companion,"* 102-3.

7. Foreword to Pankake, *A Prairie Home Companion Song Book*, xv.

8. *How to Talk Minnesotan: A Visitor's Guide* (New York: Penguin Books, 1987). Information about Mohr's career and work on "PHC" is taken primarily from letters to the author dated 24 June and 5 July 1991.

9. "Mohr's Scripts for 1985 APHC," manuscript in AMPR.

10. Gordon Mennenga, telephone conversation with the author, 9 September 1991; hereafter cited in text as Mennenga.

11. "Garrison Keillor's Home" was one of a series of "compilation" shows taken from the videotaped series that were subsequently aired by PBS television. The two other specials were "Garrison Keillor's Hello Love" (14 February 1992) and "Lake Wobegon Spring Weekend" (10 April 1992). All three were made commercially available subsequent to airing.

12. The word count is based on Keillor's untitled manuscript, which is bound together with that of Gordon W. Mennenga, "February 3, 1959," in the *1986-1987 Chronological Monologues* binder, 21 February 1987, AMPR.

13. Kline also observes that "this narrative ubiquity appears symbolically as comic synechdoche in . . . 'The Living Flag.' One can either present a red, white, or blue cap so a viewer above can make out a flag, or one can try to look up and see the living flag reflected in a mirror – in which case it disappears as the heads tilt back to see. In other words, one can be a storyteller or one can live, but cannot authentically do both at the same time; yet Keillor's shifting between first and third persons creates the illusion of doing both" (Kline, 135, 136).

14. "September 6," *A Minnesota Book of Days (and a Few Nights)* (New York: Penguin Books, 1989), 158-59.

15. *In God We Trust: All Others Pay Cash* (1966; New York: Dolphin Books, 1972), 183-96.

16. *Jean Shepherd: Shepherd's Pie: Slice One and Two* and *. . . Slice Three and Four*, four audiocassettes (1991?); Jean Shepherd, *Wanda Hickey's Night of Golden Memories and Other Disasters* (1971; Garden City, N.Y.: Dolphin Books, 1976).

17. *Understanding Media: The Extensions of Man* (New York: Signet, 1964), 265.

18. Interview with the author, 7 October 1976. For a fuller discussion see Peter A. Scholl, "Jean Shepherd: The Survivor of Hammond," *Great Lakes Review* 5, no. 1 (Summer 1978): 7-18.

19. In addition to the five of the stories in *Leaving Home* published by MPR on audiocassettes and disks by 1991 (see Appendix), at least three additional tellings were videotaped and cablecast by Disney: "Aprille" in 1986 and "The Speeding Ticket" and "Goodbye to the Lake" in 1987. The last was marketed on a videotape titled "A Prairie Home Companion: The Last Show."

20. "The Grandstand Passion Play of Delbert and the Bumpus Hounds," in Shepherd, *Wanda Hickey*, 15.

21. On the concept of the Midwest as joke see Joseph F. Trimmer, "Memoryscape: Jean Shepherd's Midwest," *Old Northwest* 2, no. 4 (December 1976): 357.

22. Jean Shepherd, Introduction to *The America of George Ade* (New York: Capricorn Books, 1961), 11. Compare Keillor on the "Law of the Provinces" in the Introduction to *We Are Still Married*, xviii.

23. Berkley Peabody, *The Winged Word: A Study in the Technique of Ancient Greek Oral Composition as Seen Principally through Hesiod's Works and Days* (Albany: State University of New York Press, 1975), as cited by Ong, 145.

24. Viv Edwards and Thomas J. Sienkewicz cite this passage from Homer's *Odyssey* (8.487-92) and note that "good talkers" (bards, etc.) often express the notion that they are "transmittors, not creators . . . by associating their song with divine inspiration and making the gods responsible for it" (*Oral Cultures Past and Present: Rappin' and Homer* [Cambridge: Basil Blackwell, 1991], 33).

25. The orator Gorgias in "Encomium of Helen" (ca. 414? B.C.) claimed that rhetoric worked like witchcraft or drugs. Havelock's "paideutic spell" was cited by Robert J. Connors, "Greek Rhetoric and the Transition from Orality" (1986), reprinted in *Essays on the Rhetoric of the Western World*, ed. Edward P. J. Corbett, James L. Golden, Goodwin F. Berquist (Dubuque, Iowa: Kendall/Hunt Publishing Company, 1990), 99.

26. David Heim, "Garrison Keillor and Culture Protestantism," *Christian Century* 104 (3-10 June 1987): 517-19. Heim alludes to Keillor's "Gospel Birds" (in *Gospel Birds and Other Stories of Lake Wobegon*). Some writers who find a genuine religious sensibility in Keillor's work include Randall H. Balmer, Wilfred Bockleman, Gracia Grindal, John E. Miller, Doug Thorpe, and James M. Wall (see Bibliography).

Chapter Seven

1. Paul D. Colford, "For Keillor, There's No Going Back," *Newsday*, 14 March 1988, part 2, p. 4; hereafter cited in text.

2. Noel Holston, "Back to the Prairie," *Minneapolis Star Tribune*, 28 March 1992, 1A, 12A.

3. For example, Michael Fedo added a postscript to the paperback edition of his biography where he opined that Keillor moved to New York because there he could best orchestrate "mega sales for his books" (Fedo, [1988], 225).

4. Keillor did not mention his role leading the anthem but expressed his sympathy for the Democrats' cause in an unsigned "Talk of the Town" piece about this visit to the convention ("We flew down to Atlanta . . . ," *New Yorker*, 1 August 1988, 16-17).

5. See his editorial "The Heart of the Matter" (1989) and the Introduction and "Reagan" in *We Are Still Married*.

6. See "Keillor, NPR Settle Lawsuit over Disputed 1987 Speech," *St. Paul Pioneer Press Dispatch*, 24 June 1988. On the Fedo biography see "My Life in Prison" (1988). On the proposed amendment see "Bush's Cynical Use of the Flag" (1989). The text of his testimony on 29 March 1990 before the Senate Subcommittee on Education, Arts, and the Humanities was published as "One of the Wisest and Happiest Pieces of Legislation Ever to Come through Congress" (1990). He targeted Quayle in "He Didn't Go to Canada" (*WASM*) and in "The Latest Quayle Joke" (1992).

7. Keillor criticized the deployment of forces in the Middle East in "Notes and Comments," *New Yorker*, 20 August 1990, 25-26. The reaction to his speech in Denmark was reported in "Short Takes," *Des Moines Register*, 27 July 1991, 6T.

8. The birth of the mayor Eloise Krebsbach's child was narrated 7 April 1990; he talked about the Gulf War on 9 February 1991 (and on several other "ARC" broadcasts).

9. Roger Catlin, "Keillor Brings Bit of 'Prairie' to Oakdale," *Hartford Courant*, 6 July 1990, E1, E12; hereafter cited in text.

10. Leslie Hulse, Viking Penguin, telephone conversation with the author, 24 June 1992.

11. Robert Barr, "Fear and Pride in Lake Wobegon: An Author with a Mission," (New Brunswick, New Jersey) *Home News*, 13 October 1985.

12. Burns had been working on the project since 1985 ("Ken Burns," *Current Biography* 53, no. 5 [May 1992]: 8-9).

13. Michael Anthony previewed the show in "Show Puts New Spin on the Old Testament," *Minneapolis Star Tribune*, 12 April 1991, 1E; Anthony reviewed it in "Keillor, Davidson Give Humorous Twist to Old Testament in 'A History of Evil,'" *Minneapolis Star Tribune*, 15 April 1991, 2E.

14. Interview with Bob Potter, "Midday," MPR, 13 November 1982.

15. *My Life and Hard Times* (1933; New York: Perennial Library, 1973), 115.

16. Answering a question about the restrictiveness of his background and upbringing, Keillor said that enforced humility and "this reticence to express affection and approval . . . may also be ethnic. I grew up in a Scandinavian-German part of the country and those people tend to withhold approval. They tend to be slightly phlegmatic" (manuscript of an interview with the *Maryland Coast Dispatch*, 31 May 1991, GKP).

17. See *A Fugitive Crosses His Tracks* (New York: Knopf, 1936), 77-78. The Norwegian first edition is *En flyktning krysser sitt spor* (Oslo: Tiden Norsk Forlag, 1933).

18. "Zeus the Lutheran," *New Yorker*, 29 October 1990, 34.

19. In one very amusing piece written after *We Are Still Married* was published, Keillor tells of an encounter with a Manhattan panhandler who tried to sell him a copy of one of his own books. "Autograph: A Transplanted Midwesterner Writes," *New Yorker*, 7 August 1989, 30-32.

20. Keillor throws readers off his scent in the original version by telling of an uncle who knew all the counties in Wisconsin by heart and by referring to his Baptist family (see "A Friend Writes," *New Yorker*, 21 November 1988, 41-42).

21. This passage was adapted for the Introduction from "A Friend Writes."

22. Lynne Truss, "Garrison Keillor: Who Does He Think He Is?," *Times Literary Supplement*, 3 November 1989, 1217A.

23. "My Name Is Yon Yonson" appeared 18 December 1988, 77-78, 96-98. Kurt Vonnegut said he was reminded of the rhyme when "I think about how useless the Dresden part of my memory has been" (*Slaughterhouse-Five* [New York: Dell, 1969], 2).

24. "Frame-Tale" consists of the line "Once upon a time there / was a story that began" printed vertically, one-half on each side of a page. The line was accompanied by a set of instructions that turned a strip of paper into a Möbius strip so the printed line fed endlessly into itself (*Lost in the Funhouse* [New York: Bantam, 1969], 1-2).

25. *New Yorker*, 25 December 1989, 40; hereafter cited in text as "Christmas."

26. Keillor, audiotape of his speech to the Public Radio Conference, San Francisco, 18 May 1989, AMPR.

27. Richard Barbieri, "Keillor Series Price up $600,000," *Current*, 23 April 1990, 1, 13.

28. The number of listeners is from an Arbitron survey reported by Tom Voegeli in a report to the MPR Board dated 18 June 1990; the number of stations was given in the 1992 MPR *Report to Funders*.

29. Noel Holston reported on theater selections and budgetary considerations of "ARC," noting that with its $2.6 million budget, which may have gone several hundred thousand in the red, "the show is the most expensive on public radio." The budget for the second season was "targeted at $3.2 million." See "Garrison Keillor Show Goes from Brooklyn to Broadway," *Minneapolis Star Tribune*, 17 June 1990, 1F, 7F.

30. Eleanor Blau, "He's Not Laughing (Well, Mostly)," *New York Times*, 16 May 1990.

31. Words by Garrison Keillor, music by Spenser Williams; ca. 1917, Edwards B. Marks.

32. The passages from Henry David Thoreau conform closely to passages in *Walden*: "Where I Lived, and What I Lived For" (1854). This monologue was titled "Thoreau on the Subway" on the audiocassette *Local Man Moves to the City*, HighBridge, 1991 (HBP 18125).

33. *New Yorker*, 25 June 1990, 23-24.

34. Manuscript of an interview with the *Maryland Coast Dispatch*, 31 May 1991, GKP.

35. *A Visit to Mark Twain's House with Garrison Keillor*, MPR, 1992. Two other recordings from "ARC" are *Garrison Keillor's American Radio Company: The First Season* (1990) and *Local Man Moves to the City* (1991).

36. David Armstrong, "Keillor's Complaint," *San Francisco Chronicle Image*, 12 January 1992, 10.

37. Lisa Schwarzbaum, "The Loneliness of the Long-Distance Lutheran," *New York Daily News Magazine*, 4 February 1990, 12.

38. Timm Storrs, "Big-City Life Far Cry from Lake Wobegon," *Compass Readings*, August 1990, 71.

39. Keith S. Graham, "Keillor Finds His Way through Big-City Show," *Atlanta Constitution*, 25 May 1990.

Chapter Eight

1. The allusion is to Andrew Dice Clay, a standup comedian famous for offensive humor (James Wolcott, "Keillor on the Loose," *Vanity Fair*, November 1991, 104).

2. "Oldies But Goodies," *Washington Post*, 10 November 1991, 7.

3. "Garrison Keillor Interview with the *Maryland Coast Dispatch*," 31 May 1991, manuscript in GKP.

4. Tim Warren, "Keillor Tells More Stories about Minnesota," *Cedar Rapids Gazette*, 24 November 1991, 2C; hereafter cited in text.

5. Letter to the author, 24 July 1989.

6. Leslie Hulse, Viking Penguin, telephone conversation with the author, 24 June 1992.

7. Diana Postlethwaite, "Is This Garrison?" *Star Tribune*, 17 November 1991, 8FX.

8. "The Air Castle of the North" reminded many Minnesotans of Minneapolis radio station WCCO: "The Good Neighbor to the Great Northwest," although Keillor denied that his novel is based in any way on that station (Holston, 7F).

9. "My Life in Prison" (1988) was reprinted in *We Are Still Married* and is discussed in Chapter 7; "That Ol' 'Picayune-Moon,'" *Harper's*, September 1990, 68-70.

10. Tom Lewis, *Empire of the Air: The Men Who Made Radio* (New York: Edward Burlingame Books, 1991), 163.

11. Ken Burns, *Empire of the Air* (Florentine Films, 1991).

12. *Of Mikes and Men* (New York: McGraw-Hill, 1951). The WLS book is an illustrated promotional pamphlet from the Prairie Farmer Publishing Co. (Chicago, 1933).

13. The names of the clergyman on station WLT correspond to three parallel streets in Brooklyn Center, near Keillor's home in Brooklyn Park. There are many such insider touches; another mentioned by Cheryl Walsh is the correspondence of the first names of the Shepherd Boys – Elmer, Rudy, Al, and Wendell – to those of Minnesota governors. See "All His Trials . . . ," *Minneapolis Star Tribune*, 8 August 1991, 2B.

14. Keillor's 1966 story "Frankie" was about another young man who may have had biographical significance.

15. Donn Fry, "Keillor Continues His 'Romance' with Radio," *Seattle Times*, 10 December 1991, F1.

16. John Bordsen, "All the News from Lake Wobegon," *Saturday Review*, May-June 1983, 19.

17. Neely Tucker, "Keillor's Charm Warms 'Radio Romance' Novel," *Albuquerque Journal*, 26 January 1992. This is a portion of a review supplied by Knight-Ridder Newspapers syndicate.

18. The notion that the Soderbjerg brothers personify Keillor's internal ambivalence toward radio was articulated by Alyn Beckman, "With Laughter and Tears," unpublished paper for my Seminar in Keillor and Twain, Luther College, spring 1992.

19. "The Sir Oracles Who Are Unable to Speak," *Minneapolis Tribune*, 19 May 1974, 14A.

20. The inventor Lee De Forest also deplored the triumph of commercialism in radio and shared with Sarnoff the belief that, ideally, radio should be a tool to elevate and educate the masses. See Lewis, 177 and 242.

21. See Plato's *Phaedrus* 275E. For a contemporary discussion of "the play of signification" in Plato's use of the word *pharmakon* see Jasper Neel, *Plato, Derrida, and Writing* (Carbondale: Southern Illinois University Press, 1988), chap. 4.

22. "Little House in the Big City: Smiling Through," *New York Times Magazine*, 8 April 1990, 8.

23. Eric Ries, "Live, From Atlanta: It's Garrison Keillor," *Savannah News-Press*, 25 May 1990.

24. David Streitfield, "Garrison Keillor: The Man Who Deserted Minnesota," *Cedar Rapids Gazette*, 31 August 1989, 1B (written originally for the *Washington Post*).

Selected Bibliography

PRIMARY WORKS

Books
Fiction and Nonfiction
G.K. the DJ. St. Paul: Minnesota Public Radio, 1977.
We Are Still Married. New York: Viking Penguin, 1989.

Fiction
Don: The True Story of a Young Person. Minneapolis: Redpath Press, 1987.
Happy to Be Here. New York: Atheneum, 1982. Revised and enlarged edition, New York: Penguin Books, 1983.
Lake Wobegon Days. New York: Viking Penguin, 1985.
Leaving Home: A Collection of Lake Wobegon Stories. New York: Viking Penguin, 1987.
WLT: A Radio Romance. New York: Viking Penguin, 1991.

Poetry
The Selected Verse of Margaret Haskins Durber. Lake Wobegon, Minn.: Jack's Press, 1979. [St. Paul]: Minnesota Public Radio.

Uncollected Writing
College Publications
"The Broadside of the Tower." *Ivory Tower* 65 (9 March 1964): 7-8. Untitled item, beginning "There was once a Zenith console radio."
"The Courtship of Eve." *Ivory Tower* 65 (13 January 1964): 18-22. Story.
"God Bless the Press and Save the People." *Ivory Tower* 67 (6 December 1965): 21.
"The People, the Game, and the Spirit." *Ivory Tower* 66 (5 April 1965): 25-31.
"Sleepers." *Ivory Tower* 65 (7 October 1963): 27. Poem.

Fiction

"Al Denny." *New Yorker*, 11 March 1991, 30-32.

"Bangor Man." *New Yorker*, 14 October 1972, 39.

"A Christmas Story." *New Yorker*, 25 December 1989, 40-42.

"The Chuck Show." *New Yorker*, 24 July 1989, 26-29.

"How the Savings and Loans Were Saved." *New Yorker*, 16 October 1989, 42.

"If Robert Frost Had an Apple." *New York Times Magazine*, 20 November 1983, 80-84.

"Letter from Lake Wobegon." *Los Angeles Herald-Examiner*, 16 March 1982, A1-A15. Recorded as "Letter from Jim." *Spring* cassette, "PHC 909," *News from Lake Wobegon*, MPR, 1983.

"Little House in the Big City: Smiling Through." *New York Times Magazine*, 8 April 1990, 6, 8.

"Lonesome Shorty." *New Yorker*, 5 March 1990, 36-37.

"A Prairie Home Companion." *Preview*, July 1972, 4-8; *Preview*, February 1973, 9; *Preview*, July 1973, 20.

"Sex Tips." *New Yorker*, 14 August 1971, 31.

"Snack Firm Maps New Chip Push." *New Yorker*, 10 October 1970, 45.

"That Ol' 'Picayune-Moon.' " *Harper's*, September 1990, 68-70.

"Your Book Saved My Life, Mister." *New Yorker*, 28 December 1987, 40-41.

"Zeus the Lutheran." *New Yorker*, 29 October 1990, 32-37.

Poetry

"Some Matters concerning the Occupant." *Atlantic*, July 1968, 54.

Play

"Prodigal Son." *Antaeus*. 66 (Spring 1991): 242-47. Published as a play in one act, it was originally aired on "PHC" 15 October 1983.

Nonfiction

"About Guys." *New York Times*, 27 December 1992, E11.

"The Boy Who Couldn't Have TV." *TV Guide*, 15 May 1982, 39-42.

"Bush's Cynical Use of the Flag." *Des Moines Register*, 4 July 1989, 8A.

"Cherished Moments." *Life*, Fall 1988, 153-56.

"The Fabric of the Flag." *New York Times*, 2 July 1989, E13.

Foreword (with Mark Singer) to *The Honest Rainmaker: The Life and Times of Colonel John R. Stingo*, by A. J. Liebling. San Francisco: North Point Press.

Foreword to *The New! Improved! Bob & Ray Book*, by Bob Elliott and Ray Goulding. New York: G. P. Putnam's Sons, 1985.

"Get Ready for Monday Night Mudwrestling – Plus Dan Rather and His Orchestra." *TV Guide*, 7 December 1985, 4-6.

"The Heart of the Matter." *New York Times*, 14 February 1989, A23.

"He Digests the Star and Finds It's a Meat-and-Potatoes Meal." *Minneapolis Star*, 4 August 1977, 1C-2C.

"He Made the Furniture Talk." Review of *Fred Allen: His Life and Wit*, by Robert Taylor. *New York Times Book Review*, 9 July 1989, 7.

"If Begonias Bloom, Can Baseball Be Far Behind?" *Minneapolis Tribune*, 1 April 1979, 17A.

"Keillor Speaks for Parents to Class of '84." *St. John's* 23 (Summer 1984): 7-9.

"The Latest Quayle Joke." *New York Times*, 14 June 1992, E19.

"Lust on Wheels." *Esquire*, July 1986, 61.

"Midnight Meeting about Secret Meetings." *Minneapolis Star*, 13 March 1979, A4.

"My Son, the Delivery Entrepreneur." *Minneapolis Star*, 25 January 1979, A6.

"Notes and Comments." *New Yorker*, 12 September 1988, 25.

"Notes and Comments." *New Yorker*, 6 February 1989, 23-24.

"Notes and Comments." *New Yorker*, 15 May 1989, 35-36.

"Notes and Comments." *New Yorker*, 25 September 1989, 47-48.

"Notes and Comments." *New Yorker*, 25 June 1990, 23-24.

"Notes and Comments." *New Yorker*, 20 August 1990, 25-26.

"One of the Wisest and Happiest Pieces of Legislation Ever to Come through Congress." *Chronicle of Higher Education*, 11 April 1990, 33.

"Onward and Upward with the Arts: At the Opry." *New Yorker*, 6 May 1974, 46-70.

"The Place to Ease the Blues." *MPLS-St. Paul* 9 (April 1981): 144.

"A Reporter at Large: Country Golf." *New Yorker*, 30 July 1984, 37-45.

"A Return to the Basics: Mealtime without Guilt." *New York Times Magazine*, 2 February 1983, C1-C8. Reprinted as "Outrageous Opinion: Eating without Guilt." *Cosmopolitan*, June 1984, 16. Reprinted as "Down with Mealtime Guilt." *Reader's Digest* (Canada), June 1984, 95-96.

"The Sir Oracles Who Are Unable to Speak." *Minneapolis Tribune*, 19 May 1974, 14A.

"St. Paul's Orchestra Pure Sunshine." *Minneapolis Tribune*, 27 January 1974, 11A.

"Talk of the Town." *New Yorker*, 21 November 1988, 41-42.

"Talk of the Town." *New Yorker*, 1 August 1988, 16.

"Talk of the Town." *New Yorker*, 13 March 1989, 26-27.

"Talk of the Town." *New Yorker*, 7 August 1989, 30-32.

Ten Years: The Official Souvenir Program for A Prairie Home Companion. St. Paul: Minnesota Public Radio, 1984.

". . . To the State of Radio-Free Wobegon." *Los Angeles Times*, 12 April 1981, V5.

"Voices of Liberty." *Newsweek*, 14 July 1988, 33.

"Where There's Smoke There's Ire." *American Health* 8 (1 December 1989): 50-53.

"Who's on the Right Track?" *Minneapolis Tribune*, 14 January 1974, 8A.

Recordings

The Family Radio. Minnesota Public Radio, 1982. Two records. PHC 606. Two audiocassettes.

Garrison Keillor's American Radio Company: The First Season. St. Paul: Minnesota Public Radio, 1990. One audiocassette. "ARC" 17332.

Garrison Keillor's Home. A La Carte Communications, 1991. One videocassette.

Gospel Birds and Other Stories of Lake Wobegon. Minnesota Public Radio, 1985. Two audiocassettes. "PHC" 1213.

Lake Wobegon Days. Minnesota Public Radio, 1986. Four audiocassettes.

Lake Wobegon Loyalty Days. Minnesota Public Radio, 1989. One audiocassette. MPR 15065. Compact disc MPR 15066. Reissued by Virgin Classics, 1989. Compact disc. VC7-92209-2.

Local Man Moves to the City. HighBridge Company, 1991. One audiocassette. HBP 1825.

More News from Lake Wobegon. Minnesota Public Radio, 1989. Four audiocassettes. "PHC" 14988. Four compact discs. "PHC" 15376.

News from Lake Wobegon. Minnesota Public Radio, 1983. Four audiocassettes. *Spring*, "PHC" 909; *Summer*, "PHC" 910; *Fall*, "PHC" 911; *Winter*, "PHC" 912. Reissued by Minnesota Public Radio, 1989. Four compact discs. "PHC" 15376.

A Prairie Home Album. Minnesota Public Radio, 1972.

Prairie Home Comedy. Minnesota Public Radio, 1988. Two audiocassettes. "PHC" 21302.

A Prairie Home Companion Anniversary Album. Minnesota Public Radio, 1980. Two records. "PHC" 404. Two audiocassettes.

A Prairie Home Companion: The Final Performance. Minnesota Public Radio, 1987. Two audiocassettes.

A Prairie Home Companion: The Last Show. Disney Home Video, 1987. Videocassette. VHS and Beta.

A Prairie Home Companion: The 2nd Annual Farewell Performance. Minnesota Public Radio, 1988. Two audiocassettes. "PHC" 2172. Videocassette. VHS and Beta. "PHC" 55041.

A Prairie Home Companion: The 3rd Annual Farewell Performance. Minnesota Public Radio, 1989. Two audiocassettes. "PHC" 14989. Videocassette.

Prairie Home Companion Tourists. St. Paul: Minnesota Public Radio, 1983. One record. One audiocassette. "PHC" 808C.

Songs of the Cat. HighBridge, 1991. One audiocassette. HBP 17398.

Stories. St. Paul: HighBridge, 1992. Two audiocassettes. HBP 17369.

Ten Years on the Prairie: "A Prairie Home Companion" 10th Anniversary. Minnesota Public Radio, 1984. Two audiocassettes. "PHC" 1212C.

A Visit to Mark Twain's House with Garrison Keillor. Minnesota Public Radio, 1992. Two audiocassettes. HBP 19387.

WLT: A Radio Romance. Penguin-HighBridge Audio, 1991. HBP 18903. Four audiocassettes.

SECONDARY WORKS

Interviews

Blount, Roy, Jr. "A Conversation with Garrison Keillor." In *Farewell to "A Prairie Home Companion*," 13-24. Collector's Edition. St. Paul: Minnesota Public Radio, 1987. The volume was published simultaneously as a supplement to *Minnesota Monthly* 21 (June 1987). With his friend and fellow humorist in the special context of the end of "PHC," Keillor gives an informal yet illuminating and professional analysis of his craft and review of his career to date.

Hemingson, Peter. "The Plowboy Interview: Garrison Keillor: The Voice of Lake Wobegon." *Mother Earth News*, May-June 1985, 17-20, 22. Published a year after it was conducted, it covers "PHC," Keillor's progress-to-date on *Lake Wobegon Days*, and how his oral storytelling differs from his writing for publication.

"Radio Is 'A Magical Country.'" *U.S. News & World Report*, 4 November 1985, 75.

Roback, Diane. "PW Interviews: Garrison Keillor." *Publishers Weekly*, 13 September 1985, 138-39. Concentrates on how *Lake Wobegon Days* was written but includes discussion of Keillor's writing career, including his understanding of the difference between the Lake Wobegon material and his other published humor.

Scholl, Peter A. "Coming Out of the Crackerbarrel: An Interview with Garrison Keillor." *South Carolina Review* 24 (Spring 1992): 49-56. Discusses differences between radio performance and writing and provides a glimpse of his life as staff writer on the *New Yorker*.

Schumacher, Michael. "Sharing the Laughter with Garrison Keillor." *Writer's Digest*, January 1986, 32-35. Based on interview in 1985, gives special attention to Keillor's early ambition to be a writer.

Wall, James M. "*Door* Interviews Garrison Keillor." *Wittenburg Door*, December-January 1984-85, 12-20. Concentrates on Keillor's religious convictions and ideas and whether his work reflects these.

Criticism: Books

Brown, Carolyn S. *The Tall Tale in American Folklore and Literature*. Knoxville: University of Tennessee Press, 1987. A historical and critical study of folklore in literature including a discussion of the tall tale elements in *Lake Wobegon Days*.

Farewell to "A Prairie Home Companion." Collector's Edition. St. Paul: Minnesota Public Radio, 1987. Simultaneously published as a supplement to *Minnesota Monthly*, June 1987. Includes selected poems, letters from Jack, mock-commercials, and so on by Keillor along with interviews and feature articles to commemorate the end of "PHC."

Fedo, Michael. *The Man from Lake Wobegon*. New York: St. Martin's Press, 1987, 1988. An "unauthorized biography" that is long on interviews and short on analysis (though occasionally the interview material is illuminating). The paperback edition adds a Postscript.

Keillor, Steven J. *Hjalmar Petersen of Minnesota: The Politics of Provincial Independence*. St. Paul: Minnesota Historical Society Press, 1987. Written by Garrison's brother, a professional historian, it explores life in the Danish-American community of Askov, Minnesota, providing (though not intentionally) a nonfiction parallel to Lake Wobegon.

Lee, Judith Yaross. *Garrison Keillor: A Voice of America*. Jackson: University Press of Mississippi, 1991. A meticulous and detailed critical history and interpretation of the radio work and writing through 1987 (with limited discussion of material into 1989), based solidly on extensive archival sources, supplemented by personal interviews with the author.

Mohr, Howard. *A Minnesota Book of Days (and a Few Nights)*. New York: Penguin, 1989. Humorous record of a year in the life of fictional Harold Mire by a writer for "PHC"; includes a septic tank story similar to Keillor's "Homecoming."

Pankake, Jon, and Marcia Pankake. *A Prairie Home Companion Folk Song Book*. New York: Viking, 1988. Foreword by Garrison Keillor. A collection of 348 songs submitted by listeners to the "Department of Folk Song" feature on the radio show. Includes music to some and lists names of contributors at the back.

Criticism: Articles

Balmer, Randall H. "Religion Helps Explain 'Lake Wobegon' Appeal." *Des Moines Register*, 9 June 1987, 7A. A historian of religion explores how "PHC" draws on Christian rituals and themes.

Barry, Nancy K. "The Last News from Lake Wobegon." *Chicago Tribune*, 13 June 1987, 17. Anticipating the end of "PHC," Barry recalls the pleasures of listening to it live on radio and deplores the Disney cable contract.

Beyette, Beverly. "Fishing for Meaning in Lake Wobegon Waters." *Los Angeles Times*, 18 September 1985, V1, V2, V3. Keillor talks about his conflicts growing up and the extent to which Lake Wobegon is based on his own experiences and feelings.

Birkerts, Sven. Review of *WLT: A Radio Romance. Chicago Tribune*, 3 November 1991, 8-9. The novel manages to duplicate the most entertaining qualities of the author's familiar radio monologues.

Bockelman, Wilfred. "Garrison Keillor's Lake Wobegon." *Lutheran*, 5 February 1986, 4-7. Relying partly on an interview, Bockelman explores Keillor's treatment of Lutheranism, finding that he is "quite deeply theological."

Bordsen, John. "All the News from Lake Wobegon." *Saturday Review*, May-June 1983, 12-19. Profile of Keillor and "PHC"; Keillor mentions his work on what became *WLT: A Radio Romance*.

Cooney, Barney. "Keillor, Garrison." In *Encyclopedia of American Humorists*, edited Stephen H. Gale, 251-53. New York: Garland, 1988. Biographical summary with brief literary analysis of the books published through 1985.

Fiske, Edward B. "Small-Town America." *New York Times*, 30 October 1982. A feature on "PHC."

Greasley, Philip. "Garrison Keillor's Lake Wobegon: The Contemporary Oral Tale." *Midamerica* 14 (23 March 1990): 126-36. Argues that Keillor's colloquial style links him with other populist writers as it celebrates the common person and urges the preservation of traditional values.

Grindal, Gracia. "We Are What He Says We Are." *Lutheran Partners*, May-June 1986, 19-23. A Norwegian Lutheran seminary professor explains why she finds "95 Theses 95" the funniest part of *Lake Wobegon Days*.

Hansen, Curtis. "New York Stories." *Minnesota Monthly*, September, 1989. Preview of "American Radio Company" and treatment of Keillor's adjustment to New York.

Heim, David. "Garrison Keillor and Culture Protestantism." *Christian Century* 104 (3-10 June 1987): 517-19. Examination of Keillor's use of religion in the Lake Wobegon saga.

Hölbling, Walter W. "From Main Street to Lake Wobegon and Half-Way Back: The Ambiguous Myth of the Small Town in Recent American Literature." In *Mythes ruraux et urbains dans la culture amèricaine*, 51-66. Aix En Provence, France: Université de Provence, 1990. *Lake Wobegon Days* is presented as a self-conscious use of the small town "myth *as* myth" and as a representative of the "new regionalism" of the 1970s and 1980s in the context of a wider discussion of the small town in the history of American literature.

Holston, Noel. "Keillor Says He's Freed His Characters." *Minneapolis Star Tribune*, 17 November 1991, 1F, 10F. Feature article focusing on genesis and aims of *WLT: A Radio Romance* (and how in 1981 Harper & Row rejected a draft and also the concept for a novel on Lake Wobegon).

Jones, Will. "After Last Night." *Minneapolis Tribune*, 3 October 1971, 6D. Reviews Keillor's morning radio show.

Kline, Michael. "Narrative Strategies in Garrison Keillor's 'Lake Wobegon' Stories." *Studies in American Humor* 6, n.s. (1988): 129-41. A detailed demonstration, based on a few representative samples, of how the broadcast monologues of the mid-1980s make use of both oral and written features of grammar, rhetoric, style, and narrative structure.

Kling, William. "Farewell to Lake Wobegon." *U.S. News & World Report*, 22 June 1987, 10. Keillor's longtime boss, the head of MPR, reflects on the "massive legacy" "PHC" produced for public radio.

Klose, Kevin. "The Keillor Instinct for the Truer-Than-True." *Washington Post*, 15 September 1985, K4. Review of *Lake Wobegon Days* including interview material from Keillor on how writing for the page differs from writing for the voice.

Larson, Charles U., and Christine Oravec. "'A Prairie Home Companion' and the Fabrication of Community." *Critical Studies in Mass Communication* 4 (September 1987): 221-44. Focuses on "PHC" monologues that were adapted for use in *Lake Wobegon Days* and examines the nature of Keillor's appeal to his listening and reading audience, arguing that he offers baby boomers a "strategy of acceptance" and encourages a self-flattering, delusive quietism.

Letofsky, Irv. "For Garrison Keillor, Fantasy Is a Lot More Fun than Reality." *Minneapolis Tribune*, 29 July 1976. Extensive profile of Keillor with candid interview material on his early life and career.

Lurie, Alison. "The Frog Prince." *New York Review of Books*, 24 November 1988, 33-34. In a discussion of his major books to 1988, Lurie locates Keillor as a "defuser" as opposed to a "destroyer" in the spectrum of American humorists.

Meier, Peg. "Keillor Has Had Enough of Celebrity." *Minneapolis Star and Tribune*, 22 March 1987, A1, A8. Explores Keillor's reasons for ending PHC and decision to leave Minnesota.

Michelson, Bruce. "Keillor and Rölvaag: And the Art of Telling the Truth." *American Studies* 30, no. 1 (Spring 1989): 21-34. Argues that *Lake Wobegon Days* reimagines the mythical history of the frontier, rendering it more accessible to a contemporary audience than in earlier works such as O. E. Rolvaag's *Giants in the Earth*, the naturalistic terms of which are redefined by Keillor.

Miller, John E. "The Distance between Gopher Prairie and Lake Wobegon: Sinclair Lewis and Garrison Keillor on the Small Town Experience." *Centennial Review* 31, no. 4 (Fall 1987): 432-46. Contrasts Lewis's unforgiving and merciless satires of the American village with Keillor's forgiving, ironic, and affectionate treatment of nearly the same places and peoples.

Naylor, Charles. "Of Mikes and Men." *Nation*, 23 December 1991, 823-24. Review of *WLT: A Radio Romance*, calling it Keillor's "first true novel" and "formally . . . considerably beyond any of Keillor's earlier successes."

Offenburger, Chuck. "For Keillor, the Surf's Up." *Des Moines Register*, 9 February 1992, 1B, 6B. Previews "ARC" show at site of Buddy Holly's last concert in Iowa.

Scholl, Peter A. "Garrison Keillor." In *Dictionary of Literary Biography, 1987 Yearbook*, edited by J. M. Brook, 326-38. Detroit: Gale Research, 1988. Critical discussion of Keillor's work and career to 1987 in the context of a biographical survey.

————. "Garrison Keillor and the News from Lake Wobegon." *Studies in American Humor* 4, n.s. (Winter 1985-86): 217-28. Historical and critical analysis of the career to 1984, concentrating on "PHC" and Keillor's theologically shaded view of comedy.

Schreffler, Peter H. "Where All the Children Are above Average: Garrison Keillor as a Model for Personal Narrative Assignments." *College Composition and Communication* 40 (February 1989): 82-85. Contends that Keillor's Lake Wobegon narratives give college students examples of how their own experience can provide raw material for writing that others will want to read.

Singer, Mark. "Meet Garrison Keillor, the Sage of Lake Wobegon." *Airwaves*, March 1982, 9, 40-41. A reliable description of the nature of the show and of the backstage atmosphere at "PHC" during one of its strongest periods.

Skow, John. "Lonesome Whistle Blowing." *Time*, 4 November 1985, 68-73. Cover story featuring "PHC"; reviews *Lake Wobegon Days*.

Smith, Amanda. "The Sage of Lake Wobegone [*sic*]." *Boston Phoenix*, 23 March 1982, sec. 3, pp. 1, 14. Review of *Happy to Be Here* with some incisive quotations from an interview with Keillor.

Thorpe, Doug. "Garrison Keillor's 'Prairie Home Companion': Gospel of the Airwaves." *Christian Century* 99 (21-28 July 1982): 793-96. Focuses on the salience of live broadcasting to "PHC" and contrasts the qualities of the pieces in *Happy to Be Here* to the tones and effects struck by the radio show.

Traub, James. "The Short and Tall Tales of Garrison Keillor." *Esquire*, May 1982, 108-17. Detailed feature on "PHC" with extensive treatment of Keillor's career.

Vander Schaaf, Mark E. "A Spark from Heaven: Garrison Keillor's *A Prairie Home Companion*." *Another Season* 2 (Winter 1983): 6-18. Argues that Keillor successfully reconciles the pastoral ideal with the city, since as host on "PHC" he manages to dwell in the city as host and simultaneously enters into the country spirit of Lake Wobegon, enabling his audience to imaginatively participate in the reconciliation.

Wall, James M. "The Secret Is Out about Lake Wobegon." *Christian Century* 102 (13 November 1985): 1019-20. A review of *Lake Wobegon Days* and an appreciation of the author's "religious sensibility."

Wilbers, Stephen. "Lake Wobegon: Mythical Place and the American Imagination." *American Studies* 30, no. 1 (Spring 1989): 21-34. The Lake Wobegon material responds to the deep need for a myth of a home, an imagined space that enables and shapes a sense of a collective identity and continuity with the past, all essentials to a nation's sense of cultural solidarity and purposefulness in a time of social dislocation and rapid change.

Wolcott, James. "Keillor on the Loose." *Vanity Fair*, November 1991, 100-104. A feature-length review arguing that in *WLT* Keillor "commits overkill," and in his "desire to shuck his homespun image" he also reveals his disgust with having become a celebrity.

Index

The Author

Peter A. Scholl received his B.A. from Augustana College in Rock Island, Illinois, and his M.A. and Ph.D. in English from the University of Chicago. He has taught at the University of Evansville (Indiana) and since 1977 in the English Department of Luther College in Decorah, Iowa, where he is professor and his wife, Diane Gabrielsen Scholl, is associate professor. His work has appeared in such publications as *Studies in American Fiction*, the *South Carolina Review*, *Studies in American Humor*, the *Great Lakes Review*, *Christianity and Literature*, and the *Dictionary of Literary Biography*.

Scholl was born in Philadelphia but grew up in the far West and has lived principally in the Midwest. He was preparing dinner one Saturday night shortly after coming to Iowa when his attention was captured by Garrison Keillor talking about shy persons on KLCD-FM, the local Minnesota Public Radio station.

The Editor

Frank Day is a professor of English at Clemson University. He is the author of *Sir William Empson: An Annotated Bibliography* and *Arthur Koestler: A Guide to Research*. He was a Fulbright Lecturer in American Literature in Romania (1980-81) and in Bangladesh (1986-87).

Twayne's United States Authors

These recently published Twayne titles are available by mail. To order directly, return the coupon below to: Twayne Publishers, Att: LP, 866 Third Avenue, New York, N.Y. 10022, or call toll-free 1-800-323-7445 (9:00 A.M. to 9:00 P.M. EST).

Line #	Quantity	ISBN	Author/Title	Price
1	_____	0805740007	WARD / *Rita Mae Brown*	$22.95
2	_____	080573967X	MERRILL / *Norman Mailer*	$23.95
3	_____	0805776400	HILL / *Lee Smith*	$22.95
4	_____	0805740074	SCHIFFER / *Richard Stern*	$21.95
5	_____	0805776389	BAKER / *Studs Terkel*	$22.95
6	_____	0805739858	EVANS / *Anne Tyler*	$21.95
7	_____	0805776427	WINCHELL / *Alice Walker*	$20.95

Sub-total _____

Please add postage and handling costs—$2.00 for the first book and
75¢ for each additional book _____

Sales tax—if applicable _____

TOTAL _____

Lines Units

Control No. [＿＿＿＿] Ord. Type [SPCA] [＿＿][＿＿]

___ Enclosed is my check/money order payable to Macmillan Publishing Company.
___ Bill my ☐ AMEX ☐ MasterCard ☐ Visa ☐ Discover Exp. date _____

Card # _____ Signature _____
Charge orders valid only with signature
Ship to: _____

_____

_____ **Zip Code**

For charge orders only:

Bill to: _____

_____

_____ **Zip Code**

For information regarding bulk purchases, please write to Managing Editor at the above address. Publisher's prices are subject to change without notice. Allow 4–6 weeks for delivery.   Promo # 78700 FC2542